The Beauty in my mess

Mr. Louise,
and the beauty...
Shawna Cook 2021

Cover design: Art and Design studio of Janna Geary
Editing: SFS Creatives
Marketing Head : Kayla Brissi

Printed in the United States of America

"WOW! Each of these women have stepped out on faith with bold courage to vulnerably share their stories of transparency, truth, tests and triumph. They have pushed past adversity, hurts, pain, disappointments and even discouragement and here they share it all. It's amazing how God can use what others go through to help someone else get through."

Mrs. Monique A. Brooks, Christian Counselor & Mental Health Advocate - Bayview Church of San Diego, Ca

"The Beauty in My Mess" is a masterfully woven collection of stories about survival, love, forgiveness, passion, strength and endurance. It's a collections that we all must experience to reinforce that there is a message in our mess and victory in our voice. I gasped, cried, and frequently cupped my hand over my mouth as lives were vividly painted out on pages before me through letters, words, periods, commas and quotes. It is a strong reminder that no matter the fight in our lives, we are not alone. God has greater, and He promised that He would never leave or forsake us. Through "The Beauty in My Mess," we can see that He was with them the whole time.

Chida Rebecca, Publisher/Editor-in-Chief Black & Magazine| San Diego's Premier Digital Black Lifestyle Magazine

"This book had me sitting there on the edge of my seat. I loved the flow. I loved the way the transparency. If you have ever doubted that beauty could come from a mess, when you read this book all doubt will be removed. There is hope for the hopeless and according to this book there is a message in your mess. Wow! You just never know what people are dealing with and what God can do if we let him."

Julia Banks, Author & Certified Life Coach at
https://www.juliajbanks.com

"Dr. Long has been divinely inspired to create this collection, this scrapbook of hope. The Beauty in My Mess is a reminder of God's constant love and His consistently meeting us where we are in our humanness; using that humanness to further His kingdom and bring Him glory in all situations."

Amanda Millette, Author and Owner of River Rock Interiors LLC

"I love this book! So timely, so freeing! It's a compilation of stories of women who have been identified, purposed, healed and restored by the perfect love of Jesus—a book truly born from the Father's heart! These strong and courageous women share their RAW and REAL journeys of having gone through life's battles, struggles, failures and deceptions yet chose to see God's beauty in their mess! This book is truly designed to give glory and honor to God! Nicole's obedience to run with this project will truly set many women free!"

Belisa Perez, Author, Online Business Coach and founder of Kingdompreneurs Unite.

FORWARD

In this day and age when the shame and stigma of sharing our stories has been lifted by the magnitude of women standing up to say "me too," Nicole Long has crafted a different narrative by allowing women to tell their stories of hope and triumph over the circumstances that tried to define them through stepping into a deeper relationship with Jesus Christ.

She's brought together women from different social, economic, cultural, and racial backgrounds that stand on the common ground of God's sacred unifying grace. They have shared stories not only of abuse, tragedy, and loss but also of how life can becoming overwhelmingly messy when events that can happen to anyone; happened to them. Their stories demonstrate how life's messiness can be an intersection to begin the journey of self-discovery that leads to genuine liberty.

The honesty and transparency of the women, including Nicole, who shared their stories removes the dividing line so all women can see that we are more alike than we are different. All women desire unconditional love and acceptance. All women deserve a beautiful life filled with the people and things that really matter to them. But the messiness of life doesn't discriminate; it comes for us all. However, it's not the messiness. But more so the beauty that we allow God to shape out of our mess that really matters.

It reminds me of the story of creation when the earth was in a mess, and God could have seen it as unredeemable but instead He saw the beautiful things that could be made if they were brought together in order and the right form. The thing is, there was a period of time in between what He created and the mess that was made of it. That's just like human life. We all come into the world innocent beings but then over time, things get messy. However, when God steps in He sees the beauty that can be made of our messes. He calls things into order and separates light from darkness, (Read Genesis 1). Nicole has brilliantly and thoughtfully shown through this collection of stories how God can make beauty out of any mess when we yield our lives to Him.

Krista Pettiford – Award Winning Author, Speaker, Women's Minster, and Host of Called Conference

Dedications

This book is dedicated to Jyiah, Jyaele, and John and the posse of family, friends, and clients who've shaken the way I viewed life. I have a deeper understanding of while we are different - we are, uniquely the same. In our imperfections is truly where the beauty lies - God loves us all.

Table of Contents

Introduction

Someone once told me that God gives His strongest warriors the biggest tests. I wish I could attribute that quote to someone, but I cannot remember who said it to me. And as ambiguous as the memory of that someone is; I wish the truth of that saying was just as ambiguous. You see, I did not and I still don't - want to be the strongest warrior who takes on biggest tests. Some people thrive on taking tests -I do not. My method of taking tests is simple. Get the test date, study for the test, ace said test and then move on. But somehow this method doesn't work in my actual life. My real-life tests are nothing like this. It seems like the tests God gives to me, I have to take over and over again. There's like versions A-Z, and even though I ace them each and every time, a new version keeps coming out. And while I have grown to know that those test have come to build my resilience, to deepen my faith, to quicken my patience; I still would rather not have to take them. I rather not be that type of warrior.

However, that wasn't always the case.

As I kid, I wanted to be the strong warrior with the biggest test and even bigger testimony. I really thought that God favored people more when they had more victorious stories and I had none. As a kid, even as a teenager, nothing extremely self -imposed – out of disobedience, nothing that altered my way of life, happened to me. And I didn't know at the time, but – that was a good thing. Growing up in the Baptist church (like literally straight out of the womb), I remember being in awe of the prayers and testimonies of the congregation. I remember always wondering why or how everyone had these crazy – pulled out from the fiery pits of hell testimonies to share and I had nothing that measured up. Even my own peers had horror stories to share and I had nothing that really compared. Frustrated enough, I asked my mom why I didn't have such stories, and she told me that it was a good thing but to just "keep living", I didn't know what that meant then but boy oh boy, I am "living" now.

As a write this introduction, I feel like I am writing it under duress.

I'm not, but it surely feels that way. Everything has been thrown my way today, actually this week, heck before the inception of this book and it almost led me to not write this portion. In this very moment, one part of my brain is like "shut it down – you're tired, your frustrated, your disappointed – you can't write this now" and then the logical side of my brain is like … "girl, finish. You've been holding on to this for too long. Use this energy to get it out and get it done." So being logical most of the time --- here I am writing. Here I am typing out another revision, each time more vulnerable than the last, here I find my words on a paper that actually exemplify my here and now; for all to read.

See, not too long ago I found myself not paying attention to the gaps in my heart. I found myself filling the void of an unfulfilled adult life permeated with new goals and aspirations of an entrepreneur. I was inundated with the hustle and bustle of business/family/ church/wife responsibilities. I was constantly in mom mode. Constantly being in business survival mode, trying to fulfill the expectations of everyone yet never measuring up. Adulting was getting the best of me and I just wanted a mental vacay from it all. It had become all-consuming and I found myself a little empty. Pouring into everyone and not having anyone pour back into me on that same magnitude.

Consequently, instead of taking the time out to really focus on self care, to dive deeper into the Word, and subsequently, the family and friends around me. I fell into a short spurt of selfishness. I missed all the signs that I normally catch about myself and fell right on in. And we know no matter how big or how small, selfishness can have a detrimental effect. And I don't mean the selfishness like taking a 10 min shower while your kiddos fend for themselves. I mean the selfishness that causes you to act out of character and ignore the nagging voice in your head. You know? That voice the tells you to cut it out before it even begins. I mean the type of selfishness that causes you to feel infallible, to entertain foolish conversations that normally didn't even register on your radar. This was the type of the selfishness that causes our "woe is me" list to triple, more than our gratefulness list. That kind of selfishness is scary and it can and will alter your life and those around you, if you don't pay attention.

Within my spurt of selfishness, came the reality of emotions. The emotions of confusion, heartbreak, let down, guilt, shame, discontent, pride and failure. The endless feelings of discomfort, uncertainty, fear of abandonment, anxiety, fear, nervousness, chaos, un-clarity, sorrow, and disappointment. The emotions also followed with a dose of feeling dumb, naïve, embarrassed, and numb. All these feelings and emotions came tumbling in at once.

I was a hot – hell – yep I said hell – I was a hot hell mess.

And when you feel a mess your mindset begins to waiver. Your foundation begins to expose the cracks. You begin to believe the lies your mean girl self tells you and if you don't catch it …that hot mess moment becomes a hot mess era. Luckily for me, God had another plan.

Almost as instant as the hot mess train rode into town, it peeled right out. Reconciliation, joy amongst the pain, retribution, healing, relief, belief and hope started to seep back in. Now don't get me wrong, there were still amends to make. There were some come to Jesus moments that had to be had with myself and with those my selfishness had impacted. But through it all, God's hand never left from me. And while it wasn't the worst of the worst, no sin is different right? Like God doesn't put it on a scale and say your cursing out weighs her stealing, so she's forgiven and you're not. No, God is not that type of God. So while there was repentance and forgiveness to be had, I knew there was a lesson for all this self-imposed mess. And above anything else, I held on strong to that fact that I am His daughter.

I am a daughter of the most High God. And God knew this very moment would come. And while I didn't know it at the time, He knew I would survive this and be even better on the other side.

I knew there was a message that I needed to grasp, learn from and thrive from and it came to me fairly quick. That message came pretty fast, as with me, God doesn't take too much time to teach. God doesn't let me get away with much for too long, without the lesson staring me smack dab in the face, like - ever. And for that I am now thankful!

See here's the root of it all, God used my self-imposed mess, lack of judgment and selfishness to show me that humility was fading from my countenance. I was checking in with Him for things I desired and wanted, but I wasn't CONNECTED to Him as my life source 24/7. When I felt lost, I didn't chase after Him with relentless pursuit.

"All of us like sheep have gone astray, each of us has turned to his own way" - Isaiah 53:6

I was too much in "I" and a dose of humility was needed to combat the sin of selfishness.

And then there was pride.

Pride where I thought pride didn't even exist.
Pride when I took not having so many life altering testimonies more than just a blessing but something to frown upon.
Pride that stirred up un-validated feelings of loneliness and discontent.
Pride of trying to appease those who had huge expectations of me in ways I really didn't feel called to fulfill.
Pride that wouldn't allow me to be ok with disappointing them while fulfilling my call.

That darn pride.

So with all this lesson learning, with all these come to Jesus moments, with all this "woe is me but shake it off anyway," God reminded me of this; He is not done with me. He reminded me that there was plenty to do and now, even in the midst of my mess, in the thick of the self-imposed mess, He would pull me out. He would bring me through because there was something bigger than me at stake. Remember, some of the most beautiful pieces of art were once called a mess. And it was my turn to seek out the beauty within my own life and leave the mess behind. There was beauty within the mess, and it was up to me to be obedient and execute it.

Retrospectively, one of the persons who was impacted deeply and the most by my selfishness was my hubby. And while, I too had to ask for forgiveness, compassion and love from him, in my perfectly imperfect mess; he too knew that something bigger than us was brewing. During the healing process for me, my hubby mentioned that something big was coming from this – God was using this as a stepping stone to something great and we better get ready. And boom! Just like that I heard these words : "Write it".

"Write what?" A letter? To whom?"

And I promise you I heard – " No dummy, not a letter. Write another book but this time bring other ladies aboard. Help them tell their stories:"

"Oh that…. Yeah, Lord, I'm still going through this mess here remember? So I'll do it when I'm better…"

"Nope. Now."

Those words, those thoughts seemed odd to me. The timing was all wrong. All I wanted to do was wallow in self pity. To wallow in a slow healing process, to wallow in the doing nothing for a little bit. And so I pushed the command, the idea; to the back of my mind.

But then entered my good friend : insomnia.

I literally could not sleep because every vision was a vision of a book. A vision of a book showcased on a website, an image of a faceless woman on the back cover. Even scarier, the faces of some of the women I knew personally, on the back cover. And as God worked on me to put my life back in order with a better and deeper connection to Him, the images still kept coming. That small voice in my head still kept talking, and that movie kept playing in my head every night for about 2 weeks.

Finally – like this moment here, in an almost coercive manner – begrudgingly, I started to do the research. I started to call around to publishers. I started to opt in for quotes and prices, for how to's, for details on how this would all work. And no one responded in a timely fashion except one. The one publisher I already had a working relationship with was ready! Like they wanted the manuscript the very next day. And so with that, it began. With that - I surrendered and said "yes".

With caution, because truthfully, I didn't know how I would be received; I began to reach out to the faces I saw in my dreams and they began to reply back with their "Yes". I was in such awe on how God was instantly at work for this book collaboration.

The women who were in agreement to be co-authors, were from all walks of life, from all parts of the world, strangers even. They began to instantly confide in me on how this was perfect timing. They shared how they knew their story needed to get out but like me, kept putting it off time and time again. They began to share what ignited in me as hope – they began to share with what was magnified for me as obedience and I knew without a shadow of a doubt – this was the blessing - the beauty in my mess.

The stories you are about to read are real life. They are gut wrenching, heart tugging, emotional barring, of your soul, type stories. But beyond the word story – this is real life. These women have been bold and courageous as they step out in faith and share a piece of themselves on pen and paper. And even greater, With You.

Cry with them, laugh with them, grow with them, learn from them, be inspired by them. Know that you too have a story worth telling. You too are worthy of a 2nd, 3rd + chance. – That you are no different than me. You are no different than any of these ladies represented here and God can and will use your mess. He can turn it into something of beauty. He will show you the beauty of it all, should you choose to be obedient and allow Him to do so.

Sometimes we endure things for our own lessons, but even more so, for the lessons others need to get by hearing and seeing our stories. When we go through our junk, our mess, we tend to think – "oops. Now that discredits me, I can't do this, I can't do that, who will listen to me? Who am I to teach?", and so on and so on. But it truly isn't the case.

Once you are privy to the lesson learned, once you truly take heed to change your life, to repent, become anew and transform; God begins to use it for His glory: instantly. There's no holding period for God to use you. Sorry. There aren't any rules in the playbook of life that state one must wait 60 days after her mess – then and only then can God use her. It's just not there. Sure, there are consequences and reactions to every action. Of course, we have to be accountable for our wrongdoings, but our wrong doings don't count us out. If God can use Peter, if God can use Saul/Paul, and so many others – He can use us. He can use you.

The emotions and feelings that derive in our mess aren't to paralyze us from overcoming. They are there to help us actually choose to get through to the other side, to fight, to feel something different and to experience life in a better way. God can use our shame, our guilt, our disobedience for His will – not to shove it in our faces but to truly make us better people.

My failures don't define me.

Your failures don't define you. They make us braver, stronger, and wiser. We can embrace the fact that victory is on the other side; when we choose to be transformed.

May our stories give you hope of a brighter tomorrow and ignite in you the fire you need to pull through. May they remind you that you are not alone. If we can survive – you can too. And know that you are loved. As one of our writers so termed it – The Beauty in My Mess is simply "Our stories for His glory".

Welcome to my obedience project.
Welcome to our beautiful mess.

Enjoy the blessing,
Nicole Long

"Amazing grace! How sweet the sound
That saved a wretch like me!
I once was lost but now am found,
Was blind but now I see."
– John Newton, Amazing Grace

I Once Was Blind
Shawna Cook

"I have been unfaithful to you for at least 10 years. I don't know how many women or how many times..."

My husband, the person I trusted more than anyone else in the world, may has well punched me in the stomach with those words. His confession came early one morning, after I found his car in a hotel parking lot. He didn't come home the night before, explaining that a night out with his friends left him drunk and unable to drive.

He brought in his 38th birthday celebrating with friends, bachelor style. He had been planning an 'all guy' night out for about a month. Before leaving he gave the disclaimer that he planned on drinking and that he may not come home depending on his intoxication level. He made plans with me that he would stay at one of our close friend's house if that happened. I wasn't too concerned because I trusted him. I mean, I have had the occasional girls night out with my friends and he never protested. Admittedly, my girls' nights have never left me out ALL night. But, I also get the danger in drinking and driving, so even though I wasn't happy about the possibility of him not coming home I understood, kind of.

That night I couldn't sleep. I was anxious and uneasy. My energy was elevated and I could not rest. I tossed and turned. I checked my husband's location through a phone sharing app. Relief swept over me when I saw he was at the nightclub he told me he and his friends were going to. I dosed off for a few hours of restless sleep but I woke up, jittery and on edge. Even though I felt guilty, I suspiciously checked his phone location again. It showed he was at our friend's house where he said he would be if he didn't come home. Great! He was right where he said he would be. I was worried for nothing. I tried unsuccessfully to go back to sleep. At 3am I checked his location again. This time it showed a different area. In fact, it was a place he was at just the night before meeting "friends" who were visiting from out of town.

I wondered what he was doing all the way over there. If he could make it there surely he could have made it home. Questions ran through my mind. I needed to know more. I decided to check his Facebook account. There I found an inbox message from him to a woman I didn't know. It said he was downstairs and wanted to know if she was ready for him to come up. Chills ran through my whole body.

This can't be.

He promised after the first time he would never cheat again. Unsure of my final destination I got in my car and drove where my phone directed me. I wanted to believe that I was driving to another friend's house where the party continued, or maybe, possibly the guys all went to an early morning breakfast. All the stories I made up in my mind were doubtful, but I was holding on to hope or maybe I was choosing naiveté. Whatever I was holding onto was released when I pulled into a hotel parking lot.

So many thoughts and emotions surged through my body. My heart raced. My body went cold. What do I do now? Do I sit by his car until he comes out? Do I find out what room they are in and knock? Do I bust the windows out his car or slash his tires? I didn't do any of those things. I was in shock. There had to be a logical explanation that I just didn't yet know. Why else would my husband have that Facebook message and why in the world would his car be at a hotel overnight? I drove off in a state of complete confusion and I tried to rationalize a valid excuse.

Even though I didn't know where I was headed I ended up at a nearby beach. I sat and watched the waves and wondered. I made up stories in my mind to explain away the obvious. I prayed.

2

After awhile I decided to reach out to him. I sent a simple "good morning" text. No response. Next I called. No answer. I called again and again. With every unanswered call rage began to replace confusion. But, I still didn't know what to do.

I drove back home in a daze. He was already home when I pulled up. As he stumbled out of his car, inebriated, I demanded to know where he spent the night. He kept saying at his friend's house. After a few times of telling the same story, I told him that besides being husband and wife, we had always prided ourselves on being best friends and that the least he could do was be honest with me. He said if he told me everything it would break my heart. In reality my heart was already broken. I raised my phone and showed him the Facebook message. I also revealed where I found his car. I was ready for his confession, or so I thought. I had no idea where it would lead but I wanted him to reveal the truth. That is when he confessed to the multiple affairs and life as I knew it changed forever. I didn't know it then, but on that day God opened my eyes to much more than the knowledge of my husband's cheating habit.

I didn't know who I was or where I was going. My past didn't make sense. My future felt unsure and unsteady. In that moment I could not imagine anything good coming out of something so dark and ugly. I was numb and broken-hearted yet, even then, God was weaving together the pieces of my life that had been torn apart.

It felt as if God abruptly pressed the pause button on my life and started me in a new direction. I now know that was just a feeling. God has always known what I did not see. This tragedy was the opening for something more beautiful than I could imagine at the time.

Not long after the confession my husband was diagnosed as a sex addict. This was a shock to both of us. The diagnosis forced him to confront deep pain within that had been buried for years. There would be a difficult and long road ahead toward the path of healing and behavior modification. His choice to change could not be about saving his marriage, our marriage was no guarantee. He had to make a decision to change for himself.

Even though many people are not aware of sexual addiction, or believe that it is real, it has the same ramifications of other well know addictions, like alcoholism or drug addiction. Sex addiction is about so much more than desiring sex. A person with a sex addiction seeks to numb painful emotions, past trauma, stressful situations and anxiety. Most people engage in sex to feel good, a person with a sex addiction engages in sex to feel less. People who are living with a sex addiction, like my husband, often live double lives.

The part of my husband's life that was on display aligned with who he wanted to be; husband, father, good employee, involved church and community member. But there was also another part that he tried to compartmentalize and control. The problem with addictions is that you can't control them. They slowly grow out of the box you try to contain them in and there is no turning back unless you address the very real, deep problems at the root. Even when that is finally done a person must still take the necessary steps toward lasting change.

The admission about his years of unfaithfulness was enough for me to disconnect and choose not to take the journey of recovery or reconciliation with him. I was so hurt by his actions that I did not entertain the idea of having compassion for what he was going through. I was ready to leave my marriage behind because the pain of staying in it was too much to bear. I decided I would rather be single and divorced than humiliated and cheated on. Even though my mind was made up that my marriage was over, God had other plans. He convinced me that this marriage was not over and that I was supposed to stay and work things out with my husband.

Although I knew I was hearing from God I was more comfortable with being defiant. I was more comfortable in saying no to his request to stay in our marriage. How could I? I could not rationalize the idea of being married to someone who hurt me by violating what I considered the number one rule in marriage. In my mind I could have taken anything else but unfaithfulness. It took me a long time to believe that my husband was suffering with a sickness and not just a desire to be promiscuous. I was defensive and knew that everyone who heard my story would understand why I chose to leave, but I didn't think anyone would understand why I chose to stay.

One particular Sunday in church my pastor said that if we do not do what we are called to do someone's soul could be at risk. I understood that. I knew there is something valuable about being obedient to God. Our life journey is not just about us. Every decision we make has an effect on someone else in some way. I looked around at the sea of faces belonging to people I knew and loved and wondered who's life would be impacted by my obedience to God. I wondered who needed to know that even when in tremendous pain God would never leave them and that His love was more than enough to get them through any difficulty. As I looked around in wonder I suddenly jumped back, startled. My husband's face appeared right in front of me. The intriguing part is that he was not in church that day.

God showed me in that moment that my husband was hurting. Yes, he was struggling with the fact that he was losing his marriage and that his family dynamics were about to change, but his pain was about something more. God allowed me a glimpse at my husband's heart. He was being tormented by something much greater. My heart broke for him. I cried for him. In that moment I also understood the reality that not only was my husband spiritually on unstable ground but that whatever we did going forward would hugely impact the lives of our three children and future generations.

Saying yes to God, even with hesitation, opened my eyes to a spiritual reality that I had been taught but never truly understood until I was in this place. Through this experience God showed me what true love is. God sent his only son to die for my sins. God knew that I would hurt him with my choices. He knew there would be days that I would turn my back on him but he loved me anyway.

God has called me to love like he loves. I have learned through this experience that love is not a feeling; it is an action. Love is enduring. It is sacrificial. It is forgiving. Which are all things people don't want to deal with in relationships. But love also protects, hopes and perseveres. Love never fails. It can be challenging to be on the side of giving love especially when we can justify why someone may not deserve it. Yet it is such a beautiful thing to be on the side of receiving love.

I realized that I am on the side of receiving unconditional love every day, especially when I don't deserve it. God loves me even though I do many things that do not honor him. He loves me when my behavior goes against the commitment that I made to him and when I don't act the way that he wants me to. When I look at God's standard of love and I look at the love I had for my husband it adjusted my thinking. The love I had for my husband was a comfortable love; it was conditional and even selfish. I loved him when he did things for me, when he was the husband that I wanted him to be, but what happened when I saw the flaws in him? What happened when I saw that his actions were brought on my a deep-seated pain that I knew nothing about? Where was my love then?

As I thought about this I also realized that the love I had for God was conditional too. I loved God when he answered my prayers the way I wanted them answered. I loved God when I was healthy and when I had money in the bank. I loved God when I got the house, car and job I wanted. But what did I think about God when things weren't going my way?

I have been asked did I stay in my marriage because of a lack of self-love. The answer is no. It is actually the exact opposite. I stayed in my marriage because I finally understood real love. I am able to love my husband because of God's abundant love for me. I learned that a person cannot give what they don't have. Once I accepted God's love for me fully I realized that I have the capacity to do the same for others, starting with the person closest to me. And that is God's greatest command, love your neighbor as yourself.

When I opened myself up to what God was teaching me about my view of love something happened. He opened my eyes to see that marriage is not only one of the greatest joys in life, but if we allow it, it can be a sacred place of great growth and transformation. Marriage is a place where we are exposed to the best and the worst that our spouses have to offer. Our masks come off and we see those things we think we can hide from the rest of the world. In some marriages it may be a short time before this reality takes place or like in my marriage the full exposure can take years.

God gave me the ability to exemplify his love, mercy, grace and forgiveness in my marriage. I thought when I said yes to God about staying in my marriage that my husband was the one who would benefit from the sacrifices that I was making. What I discovered was that God's plan included healing and growth for both of us.

I learned that I am deeply loved and valued. I realized that I had a voice and a purpose to fulfill in the world for God's glory. Before this happened I put the thoughts and opinions of others before God. Prior to this divine intervention I was scared to truly be me. Through this process all of that changed. I found freedom. I learned to be comfortable and confident being the woman God called me to be. I began to see one role I filled was wife and another role I filled was mother but that I was complete and whole before, and without those titles. God opened my eyes to see me.

This experience showed me that I was not the only one in our marriage who was hurting. Finding my husband's car in the hotel parking lot early that morning was an answer to prayer; not my prayer, but his. My husband was living with disappointments and let downs that occurred in his life long before I married him. He learned to build a protective wall around his heart that no one could penetrate, not even his wife. However, when things erupted he had no choice but to deal with the consequences of his actions.

As my husband attempted to come to terms with what his choices had done to me and what it could do to our family he looked to God. He finally surrendered, understanding that he could not get better on his own.

Being obedient to God allowed me the privilege of watching the broken pieces of his life come together. I was able to see him grow into a man who is honest and vulnerable. I could see his strength in his weakness. He learned to share his struggles with me knowing that he is not being judged for what he had done in the past or for what he struggles with in the present. He is able to confide in me confidently because he realizes that my love is not based on who I need to him to be, but it is based on who he is, flaws included.

That was big for him but also for me. Being able to see my husband like this opened my eyes to the way I saw others. People are hurting and living lives covered in the darkness of shame. Shame keeps us trapped. It causes us to spin out of control and get caught up in ugly, bad habits and behaviors that we don't like. It allows us to live in a way we don't like because we don't believe we are worth anything more. Experiencing God's love calls us out of the darkness and into the light.

Through this process God ignited the desire in me to pray for our marriage and the marriages of others. The Bible says two are better than one. Marriage is one of the most powerful forces in the world, yet marriages break up every day. My marriage tragedy opened the door of opportunity and gave me the privilege and desire to pray with other wives. I have witnessed marriages change drastically as women turn their lives, their husbands and their marriages over to God daily. I have seen shame and hurt disappear as love is released and activated. I have seen men and women mature in their roles as husbands and wives. More importantly I have seen what surrendering to God looks like up close and personal. It is a beautiful, life changing transition. Learning to love the way God tells us to love changes everything. Loving others starts with accepting God's love, loving ourselves as God's beloved children and then sharing that same love with someone else.

The saying is true, what is done in the dark will come to light. Darkness and light cannot co-exist. Light will always drown out the darkness. I was living in the dark for a long time. I could not see. Once my husband's secrets were confessed; anger, bitterness and not wanting to forgive could have ruled my life, but Jesus' light opened my eyes to something much bigger. Yes, the truth hurt, but that hurt gave way to necessary healing. I once was blind. Blind to who my husband was and blind to who I was. I was blind to what real love looked like and felt like. I was blind to the possibility of something beautiful coming from something ugly, but God opened my eyes and now I see.

"Forgiveness is not always easy… and yet, there is no peace without it".
–Marianne Williamson

Dare to Dream
Cristin Germaine

My journey began on a cold and icy February morning; I was born the third of four children to my parents who lived on Long Island. My father left my mom for another woman and when my oldest brother was 10, my second oldest brother was 7, I was 3 and my youngest brother was 1 ½, they decided to divorce.

After my parents' divorce my mom moved us to upstate New York where we started living with my step-father. In true God fashion He was already working out the story that would become my testimony and as I love to say, "My story for HIS glory!"

While attending Vacation Bible School at age five, I asked Jesus to come live in my heart. I'd love to tell you once I made that decision it was a walk in the park but that was only the beginning of some very challenging years ahead, as you see what was happening at home was my step-father was sexually abusing me. Looking back now, as a child, I had no idea it was sexual abuse.

Although my home life had its challenges, my faith stayed strong. I felt like God was the one person who stuck by my side and felt Him very close through those traumatic years. Shortly after moving upstate, my brothers and I were sponsored to go to a local Christian school. I loved it, my teachers and friends were my safe haven away from my dysfunctional home life. I was popular in high school, was very athletic and excelled in soccer and volleyball. In fact, I won the Miss Athlete trophy in twelfth grade. Through my years of attending Christian school, people had no idea what was really going on at home, in fact none of my brothers were even aware. Once it was discovered I was being sexually abused, the Pastor running the school took me to his home where I was met by and questioned by social workers. My step-father went to jail for a period of time but not too long went by before he was back in our home.

Years went on and I remember many nights where I would cry out to God because I felt so alone and neglected, yet I would find comfort through Christian music and I'd put all of my efforts into singing solos at church and in High School, music was healing to my aching soul and spoke peace to my heart.

After graduating from High School I attended Lancaster Bible College to pursue an Associate's Degree in Secretarial Studies and Bible. I LOVED my college days and the new life I found away from the dysfunction of my family. I could FINALLY be me without life weighing me down. I became Miss Popularity and would strive to know every person I came in contact with.

My freshman year I shared a dorm room with a girl who was enrolled in the counseling program. Through a conversation one night I learned what I had gone through as a child could have some traumatic effects and I couldn't push it away and under the surface. I needed to deal with the divorce and sexual abuse head on. That night my roommate said, "Cristin, you know it's not normal to tell people, 'my parents are divorced and my step-father sexually abused me,' and in the next sentence say, "And how are you?" That night started me on the path of dealing with these traumatic events in my childhood.

The day I walked down the aisle to graduate from College was a proud moment for me, as I felt like I had conquered a monumental task for the first time in my life. I left home- ready for new adventures and moved to Pennsylvania.

Shortly after I moved to the area, with only interviews lined up, I landed my very first professional job! I started attending a fantastic church, met new friends, and LOVED this new found freedom! Life was good and I LOVED living in Pennsylvania.

Like most single girls in their twenties, I prayed that God would bring the man He would have for me. It felt like it would never happen. My patience was thin. But God knew best. Shortly after my move, I kept running into a VERY handsome guy in the parking lot. It was fun to wonder when I would see him next.

One day I was in the local grocery store and I saw him down the way in my same aisle, my heart was beating so fast and I remember battling with myself, feeling quite inadequate, as my mind was saying, "Should I talk to him, should I not talk to him?" As he approached me I blurted out, "I think you're my neighbor." That was all the encouragement he needed and the two of us stood in the grocery store talking for the next 3 hours.

That day I knew my life would never be the same, one thing led to another, we started dating and fell in love. He was the man of my dreams, handsome with a good work ethic, genuinely cared for me and my welfare, was financially sound and went to church. I would describe our wedding day as one of the best days of my life! It was a beautiful autumn day surrounded by our families and friends, the venue was spectacular - we had planned the perfect event.

A year into our marriage we learned that my youngest brother who had been diagnosed with cancer in his foot years earlier as a teenage, was now battling the same type of cancer, this time however, it came back with a vengeance in his lungs. Those were hard times. To see my brother go through this battle again, definitely took a toll on my family and our marriage; and unfortunately my younger brother lost his battle with cancer at the age 27 on November 19, 2001.

I'll never forget being there with my brother in his room when he took his last breath. That was a time in my life where I started to question everything I had believed in, I questioned God, Heaven, Hell, and is also when I learned that most of what concerns us in this life doesn't even matter, it's the people and relationships that matter most. It was challenging to face my younger brother's death and even now all these years later not a day goes by that I don't think about him.

Right around the time I was dealing with the death of my brother, things in my once hopeful marriage started to fall apart. My husband took into an addiction called pornography. He would tell me that I was the cause of our issues, that I pushed his buttons and that I was the reason he looked at pornography. He would lose his temper too. I tried counseling for myself, as I wanted to learn how NOT to be a trigger to his temper and addiction. - but it didn't seem to help. so I thought OK I'll go to counseling, there I learned how to deal with my reactions, but didn't seem to help with his. Once my husband got involved with pornography it was a downward slope in our relationship.

The first time he beat me up I tried to leave, but he said he was sorry and cried about what he had done so I thought to myself, I didn't keep my mouth shut so I deserved it... I.deserved.it. He didn't hit me often but another time while I was pregnant with our son, we got into an argument in our bedroom, he ended up taking a pillow off of our bed and whacked me so hard that I fell to the ground. It was at that point I realized how dangerous he was to hit a pregnant woman.

Once our son was born I thought things would change for the better but the first day we came home from the hospital he ended up taking him and telling me I was an unfit Mother and threatened to keep our son away from me.

Let's fast forward 3 years, I slowly opened up to the handful of trusted friends who would speak into my life, pray for me and tell me I didn't deserve this treatment. I remember not feeling strong enough because I could not imagine leaving my cozy 3 bedroom home. Besides at this point in my life I was working full time at a church and being a faithful Christian with strong beliefs I had the mindset that you should never get divorced when you vowed for life to be with this person. Being a product of a divorced family - it was my heart's desire to stay married and not repeat the past.

Friends would tell me you'll know when you've had enough, that day came one morning as I was home with our son. We would alter our schedules and exchange our son in my employer's parking lot so that we didn't have to put him in daycare and since both of our families lived in New York it was the best option. He would work the morning shift at his job, I'd work the afternoon shift at mine.

At home this particular morning I needed information printed from our computer. I plugged the printer into our laptop and without pressing print it started up. I thought, "Hmmm, that's odd," until a paper, dated a few days earlier popped out with a picture of a nude woman. I remember sitting in my living room feeling disheartened because he would reassure me that he wasn't looking at pornography and yet each year I'd find it even when I wasn't particularly looking and now here we were 8 years later.

I drove to work thinking, "OK Cristin, how are you going to react?" I pulled up to my employer, my husband got into the driver's side of my vehicle while our son was in his car seat in the back. I stood on the passenger side with the door open and said, "I found some things I needed on the computer today," I proceeded to lift up the piece of paper with the nude woman and continued, "Out popped this." He grabbed the picture from me and I said, "You know I'm not mad or angry, I feel very hurt and upset."

I looked at my husband and he said, "I don't know where that picture came from, it must've come from the other computer." I knew at that moment he looked me straight in the eyes and lied as the "other computer" was not hooked up to the internet. I simply said, "OK." In my mind I then thought, "Holy Spirit, you have to convict this man because I cannot convict him of his sin, only You can."

I knew that day nothing would change unless I changed it and so that March afternoon I started planning my secret getaway.

I would make lists in my head of what I needed, opened up to friends and coworkers telling them my exit plan, all in secret. I was advised that in an event such as this, a man with a hot temper will absolutely lose it, so I planned with exact movements and strategies to leave. It amazed me how people would go above and beyond to help me. Friends opened up their home to me. My parents traveled from NY and took my son camping and I even had a car dealership that helped me switched my vehicle so that my husband wouldn't know where we were.

That September morning I left my husband. It was the scariest day of my life, although, it was only the beginning of more battles and horrible situations. From an emergency custody situation in business court, to my husband receiving supervised visits, to splitting up our assets in a very messy divorce, to learning he had been having an affair for most of our marriage. Since I had filed for divorce I had also been kicked out of the ministries I had been leading and involved with at my church. That hurt.

My life was literally at the lowest point it had ever been, but there was peace, peace in our one bedroom apartment and although I had to completely start over, I felt God's presence in the midst of my pain. I was determined to trust the Lord through this time and my favorite Bible verses would often come to mind, Proverbs 3:5-6, "Trust in the Lord with all your heart and lean not on your own understanding in all your ways acknowledge Him and He will direct your paths."

After my divorce, my son and I moved into a new home in a beautiful neighborhood. We ended up landing at a local church, and for the first time I walked in it felt like I had come home, it was refreshing and the people were very welcoming.

One Wednesday night during a business meeting, the Pastor started talking about the business at hand then proceeded to talk about single Moms and statistics. As I was sitting in the back row that night, it was like a light beam came down from heaven and I heard the Lord say, "Cristin this is your ministry - for Single Moms." I started to cry in the business meeting that night because I couldn't believe God would give me a purpose through all the pain and abuse I had just lived through and although I had no idea what that meant I trusted the Lord to show me.

The next day I wrote to the Pastor and his wife and said, "You talked about single Moms last night and I would like to help in whatever way you need." They replied, "Cristin we've been praying and we were going to approach you about leading a single Moms group."

My heart leaped that day

In 2012, we started planning a ministry for single Moms called H.O.P.E. which stands for Helping Out Providing Encouragement. We officially started meeting in February 2013 with 2-3 single Moms and now years later we have grown to dozens of single moms attending H.O.P.E.! In fact, in January and February of 2018 we expanded H.O.P.E. into two other local churches, one being in Lancaster City, the other in Stevens, Pennsylvania!

A year after H.O.P.E. was established I attended an event called Dare to Dream Single Moms' Day Out up North. I was standing in the back of the auditorium that day looking around, amazed, as there had to be at least 400 single Moms in attendance. As I'm watching the speaker I hear the Lord say to me, "Cristin, I want you to do this type of conference in Lancaster." When the Lord spoke to me that day it literally changed the course of my life forever!

The next two years, from 2014 to 2016, I planned and strategized. On July 8, 2016 the very first Lancaster Dare to Dream Single Moms' Day Out event was held at Lancaster Bible College hosting 90 single Moms, 70 children and close to 100 volunteers! This was a free event for the Single Moms so I was raising funds and my goal that first year was $10,000! When all was said and done that year we ended up raising over $11,000!

As part of this event we gave the Moms four Diva Dollars to spend at our Diva Shop where we had collected new or gently used items like purses, jewelry, scarves, and various other items. Every Mom who attended also received a gift basket or gift certificate to retailers like restaurants, stores and auto mechanics. Finally each attendee left that day with a gift bag full of personal care items like razors, soap, shampoo, nail polish, lotions, etc.

That day, as I stood to tell my life story, it was very emotional to see the vision I had received from the Lord two years earlier come to life! THEN to realize after the event, how God had used the mess of my life to touch other single moms was literally life changing!!

The next year in 2017 we hosted this free event again, this time 125 single Moms, 125 children and numerous volunteers attended. We had changed locations this time to Calvary Church in Lancaster, the event was kicked up a notch and was another HUGE success!

I'm now well on my way to organizing and planning the third annual event for single Moms in Lancaster County. My hope is to one day establish a nonprofit ministry focused on single moms helping them to Dare to DREAM!!

Never in my life did I think I'd see the beauty in my mess, but I am loving every day of my life and living the dream I had way back as a teenager. Did I imagine it as a single mom? Not so much, but God has been faithful, I'm excited about the future and I want to use every last bit of my story for HIS GLORY!!!

"We gain strength, and courage, and confidence by each experience in which we really stop to look fear in the face...we must do that which we think we cannot."
–Eleanor Roosevelt

#FaithHappens
Janis Melillo

I know that faith happens in ways we perhaps never expected. Without having my faith and spirituality to move forward, I would really be in quicksand. There have been underlying and undermining events in my life which have shaped the fiber of my being to the core. Here's a fragment of mine in my open letter to my baby sister Jan Jan

----

My Dearest Sister;

You may have taken away my title as the "baby" and as I sit here writing this letter to you for all who may read this, I laugh a little bit. You were my baby sister, this bundle of fluff who came home one afternoon and stole my thunder. Even though you did so, you were my baby sister, someone whom I grew to love, cherish and protect as I was the older sister. I sometimes watched you sleep and wondered what you would be when you grew up. Yes, as young as I was then, I wondered.

Your crinkled nose made this funny snort and whenever there was a peep coming from your crib, we all gathered around to see what you were up to. The "baby newness" eventually wore off but I always remember running toward your crib, especially when you learned how to climb out of it! As little as you were, you were strong and invincible and had such a zest for adventure.

As you may recall, we had an amazing childhood, such great memories! Do you remember Christmas time and how Mommy would dress us up both the same; the murals you drew in back of the couch with your crayons, your first cooking expedition - eggs, not de-shelled and limes - you created the biggest kitchen mess I have ever seen in our house on Elizabeth Street in Hartford,

Connecticut? Do you also remember all of the great times growing up in Cromwell? From weeding in that darn huge garden Mommy and Daddy had in the lot by their house and the little garden by the pool. How about all of our summer shenanigans, the great family picnics, swimming in the pool at night, baking and cooking, me learning how to cook some things with you to you growing the biggest pumpkin I have ever seen - the vines of it stretched across the driveway - I think you must have planted the whole package of pumpkin seeds!

You were funny, creative and such an amazing cook and at some point, not sure when or how, you once jokingly bestowed upon me the rank of "baby" of the family. I guess I was the more quiet and shy sibling and you said that I needed someone to watch or be a guide over me. We laughed as you pointed out how I just needed that reassurance or gentle push from others to move forward. You were the bull and I was well not the bull.

You were the lion and took no prisoners. I was the sheep who wanted to still protect you. As you grew older, as we all do at certain points in our lives, you made some hard decisions and hard choices that shaped you forever. You never gave yourself enough credit for the sacrifices you made and hid certain truths that eventually tore your heart apart and I believe to some extent, your soul as well.

I feel as though I have been mourning your loss for years now, and why is that? You are still here on this earth, a viable part of humanity, Daddy's youngest daughter, a Mom to your son and birth Mom to an amazing young woman who is happily in our lives. It's unfortunate that your son and birth daughter have not met yet and I pray that they do someday soon.

I pray for you and have faith that this will happen. You have to have faith, resolve and love for yourself. No one can do this but you.

Where did it all go wrong; why are you so mad - so mad that you cut not only me but other people out of your life? For whatever wrongs you think I may have done, I am truly sorry. I understand being mad or angry with someone but to just cut off your relationship with me, yes I am still devastated and despite the fact that I know you don't understand or recognize your part of what you did, I still pray and have faith in you. Faith and hope that the bull in you will know when to put the horns aside.

Do you know Daddy asked me a couple of months ago if I hated you? He said he wanted to know before he passes; as he sensed you hated me. For me as a daughter to hear our Daddy ask me this question, I can only think of what venomous hatred you must have in your heart toward me - I don't hate you and I told Daddy that too. Yes it pained me to know that our Dad felt he had to ask me, as I guess you were relaying to him how much you hated me.

I don't hate you.

I have faith and pray for you each day. I have faith that you will reach a point in your life will you will love yourself enough to move past the anger and resentment you may feel toward yourself and others. It literally is killing you; emotionally and physically, it is - I know you are not taking care of yourself and have medical issues that can be dealt with that is if you only dealt with them.

I am not perfect; you are not perfect; we are children of God and Baby, God loves us all. Be gentle and kind to yourself, love and respect where you have been, acknowledge your fears, be mad at the world if you must but know that in the end it is only you that can move you forward in life.

I forgive you, even if you do not forgive me. I have faith and pray that the love that is in your heart reaches your soul. You deserve happiness. You deserve to have a happy and healthy life. You deserve to love and to be loved.

That my sister dear is why I have faith and pray for you that you see the light and love of others, especially from your family and God. He is watching, He knows. Allow the ebb and flow of all of that light and love to bring you comfort.

Love, JanJan, your older sister

"To love means loving the unlovable. To forgive means pardoning the unpardonable. Faith means believing the unbelievable. Hope means hoping when everything seems hopeless." - G.K. Chesterton

Writing this letter to my younger sister, at first in the past tense, was a very difficult task for me to do. It felt as though I have been mourning her physical loss. I prayed for the hope, love and guidance that our Heavenly Father could only bring. By doing so, it is with the most heartfelt intention that others are inspired to do the same and take action in their own lives; to reach out to a loved one, no matter how hard, no matter if we lack the understanding of such a surmountable undertaking.

With any type of loss, in this case for me was a mourning process. Anger, sadness, frustration to name a few. I cannot change the past but I can somewhat direct my future. Only God knows what will happen. I know that he will reach out to her with love, guidance and understanding. I hope she will be brave enough to feel and embrace the gravity and shift the weight and burdens she is feeling.

I feel somewhat vulnerable as I expose a raw and very real emotional event in my life. I do this with all due humility and respect. I feel this is my only outlet to reach her and it is also my hope that by doing so that my story may inspire someone to reach out to someone they know and take action in their own lives.

I say my prayers as I always do. I pray for the guidance and strength to continue to move mountains. God has me on assignment and sends me tasks some days I don't know how to keep up. I hear a message, I close my eyes and breath. If God can move mountains, he has enough faith to guide me to do the same.

How do I know this to be true? Simply because #FaithHappens

"Giving birth and being born brings us into the essence of creation, where the human spirit is courageous and bold and the body, a miracle of wisdom."
– Harriette Hartigan

When Plans change and List Fail
Tae McKinney

I never cried so much in my life. I was devastated. I was at a loss. There was nothing else I could do but watch as my fight to be a mom was stripped from me…

You see I am a control freak. I like to be in control and I have set up my life in such a way that everything is planned out to the tee. I create list. I revise the list. I schedule my day by each hour and set itineraries that are supposed to be followed. That was me. Everything existed perfectly in my head and I was sure that though life has its twist and turns I had a plan to counteract all of that. And if life altered the direct plan I had construed… there was always plan b and plan c. And yes I had those accurately lined out too.

You see I was set to have a scheduled c section on June 27th, the day the new transformer movie came out. I was going to meet my son on that day. I had thrown out the idea of naming my future son Optimus Prime since before I could remember but I just couldn't get the hubby to agree. I mean how perfect it would be for my future son to stand up in his kindergarten class and announce, "Hello. I AM OPTIMUS PRIME!" But since we couldn't settle on the name (I mean the whole family was against it) the movie premiere day would just have to suffice.

I remember the day perfectly clear I had scheduled one of my friends to help me come and organize the kitchen. I wanted to be in tip top shape for the impending arrival of my baby boy. She cleaned and organized as I sat on the couch directing and such. Pregnancy for me hadn't been easy and my sciatic nerve was sending shooting pains up my back and all I could do was write a list of things I wanted help on. I know. I know -- again with the list.

The day was going perfectly. All the old pots and pans had been removed. The cabinets rearranged and the floors mopped. I waved goodbye to my friend from the front door and made plans to see her again on Friday. Shutting the door, I ran through my day. Laundry completed. Dishes done. Cabinets Done. I sat my tired pregnant self on the couch and called the hubby. I ran through the list of things I needed him to pick up for the house. TUMS being the priority as the heartburn I was having was ruining my entire day. Oh the joys of pregnancy!

After a detailed conversation with him, I was certain that my husband loved me but was thoroughly annoyed. Hanging up the phone, in my mind I ran through my next set of lists: prep dinner, take a nap, but first things first; I had to pee. I shuffled to the bathroom and went to pee but something was off. I looked into the toilet and my heart jumped. In my head, I ran through all the books I had read, the articles, the baby app. And then I went to everyone's favorite friend -- Google! I pulled out my phone and Google sent me straight to the insanity that is WEB MD. Because let's be honest who doesn't immediately WEB MD everything. All signs... roads... and mom blogs pointed to my Mucus PLUG! I will spare the descriptive details here.

The internet proved that it had to be my mucus plug. But that wasn't right was it? It was a little too soon right?! I talked myself down out of the panic, tore myself away from the bottomless hole of WebMD and I immediately called my doctor. She calmly asked me to go in to Labor and Delivery and get myself checked out. As I paced from my room, to the kitchen, to the living room, I looked on the kitchen island and saw the chicken I was about to cook. A deep sigh escaped from my lips as I grabbed my keys and headed out the door. Plans averted.

Heartburn still leaving a fire hole in my chest I drove to the hospital which was less than three minutes from my house. Thankful for a short drive I valet parked the car. I was completely shocked at the valet amenities and then remembered that I had yet to have the hospital tour so I had no clue where I was going. I had scheduled my appointment for the next Monday. It was scheduled.

This - was - not.

The valet man gave me directions and even let me know where the gift shop was. I immediately set up a plan B in my head. I would walk to the gift shop to see if they had tums first then I would head to labor and delivery; and by the time I made it back home the chicken would be defrosted. I would cook. My heartburn would be gone and I could enjoy the chicken pasta that I had my mouth all set on. Plans!

I walked quite a ways down the hall of the hospital until I realized it was way too far. And something in my head just kept screaming turn around. Go back. It was like my head was screaming go to Labor and Delivery and my heart was screaming you are on fire! Go get something… ANYTHING for this vicious heartburn! It was the warring emotion s of a hormonal pregnant girl; and I didn't know who would win. Ultimately, it was tired who came and saved the day. I had walked too far and was too tired to continue my search for the gift shop so I turned around and headed to Labor and Delivery.

I reached the elevator, dragged my tired belly inside and pressed the button for floor number 4. Immediately, as I the doors closed a loud splash filled the elevator. I looked down at my feet and saw the puddle of water. I did not have to WebMD this. Nope it was perfectly clear that my water broke and my baby was on his way. Almost 6 weeks early.

The elevator door opened and the nurse looked at me. Looked at the floor and immediately grabbed a wheelchair to get me checked… Nurses rushed around me. Paperwork was shoved in my face. Test where done. Monitors were set up. Husbands were called. (Well only one husband but you get the idea). Everything was happening at once. My parents arrived. My doctor came in. I was prepped for surgery. I was given a shot or multiple shots. Time flew by and epidurals were administered. I was in and out of it at this time. And the next words I remember were… "Excuse me?

Is there supposed to be that much blood on the floor?" I heard my husband ask one of the attending nurses.

What?! Blood!

As I faded in and out of a semi-consciousness. I wondered how in the world I had gotten to this place again. I vowed to never let myself get here. I was terrified the first time and here I was again having a sense of déjà vu. Another pregnancy which meant, due to my condition, another C-section. You see this was my second c-section and the first one was a surprise and an emergency. But this one. This one was supposed to be planned. Scheduled. Thought out. I was supposed to be prepared. Ready. On Time. Not early.

But blood on the floor?! That wasn't a part of the plan. That didn't happen the last time. That wasn't on my list. I tried to sit up for a moment then realized that the lower half of my body was still numb and as I felt more tugging and pulling, my nausea bubbled up and just as I was about to throw up -- with one final tug - I saw him.

I saw my baby.

And in those few seconds which felt truly like hours, I wondered if everything was okay because I heard no cry. Then suddenly, with a faint cry the baby was rushed away by another team and the other team of surgeons went to focus on me.

Familiar with the surgery process, I knew the first moments with my baby was limited as the Doctors wanted me to focus on my recovery. But after what seemed like days... alone in the recovery room... no husband, no baby, just me, and the flustered nurse who couldn't find the proper dosage to ease my pain. Finally, once I was stable, they rolled me back to my room and the silence was piercingly unbearable.

There was no baby. No crying. No cooing.

I looked to my right and my mom was there.

I looked to my left and my husband sat constantly asking me how I was doing.

Still in pain, I asked, "Where is my baby?" I didn't hear any audible words though… everyone just stared for what seemed like hours but it was truly only seconds.

During those moments… they could have very well been wallpaper because to me they weren't there. A nurse came in right away to check on me and the baby, "Oh I'm sorry. That's right. Your baby is down in the NICU. He is probably doing just fine."

"Probably?" I thought to myself as my mind raced out of control heightening my anxiety.

I believe at some point my husband showed me some pictures of our new baby boy explaining to me that our son was in the Neonatal Intensive Care Unit (NICU) being cared for. In the pictures he was hooked up to monitors and a feeding tube was attached. Then the nurse left and another one came back with congratulatory praise but I noticed her surveying the room and seeing no baby, she then checked her chart and said "Let's get you manageable so you can see your baby."

I felt empty and weak.

I know I was exhausted from surgery but something was happening on the inside of me that I couldn't handle.

I was breaking inside.

After almost 7 months with my baby inside of me, all of a sudden, I felt like everyone was keeping him from me. I felt like God was keeping him from me. That this was all some major ploy to stop me from being with my baby. Was this some type of government scandal? Where was Olivia Pope? Where was my help?! At that moment I resented everyone. I didn't trust the nurses or the NICU doctor who came in to "discuss" things. I didn't trust the medicine or the hospital. And in those seconds be it the drugs, the trauma, or the reality of it all... I felt like I didn't want to trust God.

My baby wasn't supposed to be in the NICU. Attached to tubes away from me. The reality that I wasn't even able to get to him sunk in as the surgeon came in to tell me that I had lost a lot of blood and needed to be heavily monitored. It was like the bad new kept coming.

My baby... though they kept assuring me was in the NICU to get stabilized but not in critical condition was okay. But I wasn't. This was critical. Something in my mind broke that day. Anxiety creped in and lingered like a thick fog. Confusion joined soon after. But also, in that moment arose sheer determination. Determination to do whatever I could so I could get down to the NICU to see my baby. The doctors warned me that I was too weak and I needed to recover. They reminded me that I had just had major surgery and that I was high risk due to the amount of blood I lost during the operation. They wanted me to wait. I wanted to punch them for even suggesting such a thing. Again, I asked my doctor, "what do I have to do to get to my baby?" Their response was two things. I had to walk the hallway and poop. Poop? Really, all this crap I was going through and they wanted more of it to prove that I was strong enough for my baby.

It was 6am the next morning. Not even a full 24 hours after my C-section and I was washed up and ready to see my baby.

You see I learned something that day. I learned that in me was a beast who would continue to fight for the opportunity to be there in my child's life. A mother's love is something that cannot be replaced. And I was determined to do all of what I could for my baby the best way I could. So fresh c- section scars, slowly moving, and in pain I made the trek to see my baby. It was my mission and what I was supposed to do. For me, there was no other choice but to get up and go.

A nurse wheeled me to the elevator and as I held on to my stomach in pain I winched but gritted my teeth through it. The elevator slowly descended down until we reached the designated floor. The elevator doors opened slowly and the nurse paused in front of the glass doors. This was it. I took a deep breath and read the clean glass doors that separated me from my baby, I whispered, "Neonatal Intensive Care Unit."

The nurse looked at me concerned and apologized saying, "This is as far as I can push you. Can you walk through the rest of the way?" I nodded and pushed myself to my feet. I walked into the Neonatal Unit tears steadily flowing down my face. I stood at the sink washing my hands for three full minutes; the mandatory washing time to enter the NICU.

It was the longest 3 minutes of my life.
3 minutes to contemplate.
3 minutes to second guess.
3 minutes to doubt.
3 minutes to put your big girl panties on and be a real mom.

As the water ran, in those 3 minutes, my tears dried and I was ready -- ready to be his mom. Ready to meet the little man who was determined to break out early just to teach his mom just how strong she really was. In those 3 minutes I was instantly changed.

I walked over to the curtains and pulled them back slowly and there he was. Tiny, yet strong. I reached into touch his hands, his feet, and legs. And a sweet song washed over me. And I started humming,

"Your Grace and Mercy brought me through.
I am living this moment because of you.
I want to thank you and Praise you too.

Your grace and mercy brought me through"

That day though just as strong as Optimus Prime… we named our precious baby boy Carter Gracen.

Because it was nobody buts God's grace that had brought us here to this very moment.

It was the grace of God that kept me alive through my complications during surgery.

God's grace gave me the strength to fight through the pain. The tears. The fear. To get to my baby.

It was the grace of God that gave me the motivation to keep showing up for my baby in the NICU.

And it is by God's grace that I am a woman with a horrific birthing story but a story of strength, determination, and drive. I found my purpose that day. I found the ability to stand and face the storm no matter how sudden. I did not expect this. There was no plan for this. But I was strong enough for it.

"One of the most courageous things you can do is identify yourself, know who you are, what you believe in and where you want to go."
– Sheila Murray Bethel

"A Hot Mess"
Jaclyn Glaze

'A Hot Mess' is how I would describe myself.

According to urbandictionary.com, Hot Mess is the state of disarray so chaotic that it's dizzying to look at. A mess that is beyond the normal range of disarray. Visual clutter that draws attention to itself. At 34 years of age, that's what I was—A Big... Hot... Mess... Except contrary to the definition, my Hot Mess was not visible to anyone. My Hot Mess was brewing on the inside, raging a war inside my spirit and my mind, ready to boil over.

This Hot Mess wasn't something that came on suddenly. It was actually a process that had been building for years. And I was certain no one knew my intrinsic chaotic state of disarray; however, the fact was there was One who did. It would only be a matter of time before He revealed my Hot Mess as I began to implode revealing I wasn't the self-confident woman I had tried so hard to make others believe I was.

I come from a long line of strong women. When I say "strong," I mean they exude confidence, tenacity, and determination. I would also describe them as a little high strung. I follow in those footsteps. Like the women before me, I'm a multi-tasker, someone who follows through and will get the job done. Having four young children between the ages of 2 and 7 has not slowed me down. I will take my kids to the beach, the pool, shopping, a parade in the middle of the city, or even road trips across the country all by myself. I like adventure! And well, with four little ones, a trip to the grocery store can end up being an adventure. Along with adventure, I like challenges.

But along with these strong traits comes a great amount of pressure—pressure I put on myself. I tend to be a control freak and perfectionist. I must do all things perfectly. This is what Jill Savage calls the "perfection infection." I don't want to drop one single ball while I'm juggling several at once. And heaven forbid if I do drop a ball, no one must ever know about it. My reputation as a woman who can do it all will be ruined. My pride will be hurt. Pride. Ouch! As hard as it was to admit, I have been plagued by pride and tried to avoid paying attention to the hold it has had on me.

In February 2015, my husband and I purchased Union28, a Christian marriage apparel company a friend of mine had started. After the birth of my first son in 2010, I decided to quit teaching and stay home with him. However, I wanted something to do to earn a little extra money and stay busy. I began working for my friend filling orders, replying to customer emails and after awhile, ended up running things as she and her husband lived abroad for nine months. I absolutely loved Union28 and its mission to encourage marriage, communicate a positive image of marriage and to honor the sanctity of the marriage covenant between a husband and wife. So of course, when she told me she would be selling the company, I was immediately interested. That year was intense! We already had three small children at home at the time and another one due to arrive in just a few months. We were also directors of our church's English as a Second Language Program and I was a table leader for a women's Bible study. Additionally, my husband and I were constantly running to soccer practices and games. Now throw into the busy mix maintaining a small business in your home with no prior business experience and you've got yourself a big ball of stress!

And, of course, admitting any type of pressure and stress was unfathomable. When people would ask me, "how do you manage four children, run a small business, direct a ministry at church and keep everything together?" I would simply give them the "humble" answer: "Jesus' grace and lots and lots of coffee." When on the inside I was actually screaming, "Well, I'm up really late, I'm up really early, I never stop moving, I'm a doer, I'm dedicated, I'm persistent and most importantly, I'm not a quitter!" Hmm, did you notice how every statement started with "I'm?" That's right. Instead of giving God all the glory and thanking Him for getting me through so many situations, I started to glorify myself. And it got worse. I would even do extra activities for others to notice just to hear a little bit more of "how do you do it all?" Well, as the Bible states, Pride cometh before the fall...

An important facet to maintaining the brand of Union28 involves participating in weekend Christian conferences by having a booth at these women's events. Oftentimes, I drive at least 16 hours one way to a given destination, set up for 48 hours and drive back for another 16 hours after tearing down and reloading the van. This also involves a lot of work before the conference—planning new shirt designs, advertising, tagging, folding, invoicing and adding to the inventory. Arrangements must be made for childcare and other responsibilities in my absence from home. As someone who promoted marriage as an example of Christ's relationship with his church and as a God-honoring business, I was certain Union28 would be successful. After all, I was doing my part and I was expecting Him to bless all my hard work and ambition. The stress of not experiencing the success I felt I deserved and trying to keep it all together was starting to take a toll.

While working so hard at attempting to achieve success myself, I also began to struggle with others' success. As someone who used to celebrate the success of others, I now started to feel animosity and sheer angst such as when I heard about the woman who had a side business selling makeup for less than a year, and she had already sold enough to earn a car. Wait a minute! In less than a year, this woman has earned herself a new free car? No, no, no, this cannot be true! Did I really hear that right? Yep, there's a picture showing her beside that shiny BMW along with a little blurb highlighting her successful salesmanship. I suddenly felt dizzy. I was angry. "But Lord, my business is promoting Christian values! My brand promotes marriage; you know, that thing You gave us that is supposed to be a representation of Your relationship with the church. I'm fighting for it! I'm fighting for You! You don't care about me? You don't care if this is successful? Alright, well, I guess

I'm just in this on my own because clearly praying about it is not working."

As I write this I remember so vividly the feelings I was having. These feelings ramped up and began a fast, out-of-control downward spiral of thoughts into the dark abyss that the enemy uses to trap us. "I'm a failure. I'm not good at anything. I can't do anything right. I will never be successful. I want my husband to be proud of me and instead he's probably so disappointed that all this work is for naught. What was I thinking? Who do I think I am that I can run a business? I'm only good for doing laundry and cleaning house. Heck, I'm not even good at making great meals for my family. Gosh, I'm a terrible mom. I'm a terrible wife. I'm stupid. I'm just so stupid. I hate myself."

And just like that, I began to sink farther and farther down into the trenches of depression. For about a year, I had really been struggling with depression, frustration, disappointment, anxiety, fear and now I was also overwhelmed with feelings of jealousy and anger. I was a Hot Mess. No one other than my closest friends and family would have known anything was wrong because I hid it quite well. Again, my pride would not let anyone know I couldn't hold it together. Sometime in the spring of 2017, I felt everything start crashing down and considered getting professional help for my depression.

Before this time of spiraling downward, I had felt prompted by the Lord to start journaling. Over and over again, I refused. Now once again, I felt Him tugging on my heart to start writing. In my mind, I could hardly get time for devotions, how was I going to find time to journal? I didn't even want to put in the effort. Plain and simple—I didn't want to and I wasn't going to. I can't believe I said those things to God. I was flat out saying "no" to Him and being very adamant about it. But God has a way of reaching us one way or another. Ironically, it just so happened that my gift for being a Bible study leader, was none other than, yep, you guessed it—a journal! When Andrea handed it to me, I chuckled inside and said, "Ok, God. You win."

The very next day began a humbling journey where God began to reveal Himself to me in a very real, tough, and heart-wrenching way. I decided I was going to journal my prayers to God. The first paragraph of the first journal entry included this: Sustain me through this time, Lord. I look to the King Immortal, invisible, invincible God- the only God, to be honor and glory forever and ever. (1 Timothy 1:17) What are you trying to teach me? Am I being refined? Have I been too prideful? Have I tried to do it all on my own and take credit? Have I not said, "Oh, I couldn't do it without the grace of Jesus" only to be secretly giving myself way more credit than I deserve? Being arrogant? As I sit here and think, yes, I've been arrogant, selfish, controlling, and have had selfish ambition.

If you've ever prayed a prayer for God to show Himself to you, then you know what happens next. To pray for God to reveal what has been keeping you from full reliance on Him and true joy in Christ is a very scary prayer because if you are sincere, He'll definitely show you! Exactly one week later, in my quiet time, something happened. Instead of working so hard to hide my reality, I had a need, no, an urgency to write, to be real, to expose my true emotions—my pride. My pen couldn't write fast enough.

"May 3, 2017. You've hit me right between the eyes today—my pride and its destruction. If I think about the last few years, I see myself and the situations I've been in, things I've done and many were driven by pride. I've "prided" myself on being uber-organized, maintaining a clean household and doing way more than the average person. But as my study stated, "she prides herself…" does not mean "she does a job well done to glorify God." I think others' thoughts of me have been what motivates me. How I "look" to others "doing it all" has been a huge motivation. BAM! To admit that is hard and hurtful. Hard because it's a character flaw. Hurtful because it is in the way of my relationship with God. I couldn't see it as pride because it was so big and clouding everything. I knew recently You were laying pride on my heart and that it was something that needed to be sifted. Today's Bible study lesson just gave me a talking to! Lord, I don't want the disgrace that comes with pride. I want the wisdom that comes with humility! FORGIVE ME LORD! Help me to strive to do a job well done to glorify YOU and not myself. That your name and renown is the desire of my heart (Isa. 26:8).

From that day forward, I've purposefully and intentionally sought to be changed by Him. I've had to learn a whole new way to be me in Christ! I have had to learn to let go. Let go of control. Let go of my desires. Let go of my visions for how I think something should work out. Let go of my need to be perfect. Let go of my desire to do everything perfectly. And let go of my pride. It has been hard. He's been teaching me how to live intentionally with humility and confidence only He can give. Pride and my desire to control had destroyed my effectiveness to God. But He loved me enough to pursue me in the mess I made for myself. He still saw me as worthy even in my Hot Mess. And He met me…face down on the ground…weeping. He whispered to my heart, "Jaclyn, I love you enough that I want to sift you of what is keeping you from full reliance on Me. As a woman whom I dearly love, I want you to take your eyes off your strongholds and put your focus back on Me. You've tried to do it in your own strength far too long. Now, do you trust Me? Do you really trust that I can do far abundantly more than all you could ask or think according to the power at work within you (Eph. 3:20)? Do you believe in your heart that I work all things together for good for those who love me, to those who are called according to my purpose? (Romans 8:28). I love you. I want you to trust that I will take care of you. I want your full reliance on Me." Yes, Lord. I'm exhausted. I'm relinquishing control. I need You. Need to Breathe has written a song titled, "Hard Love." God has used it to speak powerfully into my life.

> Trading punches with the heart of darkness
> Going to blows with your fear incarnate
> Never gone until it's stripped away

A part of you has gotta die today
In the morning you gon' need an answer
Ain't nobody gonna change the standard
It's not enough to just feel the flame
You've gotta burn your old self away
Hold on tight a little longer
What don't kill ya, makes ya stronger
Get back up, 'cause it's a hard love
You can't change without a fallout
It's gon' hurt, but don't you slow down
Get back up, 'cause it's a hard love
You know the situation can't be right
And all you ever do is fight
But there's a reason that the road is long
It takes some time to make your courage strong

A part of me died the day the Lord met me in my puddle of tears and the embarrassing realization of who I had become. My old self has gone through a process of being burned away. It's a hard love. But it's a beautiful love He has for me. He is transforming my life one step at a time. I don't want pride to destroy my character and who I am. Rather, let godly humility rule and take over. I pray that be a characteristic others see in me.

It's easy to think we are alone in our struggles; that no one else could possibly understand. But I believe that we as women put an immense amount of pressure on ourselves to do all and be all for everyone around us. And we especially feel the need to do it perfectly as we nearly kill ourselves to get there. But when we try to take control that only results in exhaustion and disappointment because the truth is there's no way we can be perfect. When we seek perfectionism it is essentially self-reliance and not reliance on God. We stress. Those are both born out of pride. It is us taking these anxieties upon ourselves instead of giving them to God. We know we can't do them better than He can, so why is it so hard to give it to Him? The new buzz word in society these days is "authentic."

But if we are not being authentic with God first we are still only faking it!

Here is a verse He has given to me: "The One who created me knows what to do with me. Let me run with endurance, this race you set before me. The way I do this is by keeping my eyes on you- on whom my faith depends." Hebrews 12:1-2

And the race He sets before us is a process, Oswald Chambers describes it so well: "God has to take us into the valley and put us through fires and floods to batter us into shape, until we get to the point where He can trust us with the reality of the (His) vision."

I am still a work in progress, but now knowing who I am in Christ I celebrate my new life in Him.

Reference
Chambers, O. (1935). The Golden book of Oswald Chambers: My utmost for His highest; selections for the year. New York: Dodd, Mead & Company.S

"I am not a perfect mother and I will never be. You are not a perfect daughter and you will never be. But put us together and we will be the best mother and daughter we would ever be."
-Zoraida Pesante

It is Well
Lisa Daniels

Sometimes, life has a funny way of showing you your purpose; especially when it is filled with sadness, hurt, and pain. A few months ago, "It is well" were the hardest words for me to say. I am a worship leader, so singing songs in truth and with conviction are vital to being an effective worship leader. But I did not want to say, "It is Well", because it wasn't. I couldn't say those words without tears streaming down my face, my lips quivering.

I had been struggling with one of the hardest decisions of my life; accepting that my mother may not want to be in my life after all these years. This was the basis of my struggles with depression, anxiety, and insecurity. Feeling abandoned and unloved since childhood is difficult to overcome as an adult.

I have always wanted the kind of mother/daughter relationship like Gilmore Girls. They were BFFs. They talked about everything. Lorelei was supportive, Rory trusted her. My mom was supposed to get on my nerves about my wedding because she wanted it to be perfect. I wanted her to be my birthing buddy when I had my first child. I expected to have to tear my children away from her because she would be so enamored with them that I'd never see them. Your mom should be your Shero, right? Well mine wasn't for me. All I could see was a mother who didn't seem to have any interest in me beyond taking care of my basic necessities. We never talked about the birds and the bees. We never talked about how my body would change. I wore those white ruffly Easter socks in high school with no intervention from her. And motherly affirmation? What was that?

I grew up in an environment full of brokenness, abandonment, loneliness, depression and abuse – sexually and verbally. This environment was supposed to be my village – my safe place. As I got older, I realized this environment was a cult. This church operated in every sense of the definition of a cult. I was unprotected from the detrimental, life altering actions of the Pastor, his wife and son – who were my godparents/god brother. I was repeatedly molested by both men and verbally abused and humiliated by the wife, publicly and privately. Instead of being treated as a victim, I was the seducer. An 11-year old seductress? I didn't even have boobs or my menstrual cycle!

My siblings and I were all terrorized by this family. They preyed on those who needed attention and were loved-starved. They claimed this was all in the name of Jesus. This is how my mother became involved. They showed her a life that seemed better for her. So she served them, with her life, thinking it was service to God. They did help her because they introduced her to Jesus, but the return has proven to be much greater than she thought it would be. It's almost as if we were payment for all the "good things" they'd done for my family.

Growing up, I barely saw my mother. Everyday, she would leave her full time job to go work after hours at the church. Daddy always had two to three jobs. As time passed, I learned that she believed the Lord would take care of us if she did His work. She even apologized for being absent, then she took it back. The Pastor's wife told her she shouldn't have said that to us, and that's what she told us – the very next day! I knew in my heart she didn't mean it. She was genuinely sorry, but anyone who goes against the Pastor or his wife are immediately reprimanded.

They ripped families apart if they wouldn't conform to their agenda. We didn't participate in many school or social events. Anything that pulled us away from church was prohibited. I quit the Varsity basketball team because they claimed they needed me at church on Friday nights. We couldn't visit our friends' churches. They also kept me away from other women who were sexually abused by the pastor – including my aunt. Telling on the pastor was an absolute no-no. We were all mentally enslaved to these people and we all thought we were pleasing God by staying there. That's what they taught us.

It took me a while to tell my mom and dad about the sexual abuse, because I thought I would cause the church to close. It would ruin everyone. So I wrote about it in my diary. There was a specific account of molestation in my diary that I talked about in detail. One day, I was riding with the pastor and we pulled over into a dark area. He said his famous words to me, "if you do me right, we'll go home." He started making me touch and kiss him. Of all the times we had done this, he never put his hands under my dress, until this time. I grabbed his hand and he began pleading with me to let him put his hand in my panties. He ignored all my protests until I started crying, but they weren't sad tears. I was angry and helpless at the same time. He started to ask what he could buy me to make it better. I can't remember what store we went to, but he insisted that I pick something, so I picked some random drinking glasses. I felt so humiliated. I kept thinking, "did that just happen?" He asked me who I thought the people would believe, him or me?

During the weeks leading up to my wedding, my fiancé then, Chris, was at our storage getting some of my things. Of course he stumbled across my diary and wanted to find out if I had written anything juicy about him. So he read it. Soon after, received a phone call from him. He was extremely angry and kept repeating how he was going to marry me no matter what. Of course, I didn't know what in the world he was talking about. He told me that he'd found my diary and saw that his suspicions were true. He told the pastor's daughter what he'd read. She immediately called me, at work, to tell me, "cover your pastor", meaning lie to my fiancé about what happened to me. She also knew it was true but she told Chris that I was in therapy and my therapist told me to use someone very close to me to write my story about, instead of using my "real abuser's name". So, of course I told him that it was a lie. He knew I was lying. There was nothing he could do at that point because he couldn't physically prove what he knew. The pastor had too much support. It really was my word against his.

My mom and the pastor went to the storage where my diary was packed that same day. They dug it out of the box, read through it and then mysteriously disposed of my diary. A couple of months ago, she told me that she had asked him if it was true. Like most abusers I've read about after being confronted, he told her, "no, it wasn't like that." She told me she believed him because "he was her friend." That made me wonder who I actually was to her… shouldn't a daughter be closer than ANY friend? They didn't ask me if they could go through my personal belongings, and there I was again… humiliated and unprotected by the very person I should have been able to trust the most. This is probably why I never journaled again, even to this very day.

When I finally decided to tell my truth, most of the people already knew it had been happening. No one rescued me. I was the big mouth. Can you imagine the heartbreak when the very women you thought were close to you knew that such a terrible thing was happening and did nothing except blame you? I felt like I was the worst person on earth. Why would I try to threaten the reputation of this man? After all he had done for my family, this is how I repay him? Later, after my parents divorced, I had found out that my dad went to his office to confront him and was met with a gun.

Years later, after I left the church, I decided to share bits and pieces of my story on Facebook. This made my mother very angry. She felt like I was attacking her friend. She thought that I had taken one incident and blew it way out of proportion. Not once had she investigated what really happened. She publicly defended him. My normal reaction – as always – was to hit below the belt. I wanted her to know that I felt she was a terrible mother for allowing this to happen and embarrassing me while defending him. This cycle went on and on. I thought that telling her how I felt would somehow prick her heart. It didn't.

On August 31, 2017 I shared a video on Facebook. A woman was sharing a very similar story. My mom fired back with the same, hurtful responses. This time, I didn't fight fire with fire. I tried to reason with her, almost groveling to get her to see though my eyes. She didn't. Instead she sent me a very long and hurtful text, again defending her pastor and her negligence. My response was, "ok, thank you." Another long and more hurtful text... my response, "ok, thank you." Then came the third and meanest text of them all... my response, "ok, thank you." Delete mom's texts, delete mom's phone number. Block mom and unfriend from social media. I'd accepted that I'd lost my mom and decided I would never reach out again. I said, "ok God. This is it. I don't have to have my mom if it has to be this way. She's all yours."

I have always had a little voice in the back of my mind telling me to let her go. But I couldn't. She's my mom. You only get one, no matter how bad you think she is. This is why I couldn't sing, "It is Well." I was so broken. I couldn't believe she'd chosen the abuser over her daughter – her first born. But I let her go. We had no communication for a little over a month. I tried to ignore the desire to reach out. "I've always reached for her. She never reached back. She's made her choice and it wasn't me." But one day, I couldn't talk myself out of it and I emailed her. I asked her to forgive me for holding a grudge against her and that I forgive her for not protecting me. To my surprise, didn't get the response I expected. Her words to me were, "...I'm sorry that I was so insensitive to your feelings and must ask for your forgiveness as well. You have made a very big move forward and I am proud of you. No grudge, attitude, or any such thing could ever diminish my love for you." Instantly, I melted. I read that email over and over. I was prepared to snap back at her this time, but true LOVE changed everything.

Who knew that letting go would be the best thing to do? I learned that we were both toxic. We were no good for each other in the state that we were in. I wasn't the daughter I needed to be for her. All I offered were accusations and reminders of how she didn't measure up. Love is what changes hearts and I did not offer her the love I've always had for her. Who am I to think she didn't deserve it? Why should I be the one to withhold it? I had so many unspoken expectations of her. How unfair of me to expect something she had no clue about! Not once did I try to find out about her life, her story. All I cared about was me. I assumed that since she had been abused, she knew how I felt. I never asked her how she dealt with it. I didn't even care to find out. I had become an abuser to her. Yuck… what an ugly realization.

I thank God that we've finally had the chance to listen to each other with a new set of ears. She asked my sister and I to share our accounts of abuse again. She then realized that it was not a one-time incident, but that it was ongoing for years. We found out that there was a lot she never even knew. She asked us, "what do you know about me?" We couldn't even name 5 things about her. Boy was that embarrassing! She shared stories about herself that were just as mind blowing as ours. Everything I felt about her changed that day. I made myself remember the things I conveniently forgot. I had picked a beautiful wedding dress. It was sleeveless, but we couldn't wear sleeveless clothes, so she sewed sheer sleeves onto my dress. She made all my bridesmaids dresses. We went to the fabric store and she helped me pick the prettiest fabric. She was at the hospital for all three births of my children. As kids, when we cheered for pop warner, she made the entire cheer squad's uniforms. She, my brother and sister helped me clean my filthy house while I was dealing with depression. She likes corny jokes, just like me. We're both into musicians. My mom IS a good mom. She actually is my Shero. She is resilient. She is absolutely stunning. She is gracious and soft spoken, but don't cross her!

There is no motherhood manual. She has done the best she could with the tools given to her, like all of us. I have forgiven her and she has forgiven me. I've vowed to have an open heart and to give her a blank slate. The best thing about making mistakes is that while you are alive, you have a chance to fix them. Cycles cannot be broken unless they are faced head on. So we're facing them… hearts pounding, palms sweaty. The pain of remembering is well worth the outcome.

I've learned that you've got to let go of what you think you want in order to get what you need. What I thought I wanted, I don't need anymore. I can finally sing, "It is well" in truth and its conviction, and I have a feeling we'll be Lorelei and Rory very soon.

"When peace like a river, attendeth my way
When sorrows like sea billows roll
Whatever my lot, You have taught me to say
It is well, it is well it's my soul"

"Faith is the strength by which a shattered world shall emerge
into the light."
- Helen Keller

Crippled By A Spirit
Holly M Lopez

[10] On a Sabbath Jesus was teaching in one of the synagogues, [11] and a woman was there who had been crippled by a spirit for eighteen years. She was bent over and could not straighten up at all. [12] When Jesus saw her, he called her forward and said to her, "Woman, you are set free from your infirmity." [13] Then he put his hands on her, and immediately she straightened up and praised God. NIV Luke 13:10-13

I love seeing myself in this scripture, and the imagery of Jesus placing His hands on me, a woman who has been tormented by a "spirit" for years; telling me that I am set free from my infirmity. It is the sweetest touch a soul can experience. The touch of her Father, literally raising her up in her brokenness. This scripture only tells us that she was present in the synagogue in which Jesus happened to be teaching. There was no indication that this woman believed in Jesus, or that she knew Him at all.Taking the initiative, Jesus, called her forward. He pronounced her cured, laid hands on her and then she was made straight. Upon being healed, her gratitude was to God for her healing. She was not aware of who Jesus was, but my bible commentary stated that she was pious. (MW Collegiate Dict. 11th edition: Pious - marked by or showing reverence for deity and devotion to divine worship.) It does not say how old this woman was; only that she was crippled for eighteen years.

I don't remember exactly when my spirit became crippled. I know that I confessed that my sin separated me from God at an early age, asking Jesus to come into my life and save me from myself. I grew up aware of His presence, but never bold enough to step forward to receive full freedom from the spirit that had me emotionally crippled for so long. I had placed my faith into a neat little box; one that I could carry with me and use as I saw fit. How different life would have been if I would have fully trusted what He truly wanted for me. Like so many today, we accept Jesus as our Savior, but we fall short at understanding how free we truly are in Him. Imagine the joy she must have felt when she realized that Jesus was the Son of God, and He was there to set her free.

Crippling spirits are created when we allow the enemy to tweak and twist God's truths, making them seem right, but really serving only the enemy's purpose of driving us further from God. Example: Eve was deceived by the serpent, an evil spirit, in the Garden of Eden when she allowed truth to be twisted, causing her to doubt God's truth. When we believe the diluted truths of the enemy, we no longer see His truth because we are blinded by our emotions of that trial or season. We can "faithfully" move through life going to church, doing good without ever slowing down to realize we are spinning our wheels for the enemy. He has us stretching ourselves to the point of snapping, but we think we are just moving through as it should be. Our Father never stretches us to the point of snapping. He will and does work at expanding and broadening our belief through His ability to do greatness in and through us.

As I have pondered the scripture about this woman, I have found myself wondering if she started off emotionally crippled by the weight of choices, decisions or circumstances that were beyond her control early on in her life. Then, maybe in the stress of this, she found herself slowly becoming crippled physically. From here there are the lies that come from real physical disease. Lies that tell us that we must have done something wrong to deserve such a fate. Life might have been perfect "if only" this had not happened.

I have dealt with emotional and spiritual lies for most of my life. Some days were better than others, but I never seemed to move far from them. So, when I was hit with a physical disability a few years ago, I was confronted with some lies that I had to learn how to reconcile. The physical disability was very real and very evident, but what God was after was my crippling insecurities of fear, pride, lies, failures and doubt. Like me, have your emotions altered how you deal with or see situations? Are you spiritually bent over? Broken is not how we are created to live!

Have situations in life caused you to doubt who you are in Christ? Are you in a season of despair, hopelessness, grief; or abandonment by a loved one or what feels like even God? Have any of life's misfortunes caused you to live crippled by a spirit? I have been crippled by the "spirit" of insecurity for far too long. I have been crippled by a disease that threatened to take my life but a disease that also restored so much!

"...Jesus was teaching in one of the synagogues,"
Back during the time when Jesus was teaching in the synagogues, it was custom for the front row to be seated with the wealthiest and most knowledgeable men. From there, status in the community worked its way to the back of the room. If there were no seats left, and there was room, you could stand in the back of the synagogue. That is where the woman in our scripture was standing.

Just like the times of Jesus, we live in the same world that has its own social pecking order. These social norms have caused me to believe I am not worthy of the front row over and over. I have times when I am certain I am good enough to sit amongst those in at least the second row. However, because of either perceived or real rejection, I allow one or two people to shame me to the back of the room. Yes, I have been that woman standing in the back of the room, because I chose to believe that was where I belonged.

People look down at others and judge them based on a cascade of standards, all of which are filtered through their own lens of power, pride, selfish conceit, and for many, because of their own insecurities. We live in a cruel society that uses power and authority to belittle or shame people into thinking they are not quite good enough. (That is a lie from the pit of hell, just so you know!)

Insecurity has been <u>my thorn</u> my whole life. The enemy is so cunning and crafty in how he uses his lies. My insecurities have had a direct effect on most all the relationships I have had. I respond so much differently to people when I believe the enemy's lies that tell me, I am not good enough, I am not pretty enough or that nobody likes me. I wish I could say that it was a whole group of people who convinced me of these lies, but it was not. It was only a very small number of people whom the enemy used. I remember the day I physically faced one of them, nose to nose. I faced my giant and said: no more. I no longer listened to the lies spoken over me. I saw this person as a hurt person, who hurt people. Unfortunately, this was only the first step in calling the lies a lie. Like an old record player stuck on that scratched album, the lies kept repeating. I was programmed to believe the lies that I had heard for years.

"…and a woman was there who had been crippled by a spirit for eighteen years. She was bent over and could not straighten up at all". What "spirit" could have weighed so heavily on this woman that it caused her to be "bent over"? Eighteen years is a long time to be living with a spirit so heavy that she was unable to stand up straight. Yet so many of us today live exactly like this woman. The enemy is so subtle in his ways; whispering in our ear that we are not worthy of the front row.

I know this woman all too well. I cannot help but feel the resemblance of her stature and her spirit. My crippling spirit is a lifetime of insecurity, fear, doubt; feelings of insignificance, unworthiness, and lack of trust. I have been gripped with the need to be in control of everything, but never being in control of my emotions or reality because of the blinders that believing the lies have caused. I have been crippled by the spirit of insecurity so long that I do not even recognize it sometimes.

I am approaching 50 and I still have him whispering lies in my ear daily. When I am in prayer and in His Word, I can silence the whispers, but when I get too busy to pray, the whispers become noise that consumes me. I get over a hurdle or two, then fall flat on my face. Back to prayer I go, praying longer and harder to find God's truth. I have days where all I want to do is cry and just give up, but I keep going, even if I do not fully understand. I either believe enough in God's promises, or I want to believe that He intends for that truth to be mine as well. I know I do not want the enemy to have this power over me, so I continue to fight.

I have heard a saying that goes something like, "The enemy will always fight hardest when he knows God has something great in store for us." God's Word tells me that He does not want me to live a life defeated, that our Savior has already paid the price for victory.

The enemy has mastered attacking my self-worth. I continue to realize how important it is to be equipped with the full armor of God at all times. It is what He gave us to be prepared for battle. It takes effort on our part. We cannot just ask for something in faith, we must be willing to fight for it through faith. The enemy has proven himself to be persistently pursuing us; do not be unequipped.

The Bible is filled with stories of how the enemy was persistent in the lives of people God used and wanted to use for His glory. There is the story of Samson and Delilah. Her persistent nagging was the enemy's way of wearing Samson down to the point of giving away his God-given gift of strength. There was the persistent wife of Potiphar, who tried repeatedly to get Joseph to "lie with her," which would have been committing adultery against his boss. Then there was Peter, who was terrified at what he saw happening to Jesus before the crucifixion. Then through that fear and the persistent questions of the people at the gate, Peter ended up denying that he knew Christ at all. The enemy is relentless in his pursuit to cause us to deny who we are in Christ.

When we allow the choices of our past to "cripple" us, refusing to take it to our Savior, the enemy will turn it into a season of crippling. If we still refuse to bring it to the foot of the cross, the enemy will cripple our lives with it.

I am grateful for the stories of the Bible, but sometimes it is so hard to believe that the enemy has been stalking me since I was a child. I look back at all of the mistakes that I have made; things that I should have known better. The enemy causes us to doubt that there is really anything wrong with the choices we are making daily. He loves to water down our sin. To plant seeds of doubt. Shame knocks at my door as well. Only Jesus and His truth have the power to set us free.

"When Jesus saw her (me), he called her (me) forward and said to her (me)"
In a room full of the most important people that lived in and around that town, what caused Jesus to notice this crippled woman? What causes Jesus to notice us? Every one of us on this side of heaven has the potential to be crippled by the enemy. Did she know Jesus was going to be there? Had she cried out before getting to the synagogue to be noticed? Was she ready to do whatever she was asked to be healed? We don't know for sure, but we serve a God who is always pursuing us, so I have faith that God knew her and desired for her to be set free.

Several years ago, I was at a very low point in my life. I was barking out deals with God about my marriage, because the enemy had convinced me that I was not happy, that my husband did not really love me. I had a list of all the things that I wanted changed, I was done waiting around for it to just happen on its own. I used my belief in the sanctity of marriage as my leverage against God, that if he wanted me to stay married to my husband, then He was going to have to do some major work on him by the end of that year. Like a good Christian, I let God know that I was willing to do whatever He needed of me to help in this matter.

As High school sweethearts, we married in our early 20's, and grew to a family of five before our 30's. After moving several times, we landed in Murrieta CA in 2009. Our older daughter was a sophomore in high school, our son was in middle school and our younger daughter was in elementary school. Three different schools with three different start times and three different end times! We had school sports and club sports. The craziness of being the carpool mom from sun up to sun down kept me swamped. The enemy had mastered busyness to trip us up.

My conversations, my prayers asking God to cover me had somehow become nonexistent. I only prayed prayers that dealt with everyone else. I had become that tired wife and mama that was just getting through her days; pouring out, but not being poured into. Fred and I just co-existed. We loved each other, but we were not taking care of our marriage. I had not gone to church since we had moved. No fellowship was happening with other godly women. I was not in God's Word. I was not even listening to praise and worship music. The enemy had used everyday life, plain and simple, to cause me to feel alone and without hope. I had started expecting my family to fill the emptiness I was experiencing, and because they were not capable to fill what only God could, they failed in my eyes.

Finally, Jesus saw me!

Well, frankly, I finally saw how desperately I needed Jesus. In 2010 I joined a Bible study group. The women in this group were older and wiser than I was. They took me under their wings and with their help I began to heal, to peel back some of those layers of insecurity. They gave me hope that God cared about me. While I began to spread my wings, I still had not fully realized how deep my insecurities of unworthiness really were. God was working on me, but I continued to blame my marriage, my husband, for my unhappiness. Even those of us going to church can be blinded by a crippling spirit. I do not know how I got so lost in my faith, but this is where He saw me and knew it was time to call me forward.

It was the beginning of 2011 that I barked out that deal with God. If only I could have heard our sweet Father sigh, I would have realized what I had just agreed to. Remember, I agreed to do ANYTHING. It was mid-year that I began waking up with unusual physical symptoms that eventually led me to the doctor's office. The first two doctors I saw informed me that, because I was now

40, I could expect more unusual changes in my body. (Forty is still young, right?)

It took several doctors, but in July of 2012, a year-and-a-half after making my deal with God, I had a diagnosis. I was meeting my newest doctor for the first time and it only took one simple handshake for her eyes to say it all; she knew what I had. It was scleroderma, an autoimmune disease that was affecting my whole body; specifically my skin and organs were hardening. My hands were hard, and my fingers were beginning to curl. Taking a deep breath was getting harder and harder because the lower portions of my lungs were hardening with scar tissue. The fatigue was causing me to be in bed earlier and earlier every night. Every joint in my body hurt and it was getting nearly impossible to do normal, everyday tasks. I was unable to open my own water bottles because of my deformed hands. Walking from the parking lot to the kids' soccer field or to the football field was now a real challenge. I would be so winded when I got to my seat that you would have thought I had been running.

When you get the news that you have a 50/50 chance that a disease could take your life within five years and there is no real cure, your mind goes into hyper mode. My youngest, Natalie, was now in eighth grade and my older two, Jacob and Abigail, were in high school as a freshman and senior. Visions of never seeing my Natalie graduate from high school, never seeing my kids walk down the aisle, never playing on the floor with my grandbabies, never growing old with my husband, were all flashing before my eyes. With these kind of statistics, even if you survive, what will the quality of your life look like in five years? I cried in the doctor's office that day. I cried out to God that night.

I was relieved to have finally received a diagnosis, even if it was not a good one. I remember leaving the doctor's office and calling my mom to give her the news. She was already devastated that I had been diagnosed with rheumatoid arthritis. So, the news of an even more devastating disease was hard to share with her. She has that amazing "mama gift" of hearing what I am not saying. She knew it was much worse than what I was telling her. There are just no words to describe the heartache I felt that day.

I was at a crossroads in my life in more areas than just my health. I believe that I had become so entangled by the lies of the enemy, that he was literally trying to choke me out of my life all together. If I was going to rise up, I needed to put my faith into action. I would need the full armor of God. I needed to attack the lies with truth. I do not believe that God chooses for us to be sick or have an illness. I believe that that is the product of living in a fallen and sinful world. However, the beauty of who God is, allows Him to take what the enemy uses to cause harm, and turn it into something He uses for His Glory, His Kingdom, and our blessing!

This disease threw my entire family into different directions. During this time my kids were being met with the peer-pressures of school as well as the thought that their mama was sick and getting sicker. The enemy dialed into their fears and started them each down a road of their own. For me, it was the first time in a very long time that I needed and desperately wanted my husband to walk beside me on this journey.

I clearly remember going to my Bible and reading Job's story of affliction. It would have been easy to blame God, yet I realized Job stood his ground when his friends and even his wife told him to curse God and die. He said that you cannot take the good from God, and then curse Him for the bad that happens. He did not understand why his sons and daughters were killed along with all his livestock, but he trusted God. It was that simple. And, in the end, God restored to Job so much more than he lost at the enemy's hand.

"Woman, you are set free from your infirmity".
No, I was not set free from my disease, but my disease was used to set me free. That crippling spirit of insecurity that I carried

around my entire life, that had caused me to blame my husband for my unhappiness, was now gone. I needed him more now than I could ever have imagined. I was no longer giving lip service to my prayers to fix my marriage. I allowed God to restore me and, in that restoration, He restored my marriage and my faith. My husband is my best friend, my guy, the absolute love of my life.

So, what happened in all of this? It is as simple as this: I began to trust God with every detail of my health and my marriage. I put on the armor of God. I no longer sat around waiting for God to answer my prayers while I took a back seat. He is not a fairy, or a warm and fuzzy feeling or even a good vibe. He is God, the Creator of all things. We were woven together in our mother's womb and He knew us! We are not here by chance, but instead with a purpose.

The faith we are talking about here is a verb, not a noun; which means it requires action. I had never fully appreciated that. My expectations of Fred were that he could do what only my Father was able to do for me. When I freed Fred from this, and pursued an intimate friendship, an authentic relationship with him, allowing God to be God and Fred to be Fred, I found everything that my heart could desire. More importantly, I found freedom from lies that the enemy used to cripple me. I found liberty in my disease.

Scleroderma, a horrible disease, was "my anything" that I agreed to when I bargained with God to save my marriage. God restored so much more than I lost because of this disease.

I do not know what is crippling you, but sister, be willing to go into that fire, knowing that He is pressing His hands on your cheeks as He lifts your face up to see Him eye to eye, "Woman, you are set free from your infirmity."

"...for the joy of the Lord is your strength!"
Nehemiah 8:10 (NIV)

Rebuilding The Walls
Amanda Wood

Rebuilding the Walls

My heart felt paralyzed, unable to feel and articulate anything. I felt like I was forced to drink from a fire hose, feeling extremely overwhelmed and barely able to function. I had been hurt before, but I had never experienced hurt like this. Not only was my heart destroyed, but I started to feel guilty, shameful, and stupid. How could I let something like this happen? Was I seriously that oblivious? I shouldn't have let things escalate this far. I should have known better and actually listened to what others said.

A Fairytale Made Specifically for Me

Once upon a time, a long time ago…okay, closer to a couple of years ago, I stepped into a fairytale. Through a mutual friend, I was introduced to a gentleman who was exhibiting a lot of qualities and characteristics for which I had been praying for a long time! I kept thinking I was dreaming, but I was convinced I had stepped into the plan and person God had for me. There was no flaw I could even discern in our time of getting to know each other. This man was surpassing all of my expectations and experiences from those in my past.

Things started to move in a positive direction as we found many common interests and developed a strong liking for each other. We started to take things a little more seriously, talking about the future we could have together and seeking God to see if this was what He had for us. One attribute that impressed me was the gift of discernment and prophecy this man proclaimed to have. There were times he would share with me something God told him, and it was spot on! It really was an impressive quality, one that led me to feel loved and blessed. Not only did he exhibit the ability to notice the small things, but he was an excellent communicator. From what I could tell and hearing him share often, he had a very close relationship with his mother, and it was evident in how he treated me and extended the love of Christ to me. I was truly blessed and felt like I was living out one of the most majestic love stories out there!

The friendship with the girl who introduced us started to grow as well. She knew this guy from her hometown, so I trusted her as a confidant and close friend in this new journey I was entering into. We started to get more involved in each other's lives, talking on a daily basis and including each other in deeper matters of the heart. She was someone who understood me and this new relationship, more so than other close relationships in my life. She made sense of things, and she helped me in times when I faced difficulty in my new relationship. She started to become a life long friend. I felt like things were moving very smoothly in my relationships in life, and I loved every ounce of it.

Now don't get me wrong—it's not like this relationship and new season didn't have its downfalls. There were areas of conflict, moments of confusion, and times I didn't think things were going the way they were supposed to. For example, many times I was reminded of the hurts and struggles I was walking through, which was translated into me holding full responsibility for this relationship not succeeding. When I tried to show him that we all are broken and working through things, he never really acknowledged any struggles he was working through, because he already worked through them. As much as I loved to share my heart, and all of who I am, I found there wasn't a mutual openness within our conversations. For the most part, I was told that I needed to fix my issues and just let go of the hurts I was holding on to, and once I could get through that, maybe our relationship wouldn't be full of hardships and conflict. But doesn't every relationship go through that? Because I'm a professional overthinker, I overlooked many things I thought were minimal issues. I just assumed my overthinking was the issue. It became common for me to let his word be what guided and directed the relationship, which I saw as the honorable and respectable way to treat him. Regardless of the difficulties we faced, I was honored to be going through this journey with an amazing man beside me.

Stepping into Reality

From where I stood, this relationship was the greatest blessing I could be given. I felt peace when asking God what He had for me in this relationship. I loved who I was becoming and looked forward to the future I was stepping into. I had some of the best support from friends and co-workers, especially those who knew I had been hurt in the past.

A few friends shared concerns that were not necessarily what I wanted to hear. Some remarked that I deserved more than what this man was giving me, and certainly more than what he wasn't giving. What lacked in our relationship, our limited form of communication and the segregation from others, my friends saw as red flags; and what existed, a continual delusion that what we had was okay and normal, wasn't viewed as healthy or normal. However, I was convinced that everyone outside of this relationship just didn't have a full understanding of what was really going on. There was so much that would happen that they wouldn't see, and so their accusations and concerns seemed to be inappropriate because I experienced something different than what they were observing. My inner voice told me that they didn't know the relationship like I did—they weren't part of it, so how could they make such assumptions? While these friends expressed their concerns, they still supported me, wanting only the best for me and my future.

As time went on, I was falling in love with this man. I grew excited for the future and to see God move through our relationship, as unconventional as it had seemed. We started to make some plans, but things would fall through and other circumstances would come up. Important parts of our relationship seemed to go by neglected by him. And yet, I feel for every excuse. I was convinced that this man was honest about what prohibited us from progressing in our relationship. It was after the second round of trying to make things work that I realized I was wasting my heart and my time on someone who wasn't even man enough to meet me where I needed him to. Not even in person.

Oh! Did I leave that part out? The part where I explain that, we never met face to face in our time together? In fact, we never even had a phone conversation, a Skype date, or saw each other in our entire relationship. We'd send pictures to each other and text and email all the time, but that was it. Text messages, a few photos, and emails were what our relationship consisted of.

Now, I get that there are some red flags that are fully ablaze in just that statement alone. But let me share with you the warning signs of a house fire that I ignored for many years of my life.

The first reason we couldn't talk on the phone was because "it wasn't the right time." This man told me that God had told him when the perfect time for us to talk would be so that we could take that next step forward. His reason was that he knew I was hurt in the past and he wanted to be different than any other man I had ever known. He definitely lived up to that statement. Time went on, but when the topic of connecting via a phone conversation came up it would always result in arguments and conflict. Every time we planned to meet up, he would give me dates months out in advance so we could prepare and seek the Lord. I even had a countdown with some friends for when we would finally be together in person! But whenever that date came around, he was either on a missions trip in Africa, his trip was delayed, his mother was fighting and battling breast cancer and passed away—all seemingly valid and very reasonable reasons to change plans. I believed him, but my friends didn't. I was so consumed with the idea that my fairytale was coming to life that I neglected to see that this man was not treating me like a daughter of the King. He may have been saying all the right things and meeting some desires of my heart in our time together, but he was not willing to prove that he was a man of his word.

On the other hand, things with our mutual friend were good. We became like sisters. Our friendship was so exclusive that the only other person in our little circle of friends was this guy I was getting to know, and I was okay with that. She was facing the hardest time in her life, so I felt I had to support her and spend more time with her than my other friends—including supporting her financially. I felt I could exhibit the love of Christ in ways I hadn't before. But things changed when she opened up to me a little bit more.

About a year and a half into this dating relationship with her friend from back home, my friend reached out to me and said she had some things to share about him with me. She started to tell me that the guy I was talking to wasn't actually real.

Umm…I'm sorry, WHAT?! Not real?

She explained that this guy was pretending to be someone else, and that he had come up with the idea to create a fake person to date me and that he threatened her into going along with it. She was behind this "relationship" the entire time, passing information from me to him—information that he would manipulate and use as "a word from the Lord" to me.

You can imagine how broken my heart felt, as if a bomb went off and there was hot lava that consumed by entire body from the explosion. I was wounded, numb, and intensely grieving. I could barely articulate all that I was feeling. And I could tell she was hurting too, so I did what I thought was best and extended a hand of grace to her. I knew she had been through a lot, and even if she had made a mistake, she was coming forward and wanting to make things right. We stayed friends.

Fast forward several months, and I was now trying to get to know the real guy I had been texting with. Things seemed to be going well, until I was informed that my "friend" still wasn't being completely honest with me about him. For the past two and half years, this woman had been portraying not only the guy I originally thought I had been in a relationship with, but also pretending to be his parents, his other friends, and the guy who was behind the first encounter with this relationship. She confirmed that she in fact had made everything up herself. This guy didn't exist at all.

Cue the vomit.

She created false numbers and lives for every person she impersonated. It became her life to pursue this, she put so much time and effort into creating this false life through unrealistic people by using pictures and information off other people's social media accounts. She was in continual denial until she was called out by someone else who was in the midst of experiencing something similar to what I went through. When confronted as to why she was pursuing this, she didn't really have much of an explanation for her actions.

I quickly realized that my friendship with this person was very unhealthy and codependent. I was so wrapped up in this person who didn't exist, and their stamp of approval, support, love and care that I neglected my other relationships and the reality of what was really going on beneath the surface. I was catfished.

Standing Up After Battle

After being knocked down and destroyed more than once, I came to see life in a whole new light. I became aware of the emotions, the finances, and the time I invested into what I thought was real, but was painfully delusional. I know I could beat myself up for being so oblivious to the many red flags I constantly saw: identical responses from the 'different people', being manipulated by this girl who used the victim mentality, encouraging an isolated friendship, and being condemned for not trusting the word of a 'man' I never met. But, that is not what God wants for me, nor did He sacrifice His son for me to do that.

God is so good and faithful to reveal Himself, even in the midst of walking through a thick fog that you think is a clear blue sky ahead. As I was walking through this season, I got to experience the peace, love, compassion, and tender care of my Abba in ways I never had before. Even in the midst of confusion, doubt, and fear, God opened doors for me to feel His peace. Throughout the entire time I was walking through this scam, I felt the assurance from God that everything is going to be okay. Even when I misinterpreted what God was saying, what He meant by what He told me, He still showed me what He wanted and had for me. I came to find my worth, I came to see who God made me to be and what I am deserving of. By the time I started to get the hint that this wasn't going to happen the way I thought, I was presented with some avenues to pursue God's calling on my life. Two business opportunities that aligned perfectly with the desires of my heart, and I'm still pursuing them to this day.

He gave me purpose, He gave me structure, He presented to me how He wants to bring me out of this stronger than I was going into it. I made the choice to surround myself with people who were healthy Christians and to get their help to wipe away the mess I had just climbed out of. I got involved in my church, I pursued my business', I made sure I was doing things that my heart longed for, things that were REAL and tangible in my life. I wanted to do this right, I wanted to heal and overcome this rather than stuff it down with other things. Even as I continue to walk through this, I never knew that the peace of God that surpasses all understanding would get me from heartache to a place of hope in the midst of days, even hours. I could try to explain and elaborate the victory I walked into in a short amount of time, but the only explanation that is accurate is; Jesus Himself.

Preparing to Rebuild

Throughout all of this, God has placed a specific calling on me to stand in the gap and be the voice for those who aren't able to speak up. He has shown me the warrior He made me to be. He knew I would go through this, and He knew that I would become the warrior that I felt called to be. He equip me for the unimaginable by allowing me to walk through this. Furthermore, I have come to see that He is a God who brings only good to those He loves. I never imagined my life to be so full, so purposeful, so rich after such a devastating experience.

One of the many challenges God has given me is to work on rebuilding the walls, the walls in my life, the walls of my situation, the walls in the lives of others. In Nehemiah, we read about the restoration of the walls of Jerusalem, and this story was one that God brought to my attention in multiple way. I was told once while hearing this story that the intent of rebuilding the walls of Jerusalem was to ultimately rebuild the city itself. God showed me that He wanted to do that in my life through the journey that I am on right now. He has encouraged me to gather my crew to help rebuild that wall in my life. And with that pursuit, there is rebuilding that needs to be done in the lives of others, there are cities that have been destroyed that need warriors to step in and bring hope and His love. And that is what I believe He is calling me to do as I walk through this adventure.

Now, from my heart, straight to yours. I'd like to take a moment to speak out to those who may have walked through or may be going through a very similar experience, please know first and foremost that you are a beloved child of the King. God looks upon you with such delight and He longs to see you step into the life He has created for you! In fact, He has created you in His image, in such a way that no one else can pursue or live out the plan He has for the way you can. Crazy right?! He loves you! He adores you! Your hurt and the struggles you face don't define you, or the love God can or can't give you. You are not alone in this and you are worth so much more than what could ever be imagined! Find what brings you the joy of the Lord, spend time with Him and step into the life He has created just for you!

"You may encounter many defeats, but you must not be defeated.
In fact, it may be necessary to encounter the defeats, so you can
know who you are, what you can rise from, how you can still
come out of it."
– Maya Angelou

Covered Through The Storm
Tiah Lewis

For as long as I can remember growing up as a little girl in a large family, I had always dreamed of going off and being someone successful one day. I was the middle child raised in a house full of boys whose goal was to ensure they groomed me how to stand up for myself and to not go down without a fight. I was tough and built to withstand a lot of difficult situations and challenges. We were raised in the church, and attended regularly, as my mom served as the spiritual foundation of our family. I was introduced to God at a very young age and knew him as someone who would always be there to guide me and watch over me no matter where I went. I used to dream and envision what my life would be like once I graduated high school and went off to pursue my dreams of a career in sports medicine.

When the time came for me to start my journey I relocated to Houston, TX along with my current boyfriend who was returning home after his military service in the Navy. Finally! I was going to be free to spread my wings and explore my independence as a young woman. I was hit with my first real blow in life, after just a short time, he and I couldn't make the transition together, and it was time for us to go our separate ways. It was one of the first big turning points in my life where I had to decide if I was going to sink or swim. The latter meant me staying and finishing undergrad, and carrying a full-time job to support myself. I was determined to explore this newfound freedom, this new life. And so I stayed, struggling to make ends meet and to keep transportation and a roof over my head. I was struggling so bad that during my freshman year of college my air conditioner went out in my car and if anyone knows Texas heat, that alone felt like the ultimate sacrifice.

But, proudly, three years later I became the first in my family to graduate from college with a four-year degree. It was a very fulfilling moment for me and I could finally see the dreams I had as a child come to fruition. What was next for me? I continued to work my full-time job and with this newfound freedom that is where I was introduced to partying and the nightlife. I met people everywhere I went. My entire wardrobe changed. I dressed more provocatively. I would drink and party all night long and multiple nights in a row. I knew I was attractive so I used my looks to gain the attention of well-established men, professional football players, basketball players, and anybody looking to show me a good time. I found myself dating men a lot older and more experienced. Here I was this young woman a lot more mature than most my age. I was living on my own. I was standing on my own and doing things that most 21-year old didn't do.

I worked hard but I played harder. I would party until the morning hours. I was in and out of strip clubs, house parties, and whatever else I was invited to for that week. I remember when the Super Bowl and the NBA All-Star games came into town I was right in the thick of it. I would party from Sunday to Sunday. Everything was new and so different than what I had experienced as a young girl in California. I was intrigued. I wanted to flourish in this life for what seemed like the life to have. I wanted the high life and the excitement.

One day, I was asked to model for a calendar shoot by a well-known local photographer and of course I couldn't' turn down the opportunity. In my usual fashion I mingled with the crowd, conversed with all those who attempted to name me, or who were looking to make a name for themselves. The excitement of all the attention stirred something in me. I craved the feeling of being wanted and desired. And so, I took it all in; I sought every bit of attention that I was given.

When the night was over, I headed to my car feeling a bit light-headed. I got in my car and started to make my way onto the highway where my head began to feel like it was spinning. I was trying my best to make it home before I started feeling worse but before I knew it, I had dozed off just barely scraping the guard rail, where I was awakened by the sound of my tires running alongside the highway rumble strips. I was losing consciousness and just after I pulled up to my apartment lethargic and stumbling up my stairs I arrived at my doorstep where I attempted to knock and passed out. I woke up the next morning to find myself fully clothed in my bed with a pounding headache.

My roommate began recalling for me what happened the night before and how she found me at our doorstep passed out. I had been drugged at the meet and greet party. I decided not to go through with the calendar shoot in fear and shame of what happened the night before. I was so thankful for making it through such a horrible situation that could have turned out for the worse. But even this wasn't enough to slow me down.

I continued to date the nightlife, and anyone who wanted to be a part of it with me. I eventually met someone who was all the things I was looking for, well-known, charming, respected, and well off. We dated and before I knew it I was pregnant having a child out of wedlock. I was so disappointed and upset with myself because this person wasn't the person I thought he was and I was dead set on leaving the relationship. I had reached another turning point in my life, I was responsible for raising my child as a single mother.

This is when reality set in as I knew that I now had someone who was watching my every move and how I made them. I struggled to make ends meet, to cover daycare expenses, and provide all our essential needs. I was looking for a change in my situation. Change came soon enough, when I had reconnected with an old friend who I had known from high school. We had so many things in common, from the same hometown, came from large families, and shared some of the same values, more importantly we both loved partying and enjoying the nightlife together.

Shortly after nine months we decided to marry not telling anyone including our closest family and friends. We were in love and were meeting the needs of each other at the time, for me it provided me with financial stability being a single parent, and for him it gave him someone to take care of things for him while he went off to war, and to be there for him when he got back.

We talked about the many horror stories of life over there, and even the dreaded conversations of what would happen should he not come back. The entire year I was plagued with fear of him not returning, or fear of receiving a knock at my door, not to mention the worry about his mental stability when he returned. For the first six to seven months, it was just the opposite of missing each other due to the separation, all we talked about was divorce. We talked about infidelity and everything negative that could plague a newly married couple going through its' first year being a part. Back home I was dealing with rejection from the infidelity, pain from the stress of the separation and fear of him not returning all wrapped in one andstarted distancing myself from some of the stress of him being away.

So, I returned to the nightlife and hanging out with old friends and did whatever I wanted while he was away. When it was time for him to return home, I was torn about if I wanted to remain married, or to file for divorce, but I knew that I still loved him and with him coming back from that environment, he needed a support system, he needed me. So together we battled with PTSD, we battled with commitment to the marriage, his relocation to Houston, and living in two separate residences. I was still stuck in the mindset of being a wife and raising my child while my husband was trying to make the transition back to civilian life and quite frankly living his own life.

I finally came to a breaking point where enough was enough and I filed for divorce. I felt so depleted and empty. I remember praying about us a few years prior when we first started dating and being sure that I heard from God that he would be my husband. I began to question God, as to if this was true, then why was our marriage so dysfunctional? I asked is this what marriage is supposed to look like? Heartache and pain, mistrust, and divorce? I felt defeated and I was losing myself and who I was as I came to a place of complete brokenness. My divorce was now final, and strangely, I felt as if a huge weight had been lifted off my shoulders despite the hurt and pain of the process. Late one night I received a phone call from a police officer saying that they were with my husband at his home and he wanted them to let me know he was ok. I was confused as to what was going on and what the officer was telling me. A neighbor had heard a gunshot come from my husband's home and notified them. As my husband was placed on the phone, crying hysterically, he explained to me he had attempted to take his own life. In that moment, I felt heartless, I was so emotionally depleted that I couldn't bring myself to feel sympathy for him. I felt guilty. How did I get here? I did everything in my power to try and keep my marriage afloat and our family together. I was so frustrated that I had come to this place and I had lost complete control of my life.

Shortly after I received a visit from my mom and I tried to make sure I cleaned up everything that could possibly show that I was really going through. Or so I thought. I didn't want her to see me like this, broken and in need. I had always been the strong one in my family and able to hold it all together; but, here I was. As I began to share some of the things I had been through with my mom the words that stuck in my head she spoke were "this is your life". And she was right it was, and I had to take back ownership of it and it wasn't up for negotiation.

Just a few days later I met up with my now ex-husband and watched as he got out of his car and approached mine. He looked good! He had lost some weight, and there was something different about him. He had a glow upon him. One of gentleness and peace, something I had never seen on him before. All of these emotions began to stir in my heart as I began to realize, wow, I was still in love with this man. I understood that we had issues and we had some painful memories of our past, but I began to ponder was it still possible to mend things? Could God be giving me a change of heart? I couldn't stop thinking about him. We started to talk again, daily, sometimes on and off all day. And one day I received a call from him inviting me to church and I accepted the invitation.

The invitation brought me to a small house church, where he had joined with some friends along with a pastor who were looking to start a church. I really enjoyed the service. After the service, I sat down and started talking to the pastor's wife. There was an instant connection between her and I as we laughed and shared stories about our children. We then started to share about my marriage and my current situation. I told her I was divorced, and I felt there was a shifting going on in my heart and my feelings towards him. She then began to share with me her own personal testimony and challenges she had faced in her own marriage, and I knew at that moment that it was time for me to let some things go, including my pride, how people viewed me, my insecurities, and accepting that I needed restoration and a real relationship with God.

God was calling me to a place of total surrender over everything in my life, including my broken marriage. In that moment, I got down on my knees and I began crying out to the Lord asking him to remove everything in me that was not of him. I repented of all my sins, my failures, my disobedience, and asked for his forgiveness for it all. Right there in that little house church, I accepted the Lord Jesus Christ in my heart, and from that point on my life had been changed. Jesus the one who had died for my sins on the cross had made me whole and saved my soul. My husband and I began to grow in the Lord together because the glow that my husband had was of the light that was also in him when he gave his life to Christ shortly before I did. Glory be to God!

With our new-found life in Christ, we still had to face our past, but we were not going to let it define our future. I had enough faith that despite my hurt and our differences, I knew we were nothing short of a miracle. I knew our marriage reunion was divinely appointed. What looked like the end became the beginning. I thanked God for his grace and his mercy, and what he was doing as he was putting the puzzle pieces of my life back in order. He had a master plan. He divinely set people in our lives and surrounded us with true people of faith who came into our home and counseled us. God sent people to pray for us and continued to encourage us not to hold on and not give up.

I think back to a counseling session when I was asked with the way things are now would I be able to go before the Lord and say I was happy with all the things I did for my family in my lifetime? In that moment, I had realized that so long as I have breath in my body, and able to fight through my pain, that I still have it in me to serve my purpose here on Earth. In that my real purpose journey began, it was now time for me to fight like I had learned how to do growing up, but now it was for my family and my marriage. And so, we are working through our challenges because we know that no marriage is perfect. We are a team. As husband and wife, we view ourselves as one in the eyes of God, and that meant ruling out one person more valuable than the other.

Nine months into our marriage we had our first love child, and as God has a great sense of humor sixteen months later I was pregnant again with twin girls. Whew! Can you say shock factor! We were just barely finding our happiness with two children and now we were having two more. I kept telling myself, we aren't prepared. More so, I wasn't prepared. I wasn't fully equipped as a mother to provide and care for two additional children let alone two more babies. I was devastated. More babies meant more stress and more issues in my marriage. It wasn't going to get easier and I knew that. My husband and I had been through some storms together, but I didn't think it had prepared us for this one. But God said yes, our storms had prepared us to depend on each other, and our four children would need us to be on one accord. They needed to see unity in our home, and so I had to hold on to my faith and our Christ-centered love for one another as my foundation when "giving up" was boiling over.

Trusting in God through it all has been the cornerstone that has kept us afloat during times of no sleep, and times of frustration, mistrust, and miscommunication. We needed something to hold on to bigger than ourselves. Our motto has been "teamwork makes the dream work". We carved out date nights so we could focus on meeting each other's needs. It was needed for us to sustain in the new season we were moving into. Transitioning to one income and a whole new set of challenges, I was being called home to raise my children. We had two additional new babies in our home to care for with our youngest still a toddler. I recall when our mothers came out to help us, and the two of them expressing how bad they felt about leaving because they knew how much work it was going to be to raise four children with three being so young. There were many of nights I cried out and asked the Lord my Abba Father, for pure physical strength, to just finish what I needed to by the end of the night, suffering from exhaustion. I wanted to make sure they had hot meals, they were to school on time, homework was done, and babies were put down with clean diapers and everything else in between that mothers do day in and day out that go unnoticed.

In all of this, I needed God to be there with me every step of the way and to be strong when I was weak. I worshipped Him through it all. In order to get through the struggles, I had to make time for God. Many of times we make time to spend time with our families, our church, our co-workers, but we forget to spend time with God. It is necessary for our spiritual well-being and growth. He is the source, and the provider of all things, why wouldn't it be a priority to spend time with the one who orders your steps?

I thank the many people who prayed for me, gave me encouragement along the way, or just spoke words of truth and faith when I was going through and wanting to give up not only on my marriage but on my family. It has been a source of strength for me. I began to stand in my truth, "that God so loved the world that He gave His only begotten Son, that whosoever believed in Him shall have everlasting life." (John 3:16 NIV) . And so it was, I was given life to persevere, to continue to stand even if that was all I could do. In this life lesson, I learned not to let the trials and tests you go through get you down. No matter what I go through, no matter what may come my way, with Jesus we can make it through. His grace and mercy endures forever.

I pray that in this season, God will continue to use me and my story to provide hope and encouragement to the wife, the mother, or the sister who needs to hear she is worthy, she is of royal value, and more importantly she is loved. Go forth, you've got this! Your best is yet to come. Be blessed women of faith.

Everyone has a mountain to climb and autism has not been my
mountain, it has been my opportunity for victory.
- Rachel Barcellona

Tapped: Going from Tapped Out to Tapped In
Omoni Williams

Aghhhhh! I sighed as I finally stood safely within the confines of my closed and locked bedroom door. This cannot be my life I thought for the thousandth time as a stream of tears rolled down my face. I am the wife of a soldier but I was the one who had just returned from battle. Battle? Yes, battle, an exceptionally difficult one from the grounds of my very own home.

My oldest, had just begun to calm down from his most recent meltdown. Highlights from this battle included me shouting commands to my daughter and younger two sons to stay in their rooms and lock their doors. They were instructed not to come out until I told them. Meanwhile, I combated with my oldest son who was raging mad with emotions and charged to make us feel his angst.

Before my son's meltdown, the day started out as a typical weekend afternoon. The younger three children were content playing in their rooms or listening to music as they relaxed. Unlike his siblings my oldest could not relax. He had been perseverating on the fact that his Legos had been taken away again due to bad behavior choices and he was not happy about it in the least. Unbeknownst to the rest of us my oldest basically had decided if he was going to be unhappy so were the rest of us. That afternoon the determination peaked and his self-proclaimed righteous indignation shone forth as his wrath was on full display for his siblings and I live and in living color as if we were watching a play on Broadway.

In a pitch that rivaled Mariah Carey's top notes from the song Someday, he hollered "Give me back my Lego's!" repeatedly. Initially with each screeching demand I attempted to explain that he would not be getting the Legos back that day. I further tried to convey to him that the Legos would remain taken away due to his bad behavior choices like the behaviors he was currently displaying. Despite my frequent attempts to explain to him my words fell on deaf ears.

He wanted the Lego's - that much was apparent. In his mind they were his Lego's, he wanted them and he should have them no matter what type of behavior he was currently displaying or had displayed. Just give him the Lego's period point blank he emoted.

As events begun to get more colorful, I began to record the incident. I planned to later show the video to his Applied Behavioral Analysis (ABA) therapist. Once the camera was on things kicked into a whole other level. He cannot stand being filmed. However, we use the tapes to help him once he is calm to process his behaviors with his therapist and strategize better ways to handle his emotions.

But, because the children had broken my phone several summers ago, the only way to record him was in selfie mode. This made it very apparent to him that he was being filmed. As soon as he saw me videotaping he rushed to the bathroom with his blanket and a water bottle and locked the door all while still screaming at his siblings and I for his Lego's. Opening the door a few seconds later he attempted to douse me and my phone with water. I struggled to keep recording while keeping him at bay, no easy task as someone lunges for you over and over.
Eventually, I got the bottle of water away from him but not before being doused from head to toe. My phone was safe minus a few sprinkles but I was a tad worse for wear. After the bottle was taken from him he took to using the blanket as a weapon. He attempted to use it like nun chucks and took swats at me over and over. In the very end I simply had enough and began to yell myself. I threatened to throw all of the damn Lego's away if he did not stop immediately, go to his room, calm down and not come out until I called him. He went to his room; the other kids were safe in the confines of their rooms and I was finally safely in my own. I was physically and emotionally spent. I was done for the day. In truth I was probably done for that whole weekend. I clearly needed to regroup and formulate a better strategy for the next battle to come because one surely would. That particular weekend day however

I was tapped out.

My oldest is a 5'7", 120 pounds, 12-year-old African American boy with Autism Spectrum Disorder (ASD). He, like his two younger brothers, who also have ASD, do not look any different from any of their typical peers. They are different though. They have issues at times in social settings, with personal space and they all at times lack a general sense of danger. Not to mention meltdowns like described above because they struggle managing their emotions.

The fact that they look like their typical peers but behave differently at times is concerning to me chiefly as a parent of three African American young men with special needs. I feel strongly that there are these invisible strikes against them because they are one; African American, two; male and now three; have special needs. I try very hard to especially work on social interactions with law enforcement and others of authority to help both my children and those in authority to build a bridge and help normalize their unique existence. Being completely transparent I know that even as their mother, being fully cognizant of their medical condition it is still hard for me at times to process and handle. Hence my own mini meltdown as noted above.

But, this was the reality—this is the reality of dealing with Autism. The scientific definition says that Autism is disorder generally characterized by difficulties in communication, social interactions and behavioral challenges where many notice signs between the ages of two and three years old. It is called a spectrum disorder because no two individuals with ASD are alike. ASD occurs in 1 in 68 children in the United States. In military families it is 1 in 18. Boys have a higher rate of diagnoses than girls. But, in my case, in my reality Autism was a part of our life, our family, and ever present in my boys. See, I am a military wife with 3 African American boys with ASD – and our definition changes and grows on daily, situational, and emotional basis.

I have struggled to put into words what my journey, my family's journey has been; a roller coaster with many ups and downs between diagnosis, getting help, advocating in school and in the community for them. I was not going to share my story. However, my story needs to be told. There are other families like mine who navigate this life and need support and understanding. Today, I am my children's champion. Many will say I am a super mom and by the end you may too. When we began this journey, I was simply a scared mommy with a relentless desire to make sure my baby was alright.

Here is how it all began...

It was May 2015 when this journey began to catch wind and from that day our family being to sift. My immediate family, affectionately called Team Will and I headed to Georgia to attend my younger cousin's high school graduation. I was super excited to actually be present for such a big milestone. My husband is a soldier in the United States Army. As such we rarely are close to family and tend to miss a lot of events, milestones and moments because we are too far away. We had an absolutely fabulous time that made me long to be closer to my loved ones.

During our visit, as the children were playing, the adults had a conversation about African Americans and health care. I remember the conversation highlighted the fact that many African Americans tend to not go to the doctor to seek help right away or at all for physical symptoms at times but especially mental health issues. Some of those reasons include access to health care, money and the mentality that whatever the "issue" is, is minor and they will get over it. As a military family I love that we have access to great health care. I do not hesitate to schedule appointments to make sure my children are healthy and well which is what I told the family in our discussion.

The next day we were set to leave. As we were saying our goodbyes I recall my uncle standing with my husband and I in his driveway. He pulled me to the side and told me that he wanted me to schedule an appointment to have my middle son tested. He believed he was on the spectrum. He had noticed things during our visit. As a clinical social worker and someone who works with children and families on a daily basis he saw several red flags. I told my uncle that I would inquire about an assessment at our next appointment.

Looking back, I wonder if that family discussion was a precursor or set up for the conversation we had the following day. I may never know and in truth it does not matter. My uncle opened a door and I am so glad we walked through it. It just so happened that we had an appointment with the doctor set up for the day after we arrived back home. The appointment went well and the pediatrician agreed with my uncle that my middle son may have autism and additional evaluations would be needed She then put in a referral for an evaluation with developmental pediatrician.

We had that next appointment a mere nine days later. That is unheard of in our current area. Patients usually wait at least a month, often longer to get an initial developmental appointment or follow up. I was a nervous wreck going into that appointment with the developmental pediatrician. I listened to both my uncle and the pediatrician. I knew some about autism not very much at that point. I was not ready for any of them to be correct after all. At the end of the assessments the developmental pediatrician told us that my middle baby was definitely Autistic. We were told that the doctor would have a full report ready for us in a month. Until then we were given some resources to look over and some basic first steps. I looked at her as she spoke and just broke down and cried. Sad does not even begin to describe how I felt.

When I got home I went online to connect with some special mommy friends of mine for support. I am blessed to be part of an amazing group online. I have been friends with this group of women for over twelve years now. We have supported each other through births of kids, deaths of parents, marriage, divorce and all sorts of in between. I love these women like sisters because in many ways they are my sisters. All of the ladies in our group are pretty opinionated women. Our opinions on many things are highly diverse but paramount of all opinions and conjecture is love.

Several of the ladies in this group have children on the spectrum. I knew they would understand my experience and I would be loved and supported in a way that others not a part of this special needs world would necessarily understand. I poured out my heart and told them the news. I told them my fears too. "What on Earth was I supposed to do now? How did this happen to MY BABY? Why my baby? Why me?" I had so many questions and my thoughts raced a million miles a minute. One girlfriend in particular, Ivy, told me I essentially had the rest of the day to cry but then I needed to suck it up and get to work. While we are all supportive of one another we will not idly sit back and watch each other wallow. We encourage each other to act and seek help when needed.

That day, I needed Ivy's tough love because I imagine I would have wallowed for longer than a day otherwise. I kept hearing Justin Timberlake singing "Cry Me a River" play on repeat in my mind. As I laid on my bed and cried my own river.

Nevertheless, when I got up I got to work. I knew that the developmental pediatrician told me my child needed certain therapies and interventions. With this basic knowledge at hand I took off and was on a mission to get him the resources that he needed. I started to get tapped in. I began finding places that had availabilities, scheduling therapies and coordinated the set-up implementation of the services with our insurance as quickly as possible. Things occurring as expeditiously as they did back then was nothing but God's favor in our lives. I did not know much at the time. Almost three years later, I feel I still have a way to go.

I talked with the speech therapist for the county my son saw weekly and informed her of the new diagnosis. We discussed increasing services for my son to get into a preschool classroom during the school year. We also found that in Fairfax County Public Schools, they have a preschool autistic classroom (PAC) that actually runs through the school year and a good portion of the summer as well. So of course, we hopped at the chance to enroll him without hesitation. Within those first few weeks the therapist and I were able to enroll him in the extended school year program. He was able to begin attending the preschool class that summer.

Additionally, I also scouted out recommendations for speech and occupational therapy. By the end of August my son was able to begin private speech and private occupational therapy, attend a preschool program specifically designed for children on the spectrum and begin ABA therapy within our home too.

Life changed majorly for Team Will after that diagnosis. I was running to appointments left and right. Initially we had speech three times a week and occupational therapy twice a week. Sometimes these appointments were able to be combined and done together. Other times we had to come at different times. Up until that summer of 2015 I had homeschooled my 2nd grade daughter and my then 3rd grade oldest son. We had a family meeting during the summer and decided that I needed to put more attention into helping my middle son get the help and support he needed so the oldest two children began public school.

Oh, I forgot to mention ALL of this was going while I was adjusting to life with a newborn baby boy born in January, he was only 5 months old. I was in full supermom status. Two kids changing environments and headed to public school, a new baby, a husband in the military, and trying to advocate for my newly diagnosed child with ASD. Yes, definitely a supermom! But we had no choice but to make it work. Adjusting was rough for a bit. In time we worked it out. We created a system and made things happen.

Things were running fairly smoothly, well smooth-ish for Team Will. I was managing my middle son's new treatments, including adding physical therapy to our weekly rotation due to his toe walking. The older kids were going to public school, my daughter for the first time and my husband's often crazy military work schedule seemed to all flow much more cohesively. The storm seemed to be gone and the new normal had set in. But, we were not finished with our ASD journey though.

Our oldest was having some behavioral problems and seeing a therapist. The therapist mentioned that he was exhibiting some ASD symptoms and she wanted to have him tested. I agreed to the testing but felt conflicted. Halloween 2015 my oldest was also diagnosed with ASD.

My oldest also has other co-morbid conditions. When he was a kindergartner, he was diagnosed with Attention Deficit Hyperactivity Disorder (ADHD). I distinctly recall his pediatrician saying, "Well, the good news is he doesn't have Autism!" I was floored because I had no idea the pediatrician ever thought he was on the spectrum to begin with. Since in the initial cursory overview the pediatrician did not determine my son was on the spectrum they never performed the standard evaluations or had my husband and I complete forms to see if he really was on the spectrum. To find out many years later that had a full evaluation for ASD been conducted they would have found out that he was indeed on the spectrum was a source of anger for me.

Only four months after my middle son was first diagnosed; my oldest was diagnosed at the age of 9. My oldest has struggled with school and social interactions for such a long time. His diagnosis made some things so clear to us. Had I known I could have helped him get those supports he needed earlier just as I was able to do with his younger brother. When you know better you do better. So, while I was angry about the late diagnosis, I was also impassioned to make changes I now felt should have been underway years before. Similar to my middle son, after my oldest diagnosis we added another child to the therapy rotation.

Last summer my youngest was diagnosed as well. Both my oldest and youngest sons are higher functioning than my middle son. It was especially hard getting the diagnosis for my youngest because we weren't sure if his behaviors were learned from his two older siblings on the spectrum themselves or if he genuinely had ASD himself. While my baby's ASD is far milder than the older two he seems to present with more sensory issues than others. Like the other two I have made sure to tap into therapy supports for him.

All three boys, now regularly, attend speech and occupational therapy outside of the home roughly one to two times a week, per child. We also have ABA therapist in the home two to four times a week depending on the child for a two hour block each session with all three boys. We also have regular counseling sessions for one child. Lastly, one son just finished weekly physical therapy and will move to consults to follow up and insure he is staying on track.

In between therapy we have fit in scouting, Cub Scouts for my middle son and Girl Scouts for my daughter as well as tennis and AWANA's (Approved Workmen Are Not Ashamed) for all the children. Our oldest just finished his third year of Special Olympics Snowboarding and was the first novice snowboarder at the Pennsylvania games earlier this year. We have also participated in music lessons outside of school, however we did not participate in music lessons this 2017-2018 school year due to my husband's deployment. Some days I simply had to make difficult choices when time management was stretched and there was only one parent to handle things. We may add it back into rotation when my husband returns.

Like all good parents, I want what's best for my children. As such I also tap into my community and volunteer as a room mom at the elementary school, I am a Mothers of Preschoolers (MOPS) discussion group leader, I volunteer with the Autism Society of Northern Virginia and I also volunteer with our church in the children's department and when possible with our local military community in various capacities as well.

To say I am busy is quite the understatement. I am learning that in all my advocating and championing for the children, as well as being an active part of the community, I MUST take care of myself. As you can guess with all of these moving pieces I often put myself on the back burner.

I have forgotten to eat way too many times to count, not made that appointment to get my hair done or simply not insuring I have down time to read a book, get a pedicure or just relax and watch a movie. This deployment has forced me to take care of myself more.

Thankfully though, I have an amazing community that checks in on my family and steps in to assist when we need them. Whether you have a child or children with special needs or not, taking care of yourself is vital. As mothers we need to realize that we cannot give our children or families our best if we do not first tend to ourselves. This lesson has been a long time coming for me. Slowly but surely, I am making me a priority.

I learned through all of this that we as moms need to make sure we are tapped in. Making sure I got connected has been an integral piece of my family getting the resources and care they need. Getting tapped in can come in the form of seeking help from a doctor, a friend or family member who is dealing with a similar situation or researching on the internet. Even taking the time to slow down and pray that God guides you to the right people and in the right direction you and your family need to go. Some days you may be tapped out but when you tap into those resources and community you will realize whatever you may be facing, you too can push through and come out on the other side.

For more information about Autism please check out:
www.CDC.gov Put Autism in the search engine
www.autism-society.org
www.autism speaks.org
www.autism.sesamestreet.org

"Destiny is what we think of as life, while life is the process of destiny!"
–Bertice Berry

The Redemption Of A Lost Soul
Em Desiray

The world was my oyster, and the possibilities were limitless.

I once was a girl who dreamt of a world that was manifested in a perfect destiny. I saw my future clear as day. It was bright, simple, and true.

I can never remember being hungry, sad, impatient, tired, upset, angry. Life was carefree. Even when my dad was absent; I never felt a void.

I loved everything about my life. My city. My family. Life was love; free-flowing love, and my grandmother held the key.

Then, one day, my entire world shattered and everything came crashing down. It happened so fast that I very quickly and suddenly became a casualty of love.

On March 31, 1997 – love died. I remember it like it was yesterday. This was the day that I lost my grandmother, my heart, my best friend, my love, to dreadful cancer.

The loss was sudden, surprising, and it shattered my whole world. In my mind, God snatched her from me, unnecessarily, and I was pissed. My young mind couldn't process what had just happened. Overnight I was without my best friend, homeless and helpless. Within 3 months, still homeless, I was transported to an unfamiliar environment with unfamiliar people who were now supposed to be my family. A family I had never really known. A family that, though I tried, I never fit into. By this time, I was lonely, stuck in my own grief. My mom stuck in hers. My uncle, drowning in his. There was nowhere to run. All I could do was walk in it. I stopped attending church, reverted inside myself and kept my emotions bottled up inside me.

You see, up until this point, God was Love. My grandmother was love. But she had left me, and God had forsaken me. They, love, had rejected me. If it was possible to feel that pain, and God couldn't protect me from it, what was the point in staying faithful to him? What was the point, when he was the source of my pain? From that moment on, I knew I couldn't depend on him. I would "protect" myself, from here on out.

LOVE IS…ABANDONMENT

I learned that love was abandonment at age 11. This was reaffirmed when 3 months after my grandmother passed, I found out I would be moving out of state. Not only would I now be leaving friends and family who I'd known and grew up with all my life, but I'd also be leaving a young boy who I thought I had fallen in love with. He had been my rock as I watched my grandmother slip from this earth. He was my blink of happiness and comfort in an otherwise depressed reality. And now, I would again, be ripped away from what I knew love to be. This taught me that love was not secure, and never was it ever definite. I began to move through life this way: afraid to love, afraid to attach myself to anything I knew had the ability to abandon me, afraid of commitment. "Friendships" were my "safe" place.

And in my self-professed "safe place," as I disguised my love within male friendships, I faced even more pain and confusion. I was trying to fill a void I didn't know I had, and trying to control the uncontrollable.

LOVE IS…ABUSIVE

My first "real" boyfriend was controlling and emotionally abusive. It started out as friends because of course friends weren't supposed to hurt you like love could. That was until he said those 3 magic words that again would change my life forever; "I Love you."

I was 13 and craved anything that sounded like love. What teenager wouldn't crave love and compassion after the death of her grandmother, an absentee father, and a grieving mother? So, I stayed with "my friend" for 3 years. Although we were the same age, he was much more advanced than I was. So during those 3 years, "my friend" would threaten to leave me if I didn't sleep with him; Or at the very least, if I didn't kiss him. Some days I was beautiful to him and in the blink of an eye he would say I was ugly. One day he tried to hit me with a car because I accidentally busted his lip while play fighting. He was redefining what love was to me. Now, love was not only hurtful, but abusive. And even through all of that, at 16, I willingly gave up my virginity to him. He broke up with me the very next day. So much for love.

LOVE IS REPLACEABLE…

It was in college that the self-discovery of wild promiscuity led me to a kindred spirit. I found a best friend, who for a minute, I think I momentarily fell in love with. Once we met, there was no separating us. And like me, or so I thought, he didn't want a "relationship;" just the "so-called" benefits and perks of having one. Relationships meant Love. Love meant pain. Neither of us wanted any parts of it.

We spent every moment together; Talking till the sun came up, sleeping together without touching each other. We loved the same music, read the same books, shared the same opinions. He told me about his past, and I told him about mine. We had life in common – all of our insecurities, all of our dreams seemed to be aligned. He had a grandmother, who like mine, was his best friend. She became a "substitute" for the grandmother I lost in my past life. He felt like home away from home, and for once, I thought my "non-attachment" in my quest for love was actually working.

I don't remember the first time we slept together. But what I do remember was that it was amazing. There was a connection that I hadn't felt in any of my other "situationships." I was hooked and we just, fit. I loved him, and I knew he loved me. But it was a new, unfamiliar form of love. This was my best friend. I loved him in all the ways a person could love someone. It wasn't just sexual. It wasn't just emotional. It was – Love. It was everything I was trying to run from and more.

I thought I could trust again, so I began to relax. But just like the cancer that stole my grandmother's love from me, a mutual friend and her cancerous ways set out to destroy everything that I considered safe. She wanted the closeness me and my best friend had, and at all costs, she began to divide and conquer. My best friend started to pull away. He started to believe her lies and deception. And as I watched the closeness we had diminish, he started to love her instead. The cancer was working.

Love, even in the name of friendship proved unstable. At 20 years old, I learned that my love could be replaced.

He rejected me to be with her. Love had failed me once again. What I thought was secure and stable was able to very easily be infiltrated. This was proof positive that Love, was NOT for me. I started to believe that I was incapable of being loved and nothing proved this more than what happened next.

LOVE IS RAPE…

At 23, I was raped. He was no stranger. He was someone I felt safe enough let inside my home. Someone I had been conversing with for some time. As he pinned me to the sofa, and I yelled at him to "stop," he would not. I tried my best to resist, but I couldn't move or release his grip around my wrists as his body weight collapsed on top of me. I vehemently turned my head from side to side as he tried to kiss me. He held me down for what seemed like forever, thrusting his body into mine until he released his soul – THAT'S when he released me. When he stood up, he adjusted his clothes, and cleaned up his mess. I laid there stunned and embarrassed. He looked at me with a mischievous grin. "Don't act like you didn't like it," he said to me. I was speechless, and numb.

I learned that love was aggressive, dirty and evil. I learned that love had the capability to strip your soul, and leave an empty vessel behind. I was empty.

LOVE IS AFRAID…

A few years later, I met love in the studio.

I was recording music as my therapy, a passion of mine I had since childhood. Music was always love; it had yet to hurt me, and I could always find solace, confirmation and answers within the music.

To find him in music seemed right. He was funny, personable and unlike most of the other ones, he was what some referred to as a "square." He was, what I felt, I needed at the time. After some dates, and conversations, he made me feel like I was good enough to be with him. Before him, I had been filling my days with liquor and marijuana to pass the time. It helped me get through each day without having to feel my reality; the hurt caused by love. With him, I no longer needed the weed and alcohol. Everyone else was finding their soulmates, so I had to believe that there was one for me too. I had to have hope if I was going to survive. So cautiously, I gave it a shot.

In the beginning, I thought he was different than the rest. He was attentive, giving and sweet. I knew in my heart, that no one would give me what I knew I deserved, so since he was at least making an effort (unlike any of the other ones), I figured I would see it through and reward him for it. To me, he was my answer.

That was, until I got pregnant.

My pregnancy was the turning point in our relationship. Though it wasn't planned, there was never a conscious effort on either of our parts to avoid it. The answer to my quest for love was simple. I would create a family I could love, that would love me in return. I was ready to love and be loved. And I was tired of running, and avoiding, and trying to protect myself from something I shouldn't have had to protect myself from.

I was excited. This baby for me, represented the love I had been longing for since that night my grandmother passed, and since all the failed loves that followed her death. This was a new beginning and I deserved this kind of love.

But in true form, as soon as I told him, he immediately rejected me. He was no longer my knight in shining armor, but a sheep in wools clothing. My new love didn't want the precious love and future that was growing inside of me. So be it out of fear, immaturity or just sheer evilness, he immediately started treating me differently.

One day, I called my mom to tell her that I just didn't feel right about the pregnancy. I explained that I had a strange intuition, and that I wasn't experiencing any of the symptoms I should be at the stage I was at. My back was uncomfortable, and although I was always sleepy, something just didn't feel right. Mom tried to reassure me that I would be fine, but I just couldn't buy into it.

The very next day, seven weeks after finding out I was pregnant, and after a morning of rigid lovemaking, I began to bleed. I told him what was happening, but he was not concerned. He got ready for work and left me at home to figure things out by myself.

I was rejected and abandoned yet again.

With tears in my eyes, I called my best friend and told him I needed to go to the hospital. Upon my arrival, the doctor told me I was having a miscarriage.

Another love lost.

He arrived at the hospital, and suddenly, the same love I thought I knew before the pregnancy, reappeared. He was sweet and affectionate that night. But this pissed me off because it was only then, while his baby died inside of me, that the love returned. He acted as if I was just supposed to forget about the way he had been acting for the last few weeks. As we lay in bed, him snoring lightly in my ear, I cried. I grieved the death of my child, the death of my relationship and the fact that not only had God stolen my future from me again, but love had also failed me once again. It was beginning to be a pattern, but this cycle had run its course. I woke him up out of his sleep and threw him out of my house, and my life.

At 25 years old, I learned that even love was afraid to love.

LOVE IS MANIPULATIVE…

It took me a few months to get back to myself after the miscarriage. But once I emerged from my cocoon of depression, I was a broken, damaged woman, who felt there was nothing to do but to dredge on. I thought about my angel baby every day, but I knew I couldn't just sit in my grief. It wasn't safe for me to do, nor was it productive. I missed my ex too, but my anger and hurt overpowered my longing for love. The only thing I could do was to find someone to fill the void and distract me from the pain.

He showed up a year later and found me online. He was attractive, masculine, and everything in a man I thought I could never have. This was the one I thought. And I made it my mission to do whatever was necessary to make him love me.

We started out as friends. But I made it clear to him that I didn't want any attachments. He seemed to have been cool with that, so we allowed a bond to form naturally within both of our insecurities. We were both damaged souls; that was evident. But for some reason I felt that our souls needed it each other. Maybe we could fix the issues we had together. It took a year for us to sleep together, but once we did, it was almost magical. He felt like he was made for me, and I for him. We fit perfectly. But I ignored the signs.

Three years into our relationship, the once attentive friend was now distant and unreliable. His words no longer matched his actions, and he seemed to have become dependent on me, both emotionally and financially. I ignored the fact that he was now asking for more than he was giving.

I loved him.

I knew I was in the danger zone, and the only thing left for me to do was to either run or see it to the end. Loyal to a fault, I chose the latter. By year 5, he was no longer hiding his philandering and he no longer respected me or my feelings. He didn't even acknowledge them. I had given up so much of myself that I had forgotten who I was without him. I needed to find her again. I missed her. That's when the epiphany happened. I needed to find love for me.

Tired of being used and abused, tired of being the only one trying to maintain the friendship that once existed, and tired of trying to make him see the value of my presence in his life, I finally found the courage and strength to leave. I realized that love hadn't been failing me all this time. I had been failing it.

All those years the biggest mistake I could have ever made was trying to find love in a man. I knew for a long while that I had to find love, not only within myself, but in the spirit that gave me life.

I realized that it had been fear all along, that kept me from love. Fear of the realizations I would need to make and fear of the work that would need to be done to overcome them.

I realized that the only reason why love had never worked in my favor, was because I was doing it alone and looking in all the wrong places. Love had always stared back at me in the mirror. Love had always been within. It was in the memories of my grandmother, the love of my family, the love of my friends, but most importantly, it was Love that allowed me wake up each day.

At 32 years old, I remembered that Love was God.

WHAT LOVE ACTUALLY IS…

I heard a saying once, that in Corinthians Chapter 13, if you replace the word "love" with the man's name, and he meets the criteria, you know you found the one. Try it now:

"4 Love is patient and kind. Love is not jealous or boastful or proud 5 or rude. It does not demand its own way. It is not irritable, and it keeps no record of being wronged. 6 It does not rejoice about injustice but rejoices whenever the truth wins out. 7 Love never gives up, never loses faith, is always hopeful, and endures through every circumstance."

Does it work? See, God had already laid out love's true definition, but I had consistently chosen to ignore it.

Healing is never easy, but I came to realize that you cannot heal until you make the effort. I knew I had to learn to forgive myself for being angry, hurt, naïve, insecure, selfish, rebellious and afraid. I realized that most of my pain was self-inflicted, and I would have to re-examine the choices I had made in order to heal from them. I also had to forgive all of my failed loves for not having the ability to love me through their own pain. But most importantly, I knew that I had to heal my relationship with my Creator. I had to stop blaming him for the pain I had endured since that tragic day in 1997. I had to "forgive" him for "taking" my grandmother's life, and accept, that being the true angel she was, it was simply time for her to go home.

I had to find my peace.

I had strayed from my foundation, that God would never leave nor forsake me. I had to regroup and remember that though I had been choosing to for so long, I did not have to walk alone – that I was never walking alone. There were always two footsteps in the sand – three if you count my grandmother.

It had taken me 20 years to realize that all I had to do was surrender to him and allow him to bestow his grace upon my life. All I had to do was let go and let God.

I finally understood, that until I could accept the fact that the battle was not mine to fight alone, I would not win.

My story is not over, and that's the beauty of this life. Every day is a new beginning. And while I'm still a work in progress and have not yet reached the end of my journey, I have come to realize that no man is strong enough to carry the burdens of this world alone. There is a lesson in it all, and the lesson I learned is that there is no testimony without the test.

This is my testimony.

Love did not run from me, I ran from it the day my grandmother left this earth. That was the error in my juvenile ways that lead me down a path of confusion. And I've been lost ever since. I've come to realize that if I continue to look for love in a man, I will fail every single time.

LOVE IS GOD… and God is Love. And I have to trust that he will guide my footsteps in the right direction.

Now, I'm ready for whatever LOVE brings.

I just have to be open to receive it.

I am redeemed

God is our refuge and strength, a very present help in trouble.
Therefore we will not fear, though the earth should change and
though the mountains slip into the heart of the sea; though its
waters roar and foam, though the mountains quake at its swelling
pride. Selah. The LORD of hosts is with us; the God of Jacob is our
stronghold. Selah.
Psalm 46:1-3,7

Wings Of Faith
Joy Ada Onyesoh

I had feelings of great excitement and joy getting married. I come from a family of four excluding our parents. I desired to have a daughter but prayed that she would come last so that we all could dot on her. Not too long after I got married, I remember vividly one night standing outside staring into the skies and admiring the constellation of stars and suddenly a shooting star appeared from out of nowhere and was moving quickly through the skies. I made some wishes, for my future, the number and sex of the children I wanted and for my husband. I felt so excited sighting the shooting stars. Many years down the road, I still recollect that night and wonder what made me believe so firmly in the myths of shooting star. I realized that I was unconsciously seeking for a reconnection with God and saw His presence in the beautiful creation of the stars and the moon. My faith in God became my solace and strength in the years ahead.

In July 2005, I found out that I was pregnant. The feeling of happiness and accomplishment enveloped me. The conception, pregnancy and delivery of my other two kids were uneventful; I was looking forward with excitement to this third pregnancy and also praying that she would be a girl. The counting down to when I would know the sex of the baby began and I felt the months were moving at a snail's speed. I was almost impatient to confirm the sex. You can then imagine how elated I was the day I got confirmation that I was expecting a baby girl. My excitement knew no bounds, I felt like I was literally walking on the clouds. I was busy planning in my head, colors, activities and all the works. We had decided that we would have three children and having my little girl as the last child was the icing on the cake for me.

Walking Through The Valley

I arrived in London, United Kingdom. This was 10 weeks before my expected date of delivery. I got myself registered in a hospital for antenatal care. Then, I started having all these weird thoughts of my baby dying or myself dying after delivery. At times the thoughts would be so strong that I would break down in tears. Sometimes, while in the store trying to find the clothes to buy, these depressing thoughts will take hold of me I would leave the store crying without buying anything. I was dealing with these depressing thoughts alone and couldn't bring myself to share with anyone.

After nine months of pregnancy, on the 21st of March 2006, I went into labour. I picked up my packed bag and headed to the hospital. I was checked and admitted into the hospital. My labour intensified and after a while the labour pains subsided and my dilation stopped. After 24 hours of no progress, the doctor suggested that I go back home until the labour progressed. I accepted and went home. When I got home and dropped my bags in the bedroom, I sat on the bed and had this prompting in my spirit to worship God. Now this wasn't something I had done much of in the recent past. Yes, I attended church when convenient and sometimes prayed but I didn't have a personal relationship with God. So, when I got this prompting it felt a little bit awkward. However, I got on feet and as I did, I was led to say a prayer of forgiveness. After praying I burst into songs of praise and worship. The songs just kept coming, rolling over my tongue; I found myself completely broken in spirit yet I felt this comforting presence all around me.

When I obeyed the promptings to pray and worship God, some of the depressing thoughts that I used to have left. Calmness began to flow through my mind and this time I wasn't scared or sad. I started to speak positive thoughts out loud. It then dawned on me that perhaps, I needed to have done that worship session to get me on track and prepared mentally, physically and spiritually for my delivery. I was in mediation and worship mode for hours and late into the day. On the 22nd of March, the labor pains started and this time with much intensity. I knew this was for real. I picked my hospital bag and off I went again to the hospital but this time,

I was convinced that I wasn't returning without my baby girl. I arrived at the hospital, went through the usual procedures and got admitted. The dilation progressed very quickly and within an hour of being admitted at the hospital. In the early hours of the 23rd of March 2006, my beautiful angel came forth. It felt like a fairy tale. As I gazed into the beautiful face of my daughter, I felt this surge of love, bond and commitment like I had never felt before. I told myself, life can't be anymore perfect, two sons, a daughter and a doting husband. What more can I ask of God?

We were discharged from the hospital two days later. As we were en route home, I couldn't help but be in awe of my princess sleeping so peacefully. I knew this was of God. We got settled in as soon as we arrived home and I decided to take a nap since my bundle of joy was also sleeping. By nightfall my daughter's consistent cry woke me up. I breastfed her, cuddled her but to no avail, she kept crying. Then I had an intuition that something else must be wrong with her. As an experienced mom, I started the elimination technique. I changed her diaper. I moved on to body parts and at the touch of her right leg, her cries became more intense. The sound of her cries, felt like my heart was being sliced into a thousand pieces. It was already late into the night, but I knew that we needed medical attention quickly. I had to call a friend, and we took my baby into the emergency room. The doctor came in and asked me several questions. I was just responded mechanically. Looking back at that night, I shudder at the amount of pain we had inflicted on my sweet princess. I can still vividly picture the examination room that night and her cries still rings clearly in my ears. This was just one of the many cries that we would experience.

We were discharged and given an appointment at a children's specialist hospital. By the next morning her right femur was visibly swollen, I was scared to my bones; little did I know or understand the severity of the situation. I knew that I couldn't wait for the specialist appointment, which was three weeks away. I quickly called a general practitioner, who happened to be a family friend, and he asked me to quickly bring her in. I swaddled my daughter and carried her carefully over to the GP's office. He was more careful than the doctor who saw us at the emergency room the previous night. He gently and carefully examined her. He asked me series of questions, the calmness he exuded, gave me a lot of comfort. My heart was almost popping out of my chest. I was faced with a situation that I didn't have an understanding of and that was the scariest bit for me. The doctor gave me a referral letter to the specialist unit of the hospital where I had her. He told me I should go straight to the hospital. So there I was recently delivered a new baby; running around in cold London. I just got overwhelmed by emotions while I was in the bus and broke down crying. I was so scared; I hadn't experienced such fear in my life.

We got to Jack's place at Northwick Park Hospital. I didn't know would be my home for some weeks to come. I got to the reception desk where I presented my referral letter. I explained all the doctor told me. The nurse asked me if I had an appointment and I said no. She asked me to wait while she checks out with the consultant on duty. I guessed then that it wasn't the usual practice to just walk into the place and present a referral letter and asked to be seen. Obviously, there were lots of kids in that particular ward that also needed urgent attention. I was lost in thought. Sitting helplessly in the waiting area, when a female doctor walked up to me, she had spoken to me for almost a minute before. I knew that someone was talking to me. She was trying to explain to me that I needed call a certain number and if it's an urgent case, I need to go to the emergency unit. I didn't hear most of what she was saying. As she was still talking to me another male doctor walked pass, turned back and approached us. I guess he was struck at how lost I was looking and the sadness written all over my eyes. He stopped right in front of me, asked to see my baby. He looked her over and said it's not the usual practice, but he would write a note for an x-ray to be done on her. He would see me immediately after the x-ray. It was at that point that I knew he was the consultant everyone was referring to.

My princess had her first of many x-rays at three days old. I remember thinking, how tiny and helpless she looked as I placed her on the x-ray couch. Finally, we got the results, and the consultant confirmed a fracture. Then another nightmare begun, I became a suspect! I was suspected of manhandling my daughter! That broke me more than anything else, as I carried her in my arms walking down the passageway to the orthopedic department; blinded by my tears. I had cried so many tears that day and I was already feeling physically and emotionally exhausted. We got her fitted into a harness and referred back to the ward and the consultant informed me that we would be admitted. We got our room. I nursed her and she settled in to sleep, the first restful sleep in her three days of life and after settling her in her bed, I sunk into my bed. I was drained on all fronts but I felt comforted that my princess was looking so peaceful.

I sat on my bed watching my princess sleep, a nurse walked into the room to introduce herself as the nurse on duty. We exchanged pleasantries, and she could immediately see how distraught I looked. She encouraged me to go for a cup of tea. It was at that point I realized that I hadn't eaten for the last two days. The nurse promised to pop in periodically to look in on my angel and encouraged me to go get some fresh air and a cup of hot tea. As she walked out of the room, I reached out for my jacket in the wardrobe. As I was wearing my jacket, I heard a quiet voice very clearly say, " Don't Go Out"! In confusion, I stepped backwards and quickly sank into the bed behind me. I looked at the bed in which my daughter was lying in, and it struck me that she was suddenly beginning to look dark. I stood up from my bed. I briskly walked across the room to her bed and gazed intently at her face. I saw that the dark color was slowly spreading from her forehead over the rest of her face!! I let out a very loud scream that got the nurse rushing into my room. She took one quick glance and all I could remember was the alarm going off, doctors and nurses rushing into my room. It was all happening so fast.

All I can remember is how my heart was literally hurting as if it was being torn from my chest, tears were pouring down my cheeks. I guessed I must have made some involuntary noise that got one nurse to take notice of me. I can't remember what she was saying but all I can remember was my whisperings to God, "Father, please don't let my princess die, please Lord have mercy on me, don't allow me go back home empty handed!!!" I didn't know that God heard a mother's cry of pain at that instance. I can't remember all that happened after then, I guessed the whole trauma of the last two days hit me real bad and I may have passed out. I woke up to see my daughter fixed up on all kinds of funny noisy gadgets. As I looked at her and I couldn't stop the warm tears from running all over my face!!! I later learnt that she was reacting to the morphine that was given to her as a pain reducer before putting her in the harness. I spent the night anxiously peeping at her to be sure that she was still breathing. How I survived that night I just can't begin to describe.

.

Wings of Faith

The next morning, the consultant came to see us. He told me that I was cleared by social welfare. I responded to him that I won't have any records because I don't live in London but in Nigeria. I also informed him that I waited and prayed for a daughter such that I am not capable of hurting her. He responded that when the GP (General Practitioner) was called during the investigation into the cause of my daughter's fracture that he backed my story. They knew I hadn't harmed my baby.

On her seventh day of being on this beautiful planet earth, she had another fracture. I asked myself if it could get any worse than that? I cried so bitterly. Crying and lamentation had become my pastime. So in seven days my princess had experienced two fractures. Seeing her in so much pain and knowing that I couldn't do anything to stop the pain killed me time and time again. The consultant requested that she have a complete x-ray of her entire body. When the results came out, he came to see me with a team of doctors. I can still picture him talking, looking grim; as he tried to prepare this young distraught mother for the news, he was about to tell her. He explained how they suspected that she might have a rare condition called Osteonegenisis Imperfecta (Brittle Bones). He said that they had sent in her x-rays to Great Ormond Street Hospital where they would have a specialist study her x-rays. The report came in a few days later confirming that my princess does have a very high chance of having this rare condition. I was daunted. I felt betrayed by God. And I was in denial. Prayerfully, this marked a turning point in my life. The consultant Dr. Benjamin Jacob showed us so much patience and took the time to explain how to care for my daughter and what to expect moving into the future. I had no choice but to show up in my reality.

I made friends with a large hearted nurse Jennifer, She was so supportive. She linked me up with her pastor who began visiting and praying with us at the hospital periodically. My personal journey with God started in earnest. I would go to the chapel each morning to pray and to ask God of all manner of miracles. Looking back at those chapel days, I laugh very deeply. We were in the hospital for two weeks before we got discharged.

We started our walk of faith with God. This was not easy in the beginning, because I was expecting some quick fix miracle from God. Slowly as my relationship with him deepened, my resolve and commitment to ensure that my daughter had the best grew. It was a slow walk of faith, I learnt to let go and allow God to take control. I can't even remember at what point my fear disappeared. I, however, do know that as I learnt to hold on to God's promises, I became a happier, more focused and determined person. The book of Psalms 23: " Yea, though I walk through the valley of the shadow of death, I will fear no evil: for thou art with me thy rod and thy staff, and they comfort me", holds great significance for me till date. My princess has had over 30 fractures, a number of tractions, been in and out of hospitals, had sleepless painful nights but we have rode on Wings of Faith. Yes, I did walk through the valleys, but it was the Lord that kept us, comforted me and made sure that we never lacked or tipped over. He has always provided a soft landing. Gradually each year would come and pass. I didn't know what the next year had in place, but I was sure that I could do all things through God who strengthened me. I held on to His never failing promise that his gift added no sorrow but giveth joy and I was determined that we would experience the joy of the Lord to the fullest.

My princess turned 12 years, on the 23rd of March 2018 and I can't but be amazed at how far we have come. The future looked so bleak when the doctor announced her condition to me 12 years ago, little did I know what the Lord planned for us. We've traveled down paths of pain, despair, frustration and helplessness. We've lived through it all. But because of His mercies, our dawn broke forth and the darkness disappeared into oblivion. Our tears and pain became building blocks for living a purposeful and impactful life. My daughter is one of the happiest, self-confident and independent children you can ever come across. We didn't allow the pain to stop us from breaking out loud. Instead, it rather drew me into a more personal relationship with my Creator, and this led me into carving my pathway in life. Life threw me bitter lemons, but I have made lemonade out of it. We've built our future anchored on our faith in God.

"…You must slow down and look ahead for crossroads, direction signs and you must have a road map and a GPS relationship. The GOD PERSONAL SAVIOR (GPS), He is your personal life coach, teacher, and guiding light. He comes fully equipped with salvation, security and protection. Affirming life purpose in Christ means simply believe and receiving (in your heart), and abiding in agreement journey with Jesus.

'And we know that all things work together for the good of them that love God, to them who are called according to His purpose'
– Romans 8:28 "

Excerpt taken from THE PURPLE WOMB
BY: ETHEL SIMS

God's Miracles
Teresa Shindle

From as far back as I can remember, I have felt God's presence in my life. I've battled obstacles in my path that taught me lessons and promoted growth both personally and spiritually. I wouldn't be the woman I am today without him by my side. Honestly, I may not even be here today if it weren't for his overwhelming love and forgiveness.

I am a confident, beautiful and strong-willed woman. I can say these things with conviction now, but I didn't always think this way. Self-worth and respecting my self-image had been a struggle since I was a young girl. I remember those times in school the boys teased me about how short I was or about my hairy monkey arms and insane overbite and calling me ugly or that one girl who told me I looked ugly when I wore yellow. Those words cut deep when you're so young and have no self-confidence. I was such a shy and quiet girl and although it seemed like I had many friends, I always felt awkward and that I didn't quite fit in.

I felt so alone all the time.

Teen years were some of the hardest ones. I was so insecure about myself. I hated the way I looked, hated my stringy brown hair, hated my braces, and hated my clothes. I always felt like an outcast. I was resorting to boys as my outlet to feel empowered. I became a terrible statistic and lost my virginity the day after my 13th Birthday.

Thirteen was a tough year for me. I felt so lost in my purpose for life. Struggling with feelings of anxiety and depression, I began thinking about suicide. Actually, I thought about it quite often. I remember a night dropping to my knees, sobbing as I held a knife to my wrist. As I knelt there crying, all I could do was pray. "God, please stop the hurt. Let me die, I don't want to live like this anymore."I was thinking of all the reasons I wanted to end my life and how much I wanted this heartache to go away, but a little piece of me felt such guilt. I started to think about my parents and my siblings. "Would they miss me?"

My mom and I have always been very close, but I never let her into the dark or depressing side of my life. To this day, she still doesn't know most of these things about me. As guilt flooded my heart I felt a warm presence around me as I continued to pray. I kept praying to end my life, but for some reason I put the knife down and began to feel a sense of relief and comfort. I should have reached out to my parents for help, but I felt so embarrassed and ashamed of what I was thinking. I started attending a support group at my school with one of my favorite teachers. She helped me turn my life around. I am so thankful for her support and words of encouragement. I will never forget what she helped me get through.

The summer before high school we received some devastating news about my Dad's health. One afternoon I saw my dad sitting at the kitchen counter with tears in his eyes. This was the first time that I ever saw my Dad cry. It was the first time I heard the words, "I'm scared," come out of his mouth. He hadn't been feeling well and recently had surgery for a ruptured appendix. When they were in there doing the surgery, they found a golf ball sized lymph node in his lower abdomen. After testing, they discovered my Dad had stage 3 Lymphatic Cancer. I never prayed so hard in my life after I heard this news. I felt so broken inside. To see my father cry and admit he was scared made me so sad. I prayed day and night for him. If God was able to protect my life at 13, I knew he could help get us through this tragic diagnosis. With lots of prayers, chemo therapy and medications, my Dad went into remission after a year of treatment.

Years had passed and I was so excited to begin my freshman year of highschool. It was so nice to reconnect with old friends I had lost along the way. I even started dating someone and later married him at the age of 19. We were inseparable, spending every waking moment together until the day he left for USMC boot camp. Life after that changed so much. Lies, betrayal, abuse and deceitful behavior began. We spent most of our marriage apart and grew up without one another. He was living life in California and I was still living with my parents in Arizona. We had a rocky start to our marriage by being apart and decided to call it quits for a short time.

Growing up not having that confidence I needed in myself, and not having a supportive husband by my side; I fell victim to alcohol abuse at the age of 21. I began drinking every day, even at work. Partying every night and I knew moving out on my own would solve all of life's problems. I remember a morning waking up on my couch with the worst headache of my life. I couldn't even remember how I got home. I ran down my apartment stairs and looked for my car. There it was, safe and sound in my parking spot, not a scratch on it. I couldn't believe what careless decisions I was making. To continuously drive while intoxicated and put other lives at risk was beyond wrong. I knew I needed to stop this abusive behavior. I called my husband and told him I needed him to come get me. We worked through our issues and soon found our way back to the love we had at 15.

Still struggling in my mid 20's to find myself, I thought plastic surgery was the answer. I thought it would give me the confidence I kept craving year after year. I was always striving for perfection. But who defines what is perfect? I was letting the world around me once again depict what was beautiful. Getting pregnant was a major struggle for my husband and I. I had endometriosis and was told by several doctors that I would likely never be able to have children. Once again, I prayed about my desire for children and specifically prayed for a little girl. I asked God that if it was in his plan to make me a mother, that he do it by the age of 24. I became pregnant at 23 and delivered three months before my 24th birthday. It was a complicated pregnancy. I developed a severe DVT just 2 months before getting pregnant. The DVT (blood clot) extended from my groin to my ankle with no blood flow. During my initial consultation in the emergency room I was told I would have to do twice daily injections of blood thinners into my stomach. They proceeded to tell me that my leg may have to be amputated if the clot did not start to break down and heal with treatment. I was terrified! They told me one other thing, "DO NOT GET PREGNANT!"

I prayed day and night that this clot would leave my body. I became very depressed about my life. I was in constant pain, my leg looked terrible and I was on strict bed rest. I began abusing narcotics to numb not only my physical pain, but the emotional pain as well. I would sleep the days away in hopes this would all just go away. As the weeks went on I started feeling nauseous and kept getting migraines. I assumed it was withdrawal symptoms. I began taking more medication, but I kept feeling worse each day. To my surprise my period never came that week either. I panicked. I rushed to the store and purchased a pregnancy test and raced back home to take it. I waited for what seemed like an eternity. When I looked down, I couldn't believe what I was seeing. My heart sank into my stomach. I began to cry tears of joy and tears of fear. I prayed for this little miracle to happen, but during these last few weeks, my abuse of narcotics was out of control. I had no idea what damage the drugs could have caused. I called my doctor right away and they got me in on an emergency visit with an OBGYN. The first words out of the doctors' mouth were, "didn't they tell you not to get pregnant?" I felt like a child that was being scolded. I began to feel so guilty for not listening. The doctor told me it was best to abort the pregnancy at this point. He said with the use of narcotics, the baby probably would suffer major birth defects physically and the heart may not form properly.

I didn't even know what to feel at this point. I left the doctor and just sat in my car and cried. I never believed in abortion. I never felt it was fair to make that choice to end a life. I couldn't shake the feeling that something could be wrong. But I couldn't stop thinking that the doctors could be wrong and that my baby would be just fine. I decided to continue with the pregnancy and trust that God had a plan for it all. I prayed all throughout that first trimester and baby and I made it through just fine. I was asked several times throughout the pregnancy to abort, but I refused. It wasn't until 27 weeks that we received the news that our precious BABY GIRL was in the clear. She did decide to make an early entrance by 5 weeks, but she was so perfect in every way. During the delivery I received a tubal ligation. The doctors felt it was medically the best decision as a future DVT and pregnancy would be too risky for myself and the baby. For such a tragic event in my life with the DVT, God had his plan for it all. He gave me my precious baby girl I had prayed for.

Life went on as usual as a new mom, but my marriage was beginning to struggle. This is when bad choices entered my life yet again as I began a short crazy career in the internet pornography industry. My life at this point had hit an all-time low. I was racking up debt left and right to try and fill this hole in my heart. I tried year after year to buy my happiness. I was in the midst of divorce and trying to be a mother to a beautiful two year old little girl. Not having the support of positive things in my life, my world felt like it was crumbling all around me.

Sometimes life brings you those that bring out the best in you and those that bring out the worst. I had to make a choice to leave some behind and carry on with new positive people in my life. Surrounding yourself with positivity and losing negativity can be a breath of fresh air.

Finally, at the age of 26, I met my soulmate. I knew it the moment we shook hands. I just wasn't sure how it was all going to work out. I had never felt such a strong, immediate connection to anyone before. You see, we were neighbors, he lived just 3 doors down from where my then husband and I were living. Morally it felt so wrong to have these feelings for someone I just met, especially being that I was still technically married, but something felt so incredibly right at the same time. He tried to help my husband and I from separating and proceeding with divorce. He tried to give advice, but the more we talked, the more we shared, the more I realized we were so alike. I felt like for the first time in my life someone finally got me. Someone understood my OCD issues and my worries. Our thought process about life was exactly the same. To him I didn't seem so different. We shared our life dreams and goals and to him they seemed attainable. He opened my eyes to a whole new world I never knew existed. I proceeded with divorce and moved on with my life.

In January of 2010, he invited me to attend church with him and that is when I finally found the eternal love I was missing. I'll never forget the way I felt as the pastor stared in my direction as he spoke. It felt as if those words that rolled of his tongue were meant just for me. It's amazing how God finds a way to teach you lessons and tell you what you need to hear at just the right moments in life. I finally filled that hole in my heart. God's love and forgiveness is what really saved me. He was there all those years I needed him most, but I knew I needed him there every day.

As the years went by little did I know more of God's miracles were in store. In August 2011, I married my soulmate. When we met I told him I couldn't have any children. I told him about the DVT and the tubal ligation, and he was completely OK with it all. We went on with life as a newly married couple, but always wondered what life would be like if we could have more children. He was such an incredible step father to my daughter; I really wanted children of our own. At a routine visit with a new doctor, we discussed options to treat the endometriosis that was starting to return. We were talking about an IUD and the doctor told me once it was removed I could begin trying to have children right away. I told him I had a tubal ligation, and kids were nowhere in my future. He looked through the chart and apologized for missing the note about the tubal ligation. He then proceeded to ask if I wanted more children and if I knew about all my options for it. I was told that during the tubal ligation they cut, tied and cauterized the segments, so no repair could be done. He told me to see a specialist and be optimistic about it all if it was something I really wanted. I rushed home and began researching about tubal repairs and their success rates. I found a doctor in Beverly Hills that would perform an exploratory surgery. If the segments were long enough he would do the repair, if not, I go through surgery for nothing. I was willing to take the risk. I began to pray every night for more children. I was scheduled for the surgery a few weeks later. When I woke up the doctor said surgery went well and I would have a 75-85% chance of pregnancy. I couldn't believe it. It only took five months and I was pregnant with our first little boy. I was able to get pregnant again but miscarried at five weeks. Just one month after the miscarriage, I found out I was pregnant again with our 3rd child. Again, it was another boy! We have been beyond blessed.

God had another obstacle to help me overcome just three weeks after my last son was born. In February of 2016, I received word from my mother that my father wasn't doing very well. He seemed depressed and forgetful. He wasn't eating, wasn't talking much and started losing weight drastically. My worst fear was that the cancer had returned. He was refusing to go to the hospital to be checked out. I prayed one night before going to bed. "Dear Lord, please help my father. Please get inside his head and make him agree to go to the hospital." My mom called me that next morning and told me they were on their way to the Emergency Room. She said, "I asked him one last time this morning if he would like to go to the hospital and he shook his head yes." I started to cry. God is good, He is so good, but I knew this was just another beginning to a rocky battle ahead of us. They ran several tests and an MRI of his brain. They discovered he had a golf ball sized tumor on the front lobe of his brain right above his left eye. He was scheduled for emergency surgery. I flew out to Arizona to see him and celebrated my birthday in the hospital the day after the tumor removal. God couldn't have given me a more amazing birthday gift. My father survived the surgery and has fully recovered.

Well, here I am now saved, loved and teaching every Sunday about God's grace and eternal love. I have confidence, and a loving, supportive husband who wants nothing but the best for me and our children. I choose to be a positive and impactful role model for my children and the children I teach every week. I will always believe in the power of prayer. Through God's words and through his love, I was able to find peace and acceptance. I was able to forgive and move on. I truly wouldn't be the woman I am today if I never let Him in my heart.

"The most beautiful people we have known are those who have known defeat, known suffering, known struggle, known loss, and have found their way out of the depths. These persons have an appreciation, a sensitivity, and an understanding of life that fills them with compassion, gentleness, and a deep loving concern. Beautiful people do not just happen."
— Elisabeth Kübler-Ross

I Found Life
Chou Hallegra

I FOUND LIFE...
AFTER CONTEMPLATING SUICIDE

I was at the end of my road. I had hit rock bottom. I wanted the pain to end. I wanted the struggle to cease. I wanted to disappear. It was February 2008 and I remember being in my room, all by myself, and feeling as if life didn't matter anymore. In that moment, it felt like there was nothing to hope for anymore. As I sat on my bed with a bottle of newly prescribed antidepressants; I just wanted to take all the pills and be done with it all - to be done with life. I wanted to die... or did I?

I was a young first-time mother. My daughter was 22 months old. She was at the childcare center that afternoon. In that moment of despair and agony, a picture of her came into my mind. That was the instant that changed it all! The thought of her having to live without me crushed me more than depression, anxiety, and trauma combined.

In that second of enlightenment, I remembered that somebody needed me. That even in my depressed, anxious, and traumatized state; my daughter needed her mother. I was the only parent she was close to, her father was living in a different country at the time. My biological family lived in the same state but were not emotionally connected to her. Up to this point, nobody else on earth took care of this kid like I did. I could not die. I had to live, if not for me, at least for her.

<u>The Wake-Up Call</u>

I had recently started taking antidepressants for the first time. I was on the waiting list to see the psychiatrist and while I was waiting, my family doctor prescribed some psychotropic medicine to help me. I started taking those prescribed medications and less than a week later, I became suicidal. There were no triggers. There were no new stressors in my life. Nothing had happened the day before or the week before that made me want to give up but in the midst of seeking help I felt even more helpless. Instead of feeling better, I felt worse and that didn't make sense to me.

I wanted to overdose on my medication and die; and that wasn't like me. In that moment when my brain told me that I should just die, my heart was telling me to live. I wanted to be there for my child. I also had dreams and hopes for the future and I wanted to see them fulfilled in my time on earth. I didn't have the strength to live but I didn't have the desire to die either.

I was coherent enough to realize that those suicidal thoughts were not mine. It was as if I was having this out of body experience. My brain was functioning outside of my own desires. I knew what my heart wanted, and I knew what my soul wanted. I knew that I wanted to live. There was a disconnect between what my heart wanted, and what my brain was telling me and I'm glad that I had already had help. I had started counseling a few months prior to this incident, so I picked up the phone and called my counselor. I told her what was going on, and she recommended going to the nearest emergency room immediately.

After I got off the phone with her, I made some arrangements for my daughter's care and I drove myself to the emergency room. From the ER, I ended up spending a week in a psychiatric hospital. While there, I told myself this wasn't how I wanted to live. I knew I wanted to live. Deep inside of me I hungered for life, real life, meaningful life.

Depression and anxiety had sucked the life out of me. I did what I could to make it through the day, what I had to do to take care of my daughter, go to work, go to school. I did it day in and day out just to show up, perhaps to even show up for life, but I was not showing up alive. I wasn't showing up for me. I had checked out of life a long time ago. Deep inside of me I wanted to live, and I didn't want to take those pills but depression had pushed me out of my life a long time ago and I was simply going through the motions for at least a year and a half by then.

While in the psychiatric hospital I realized that once I left the hospital, I was going back to survive like I did before instead of living life fully. Nothing was going to change unless I made the choice to change. Nothing was going to be different unless I chose to make a difference in my own existence. That was my wake-up call...but I didn't know how to make that, I didn't have the means to do that. I just knew that I wanted to live the abundant life that I was created to live but all I knew how to do was survive. Surviving in pain felt more like torture rather than living.

The Road to Wellness

I came out of the psychiatric hospital and I went through different counselors and I tried a few medications. Some worked, some didn't. It's been 10 years since my psychiatric hospitalization and I can honestly say that I am well. Not only it is well with my soul, my heart is at peace. I truly am well mentally and emotionally. I have not needed to see a psychiatrist or a counselor for at least four years now. It took lot of prayer and work for me to be well. Here are some steps I took to get there. And I want to share some of those steps with you...

1.   I asked for help
I picked up the phone and called for help. I realized I needed help. The first call I made was to request counseling in the Fall of 2007. When I became suicidal, I already had someone in place to support me. Someone I trusted, someone who knew me. She understood me and knew how to help me calm down so I could drive myself to the hospital and make it there safely. I had to do some research in order to find this particular counselor. I wanted a counselor who not only respected my values but who actually

understood how important my faith was to me.

After this particular counselor left the practice where I was seeing her, I had to shop around. I have met counselors who were very knowledgeable but couldn't connect with me in a meaningful way. I had no problem searching for the right fit, and I didn't stop until I found it.

2.   I advocated for myself

I quickly came to the realization that I had to voice my needs and concerns in order to be well. I have had to speak for myself every step of the way, not in arrogance but in self-advocacy. Depression and anxiety are such internal struggles, that it became difficult for others to support in ways that made sense to me if I didn't share with them what I needed or what I didn't want. I had to do this with friends, family members, doctors, counselors, and other service providers.

3.   I became an avid learner

The more my counseling sessions and other services left me wanting more, the more I felt the need to advocate for myself. The more I advocated for myself, the more I wanted to learn. I then decided to learn more about mental health in general but most specifically how it was affecting me.

For my bachelor's degree I studied psychology and Christian Counseling. Then for my Masters I focused on Human Services. I also pursued additional certifications to increase my expertise in specific topics.I became a Board Certified Christian Counselor, a Certified Cognitive-Behavioral Therapist, a Certified Christian Life Coach, and I'm in the process of becoming a Certified Family Trauma Professional.

The more I learned, the more I became passionate about mental health, and the more I applied what I learned into my own life and saw its effectiveness. I couldn't keep it all of this to myself. Once

I achieved wellness, I started helping others do the same.

<u>Lessons Learned</u>

I learned a lot of things on my road to wellness and I'm sure I will keep learning as I continue my journey on earth. Here are some of the main lessons that I cherish:

1.   I am not alone.
I met so many people on this journey who have dealt with similar things as I have. More and more people are dealing with depression, anxiety, and trauma than ever before. I even discovered that my experience with suicidal thoughts is not so uncommon. Many people with mental illness struggle with suicidal thoughts on different levels. Some experience their first suicidal thoughts after starting new medication, just like I did. Finding the right psychotropic medicine can be a very daunting task of trial and error and many of us have experienced the unpleasant side effects of some of these meds. However, they're also benefits once the right medication is found, especially when it's needed.

2.   Hiding in my pain only increases it.
Many things contributed to the depression, the anxiety, and the trauma. I have a history of sexual and emotional abuse. I also know the pain of loneliness of being in the new country with very little support. I've had a difficult marriage that eventually ended in divorce. I had to raise three children with developmental and medical needs. I've had to experience the toll of being their sole caregiver, added to the fear of almost losing one of them when he was just three weeks old. Needless to say I was carrying a lot. I had a lot of emotional baggage. Being the independent woman that I am, I did everything I could to manage. Keeping my head above water turned into surviving and that was not living. I wanted to thrive.

The more I tried to work it out on my own, the worse it became and the worse my symptoms were. This led me to understand that healing only happens in community. No man or women can heal on his or her own. You can lock yourself in your room and take as many medications and watch as many videos as you want but you can't heal without connections. It is when people connect with each other and get past themselves that they start to heal.

3. People are uncomfortable about what they don't understand.

There's a lot of stigmata around mental illness because people are uncomfortable with this topic and people are uncomfortable with it because they don't understand it. Because people don't know what to do about mental illness, they feel uncomfortable and that feeling creates a stigma. Unfortunately, the stigma is what keeps people from getting help. Often when people hear you have a mental health diagnosis, they fear that you are someone who is going to hurt them or yourself. Not everyone with a mental health diagnosis is an unsafe person. Stigma keeps us from opening up. We make the stigma bigger when we stop talking about it.

We need to talk about it despite being uncomfortable. Let's not just talk about it when we are in the midst of a crisis. Let's not wait until we are sitting there with a bottle of pills, thinking about suicide and wanting to overdose. Let's talk about it when we are going through that break up and our heart our hurting. Let's talk about it when our kids are sick in the hospital and we think they aren't going to make it. Let's talk about it in everyday life when we are going to school and a test is giving us anxiety.Let's talk about it like we talk about heart failure or diabetes.

4. Mental health is health.

A few months ago, I went into the hospital for a schedule hysterectomy that was successful. However, a few hours after the procedure, I had a vascular spasm in my brain that affected the left side of my body; mobility, chewing, swallowing, vision, my cognition, and my speech. I had suffered a stroke at the age of 33. People have been more compassionate and more supportive since I had my stroke, perhaps because the impact is visible. I couldn't walk at first and now I'm using a walker. I'm recovering well. I am learning to walk. I am talking and writing better. I am doing many other things that I couldn't do just three months ago but in many ways, my depression was more debilitating than my stroke.

I struggled with depression and anxiety for years and felt like life was passing me by. Getting out of bed was so hard at times. Seeing past today was almost impossible. Yet, my struggle was not as visible as the effects of my stroke. With the stroke, people could push me in my wheelchair or cut up my food for me. With depression, they couldn't understand that an appealingly "healthy" young woman wouldn't shower for a week or not bother to eat. With the stroke, it was easier for people to make sense of my need. With my mental illness, people didn't understand what they couldn't see. We all forget that our brains control the rest of our bodies. And when our mental health is affected, the rest of our bodies cannot operate in their optimal capacities. Mental health is health!

When we are struggling mentally or we're emotionally drained, all we need is to have at least one person who says "I will be there". They may not understand but they will be there. We all need someone to be there just because they care.

5. Our health system puts people in a cycle where they never get well.

The medical staff who were caring for me after my stroke assumed that because I had PTSD and I had a stroke that they were related. They didn't bother to explain things and give me reports because they assumed that I wouldn't understand, yet I was understanding everything that was being said. Even if I couldn't speak, I could write my thoughts and comments. There is a correlation between physical and mental health but let's start treating people like humans first.

The mental health system and our systems of care as a whole can make you a patient forever. Once you have a mental health diagnosis, you are treated as if you'll have that forever. At the time of my stroke, I have been mentally and emotionally healthy for years without needing to see a psychiatrist or a counselor. However, because I still had depression, anxiety, and PTSD on my health record - almost every doctor me treated like I was in acute mental health distress. Nobody asked me questions about my current mental health status, but everyone treated me as a mental health patient.

I had to get a full psychiatric evaluation to prove that I was well. My word was not enough. The record of my wellness in the past four years were not enough. Because of my mental record, the doctors focused on that instead of giving me the proper care that I needed to recover from stroke. My mental health history became a barrier for me to receive proper medical care. After this recent psychiatric evaluation my mental health record now reads history of "recurrent depression in full remission." FULL remission!

6. The church can be an uncomfortable and an unsupportive place for people with mental illness.

The church is just like the rest of society, it doesn't know what to do about mental illness. People are often told to just pray about it, as if they were not praying enough. Others are told to "cast out those demons." I believe in the power of prayer and the importance of bounding things in the spiritual realm. I also know that people need a place where they can be supported. People need a place where they can heal. They need a place where they can come broken, hungry, dirty and still feel at home. It shouldn't be a place where they are judged because they are not "normal" but a place where they can be themselves. Normal is overrated. People with mental health challenges have a great role to play in and outside the church in helping others better understand mental illness. We can be beacons of hope!

7. Wellness is a journey and not a destination.

I may have been cleared from my mental health diagnoses, but it could take just one life crisis to pull me down again. I have to continually work to maintain my mental and emotional wellness.   Just like we have to work out our salvation with trembling and fear, we also have to take daily actions to achieve and maintain wellness. If we see wellness as a destination, we will soon stop taking care of ourselves and before we know it we will end up right where we started. Since it's a journey, then we keep working at it.

A Greater Purpose

Although my road to wellness might have felt long and lonely at times, it's not my own. It has a greater purpose. It can be used to help others learn and grow. Everything that comes my way allows me to comfort others with the same comfort that I received from God, just as it's written in 2 Corinthians 1: 3-5.

The depression, anxiety, and trauma that I experienced were training grounds to better equip me in helping others. If I didn't have this journey, I wouldn't be a Counselor today. I wouldn't have known that I had this calling in me. That is why I thank God for my depression. I am blessed to have had this experience. When I counsel people, it's not just from head knowledge but also from heart knowledge and that's where life comes from. I thank God for this amazing ministry that I have helping women be whole and live abundant lives

Whirlwind of Life

In a whirlwind of exhaustion
She allows the wind thrust to carry her
Weary, overworked, and under-appreciated at times,

She struggles to take in another breath
So none tasks is left undone
She loses sight of herself
As the rapid wind propels her forward

She is a mother, she is a wife, she is a daughter,
she is a friend, she is a lover
A mother to her offsprings
A wife and lover to her king
A daughter of the SaviorA sister to her friends

She screams from the top of her lungs
"Peace be Still"
The wind obeys and lose momentum
Her vision is no longer a blur
Her clothes are tattered, her hair's a mess
She realizes she looks distress but she isn't alarmed

She picks herself up and write on her list
Don't ever forget to take care of yourself

Written and Humbly Submitted by
Cylnthia Rochelle Long

In The Middle
April Johnson

I'm having a very in the middle kind of day, so I think it's the perfect time to get this started. According to Webster's Dictionary, middle can be used as both an adjective and a noun. In adjective form, it means at an equal distance from the extremities of something; central. As a noun, the definition remains fairly the same, the point or position at an equal distance from the sides, edges or ends of something. There are many phrases containing that word, middle. Stuck in the middle, middle child syndrome, monkey in the middle, middle of nowhere, "Monie in the middle, where she at, in the middle." Being in the middle can be a frightening experience. All those adverse emotions - not knowing, worry, frustration, anger, fear, isolation, each of these twisting and turning until, ultimately, coalescing into what seems to be an insurmountable mountain range of negativity, replete with emotional peaks and valleys. The middle can conjure feelings of ineptness, unworthiness and lonesomeness.

But did you know that there are lessons in the middle? That in the middle you can find not only resilience, strength and peace? Peace, you ask? Absolutely! God can use your middle time. He will sometimes intentionally put you in a middle time, so He can have full access to you. Full access to your heart, your soul and your mind. Sometimes you are never more emotionally open than you are when you're in the middle of a maelstrom.

The middle is a season of which I am intimately familiar. It's a season that I'm currently in and have been for the last almost four years. Yes, you read that correctly, 4 years! And to be completely honest, I've bucked against it. I've allowed my own discord and dissonant thoughts to drown out what God is trying to impart. What He wants me to learn and in turn, HOW He wants me to grow with that knowledge and ultimately share it with others.

Remember I said I've been living this middle life for almost four years. If you don't mind, I'm going to take you on a little trip down memory lane. It was a beautiful July day in the summer of 2014. The sun was ablaze, nary a cloud in the sky and my kids and I were on our way to a friend's house for a pool party to celebrate her daughter's birthday. Fun, right? Doubly fun as it was also my son's 6th birthday, so it was like two birds, one stone. We arrived at my friend's home, laden with pool toys, excited to spend some time in the backyard shade and have some pool fun. After a few moments in the backyard, my daughter was already in the pool with her friends, and I was assisting my son with his goggles so he could join in the fun. My friend tapped me on the shoulder and asked, "Is Kayleigh alright?" I quickly glanced at her and replied "Yes, she's fine. She likes to put her goggles on and look under the water." I went back to helping my son, but something told me to look again. Thankfully I did, because upon closer observation, I realized my daughter was floating on top of the water, completely unconscious.

Without a second thought, I jumped in the water, arms flailing, to reach her. With the help of others, we hefted her wet form to the side of the pool, completely unconscious, seemingly lifeless. Not knowing CPR, I pushed and pounded on her chest, trying to resuscitate her. Thankfully, the neighbor heard the commotion and rushed over. She was a paramedic, so therefore versed in the proper CPR technique. She promptly turned Kayleigh on her side, which caused her to begin foaming at the mouth. The terror that gripped me was absolute. My baby, who I should be able to protect was laying on the ground, in a wet, unconscious heap. My son, looking on in horror at his sister, his best friend, listless on the ground. I began to wail, literally wail, to the Lord. As I laid hands on my child, calling out to God to save her, the ambulance arrived.

As we're careening down the street, lights flashing, sirens blaring, my thoughts and prayers are a jumbled mess. Please Father don't take my daughter. My husband is going to hate me for failing our child. If only I had been paying closer attention. How long had she been under water? Had she been scared? Will she be alright? Why hadn't I gotten my children swimming lessons yet? That's right, my children didn't know how to swim. It had never been an issue in the past as they'd only been in pools that clearly delineated the depth. Erroneously, foolishly, I assumed they'd be alright since I was right there. I was RIGHT there. But no matter the proximity, I'm a living witness that tragedy can strike, that in just a matter of heartbeats, life can drastically change.

To make an emotionally long story short, she was rushed to a local hospital. But then she had to be life lighted to the nearest Children's Hospital as they were afraid of secondary drowning. She had to travel via helicopter, without either of her parents, to a hospital an hour away. But thanks be to God, after 2 days in the hospital, she was released. No brain damage, no further risk of secondary drowning, nothing! And to top it off, she doesn't remember the accident at all. The last thing she remembers is us arriving at the front door. I just knew she was going to develop a fear water, but not so. She went on to be baptized the following weekend.

Through that ordeal, in the middle of that ordeal, I went through the gamut of emotions. But, pushing its way to the forefront was joyful gratitude. The Lord had seen us through! Through tragedy, our faith had been tested and we came out victorious. I thought to myself, everyone has to go through that one major faith testing ordeal, that one horrifying experience that provides the Lord an opportunity to show His amazing grace. That one moment in life where you have to go through something, be in the middle of a storm, in order to have a true testimony of God's power. We'd gone through ours and come out on the other side victorious! Our friends and family had rallied around us, surrounding us with their prayers and positive thoughts and we had prevailed. God's will had been done, His kingdom strengthened because our faith had been strengthened. While I was correct in the fact that God had brought us through, nothing could have been further from the truth regarding this being our only awful experience.

In 2015, my mother was diagnosed with Wernicke-Korsikoff syndrome. Her illness necessitated that she be placed in a nursing facility as she required around the clock care. She couldn't walk, had severe memory issues, suffered from hallucinations along with a host of other issues. It ultimately had to make the decision for her to return back to the state of her birth, Louisiana. Here she could be looked after by other family members. That in and of itself was traumatic. We went from living directly upstairs from her to my children having complete access to her. To then driving thirty minutes to visit her in a nursing facility, to now moving her nineteen hundred miles away. Unfortunately, that acted as a catalyst to our next middle moment.

While dealing with my mother's illness and petitioning the Lord for her healing, we were served with a thirty-day notice. Both our condo and my mother's condo were owned by the same individual. We weren't behind on our rent and even knowing the situation with my mother's health, he elected to serve us with papers anyway. We unfortunately didn't have much recourse as we were in a month to month lease. So, burdened with worry for my mother, the search began for a place to call home.

We'd been in this type of predicament before, having to find a place and move in a specified amount of time. Each time, the Lord had shown us favor. This time, however, was different. Weeks passed and nothing. Absolutely nothing. With about a week left, we had to make a decision. We either live in a hotel in order to stay in the city or we take our friends up on their gracious offer to reside with them temporarily. We chose the latter. My husband and I figured we'd need approximately four weeks to save up enough money to move into our own place. Well, you know what they say about the best laid plans.

Two and a half months.

It took us two and a half months to secure a place. You may be thinking to yourself, two and a half months, that's not too bad. And you're right, in the grand scheme of things, it's not that long. Our friends weren't pressuring us to leave quickly; our kids had a place to lay their heads. We were thankful for that. But, we were living an hour and fifteen minutes away from our life. That translated to waking up at 5 AM every morning in order to get the kids to school on time. If I had to work that day, I had to drive an additional hour to work. If my husband had clients in San Diego, he would have to drive back another hour and a half and once he was done, get back on the freeway for another hour and a half. It meant frequenting a variety of fast-food establishments as we didn't arrive back to the house in time to cook. It meant our children changing for football and cheer practice in the library and Target bathrooms.

Do you know what it does to you mentally when you're not able to provide for your children? When you have to rely on the kindness of friends? To turn the key in the lock of someone else's home? To see the look in your children's eyes when they ask when we're going to have our own place again? It's devastating, absolutely soul crushing. Yet through all this, in the middle of all this, we had to keep our faith. We had to continue to stay the course of righteousness, allowing the Lord to work, even if it didn't seem like He was. We had to shelve those negative emotions and remain rooted in knowledge that the Lord was going to see us through. As the songs said, "If He did it before, He can do it again. Same God right now, same God back then."

And He did. A friend of ours shared with us that her landlord was renting out a house. She gave us her contact information and the following week, we were approved for the house. Praise God! We could finally return to where our life was. God had done it again. We may have wavered, but we had not broken. While we were in the middle of this situation, we maintained our faith and the Lord blessed once more. Surely this was it. I know that there will be problems to face; such is the nature of life. But surely, we were done with the large tests. This had to be the last one.

It wasn't. The most middle moment of our lives was looming large and we were completely unaware. In November of 2016, we decided since I had five days off in a row for the Thanksgiving holiday, that we would do a turn-around trip to Louisiana and Texas to visit family. We packed up and ~~we~~ were on our way. Although it was a quick trip, we had a great time. We saw both sides of the family, had a road trip with the kids and created memories. We returned on a Monday, had lunch with friends on Tuesday and I returned to work on Wednesday. Wednesday evening, my husband and children came to pick me up from work. Earlier in the day, my husband complained of a headache, so I elected to drive home so he could sleep in the car.

Neither of us felt up to cooking that night, so we went to Panda Express for our daughter and for ourselves, we choose Subway. As we were on our way to Subway my husband said he couldn't feel his arm. I quizzically looked at him and asked, "What do you mean you can't feel your arm?" He reiterated that he couldn't feel his arm and attempted to get out of the car. He then said he couldn't feel his leg. That statement jolted me into awareness that he was having a stroke. I pushed him back into the car and rushed to the nearest hospital, where they confirmed that he had indeed suffered a massive hemorrhagic stroke. Completely oblivious to what a stroke actually entailed, I prepared myself for the arduous task of sitting by his bedside, praying and willing him back to health. I just knew that if I prayed enough, got others to pray along with me, that he would be healed and our testimony would be amazing.

Unfortunately, I can't tell you that's what happened. My husband spent five weeks in the hospital and another five months in a nursing facility. He wasn't able to speak for two and a half months. He had to be fed through a tube in his stomach and had to breathe through a hole in his neck. Yes, thankfully he's able to speak again, the tube has been removed and the hole has closed in his neck. But he's completely paralyzed on the left side, along with a variety of other health issues. I've had to leave my job to become his full-time caretaker. Our children have had to watch their father, a man, fully present and ensconced in their lives, become bed ridden and wheelchair bound. They have to watch their mother juggle being there for them and being there for their father.

Middle. Right now, my family is in the most middle moment of our lives. I've experienced every emotion that can be felt; fear, anger, despair, desperation, heartache. I've railed against this situation, asking God why us, pleading with Him to fix it, feeling hopeless when I felt my prayers go unanswered. But what I'm learning in this middle moment is that God can find you there. I've learned that it's acceptable to feel those emotions. God knew you would, because He created you. We are human, so feeling and experiencing human emotion is natural, expected. The problem arises when we wallow, when we allow those negative thoughts to take root in our soul and we continue to water them, to the point where they become a part of our spiritual DNA.

Middle. Not only will God meet you in the middle, He'll use you in the middle. Transparent moment? That part is HARD! How dare He want you to work for Him, to build the kingdom, when you're feeling desolate and alone? When you're at your lowest point and you barely have enough faith to get you through the next second? I remember when my husband was still in the ICU and the Lord told me to walk up and down the hall and pray for the other patients. "What Jesus? You want me to pray for others? I don't have any prayers to spare. I don't know if You noticed, but we're kind of in a crisis here." I obeyed, but it was a struggle, let me tell you.

Middle. We're still in this middle. And I don't know how long this middle is going to last. What I can tell you with certainty is that God has not left me alone, even when I've felt like He has. Don't get me wrong, I still have those negative feelings sometimes. Remember, I'm only human. But, I don't stay there. I visit, often, I'm sad to say. I set up camp on that mountain range and allow those thoughts to crowd me. But, eventually, a tremulous ray of light beckons me back. And I pack up and follow.

Middle. Allow God to meet you in your middle, whatever that is for you. He wants to and you need him to. Further, there are others counting on your obedience during your middle. They're looking to you to see how to handle their own middle. You are never alone in your middle. Isaiah 41:10 says, "Fear not, for I am with you; Be not dismayed, for I am your God. I will strengthen you, Yes, I will help you, I will uphold you with My righteous hand." He is your God. That's personal. You're important to Him. You were fearfully and wonderfully made by Him. He's counting on you. We're counting on you. And whether you believe it or not, YOU are, counting on you too.

"The Lord your God is in your midst, a mighty one who will save;
he will rejoice over you with gladness; he will quiet you by his
love; he will exult over you with loud singing"
Zephaniah 3:17

Daddy Issues
Crystal Dixon

I was having a conversation with a friend and while we were sharing and trading stories about dealing with insecurity, she said, "Oh! That's just because of your 'daddy issues'! Everyone's got mommy or daddy issues."

That really caused me to start thinking about some things. Do I really have "daddy issues"? Are issues such as the ones we were discussing really have to do with my relationship (or the lack of a relationship) with my dad?

See, I knew exactly what she was referring to. She was insinuating that because I grew up with no father that these particular parts to my story such as promiscuity in my teenage years, being jealous of the attention my children got from their father, the recurring feelings of wanting attention, affirmation and affection... That all of these issues were "Daddy Issues"

But you know, I'm confident that any women can relate to stories very much like mine...
...Struggling in finding your identity
...Being in conflict within your own home due to not knowing how to define clear roles of "mother" and "father", or
...Sitting in a presentation shared by a colleague and asking..., "Huh??? Masculine energy is not the only energy there is????"

I gathered enough courage to conduct an Internet search just to read about "children growing up with no fathers" and the results I got tied my nerves in knots. The studies were so sad. Most sources shared information such as fatherless homes leading to higher chances of alcoholism, poverty, depression, and more.

While we can share many woes of what challenges occur when you're raised in a home with no dad, people fail to talk about the wins that can happen as a result of those circumstances. What wins occur when there isn't a father in your life?

Before I begin to share my take on things, I would like to say as a disclaimer, I do understand that many of these lessons could simply be learned no matter who is in your home, but I am sharing my story for anyone who may be able to relate to my experiences.

Lesson #1: Others in your village rise to the occasion.

I was raised in a home with my mom, grandma, an aunt, and uncles. (After one uncle graduated from high school and went into the military, another uncle came home to stay.) It was common for us that I was cared for by my grandmother while my mom was at school or at work. It was common for us that an uncle would offer to help pay for extracurricular activities such as swim lessons. It was common for us that I had to change my daily routines when other grandchildren came to visit my grandma. It was just the way things were. They stepped up to make sure my needs (and even many of my wants) were met.

I remember becoming close with a friend who had both parents in her home. I was invited to attend dance class with her to observe. I fell in love within the first minutes and was told by the teacher that I could easily join in the class next week and begin lessons. I remember going home to ask my mom if I could be a part of the class, and she made her standard replay...

"I'm not sure, Crystal. Most kids have their mom AND dad to help pay for this kind of stuff. I'm not sure if we will be able to do that or not."

I had heard it many times. BUT guess who was in class the next week! I danced for years afterwards, and have taken a part in many other activities. I know that it was part of the village that always made sure opportunities like those were open for me.
Growing up, I was taught so many lessons in my home from so

many different backgrounds and age groups. I learned things like "God protects babies and fools" from my grandmother. My uncle John, who studied psychology in college, helped me to justify my tween emotions that were wanting to argue with my mom three or four times a day. He made sure that we knew how to communicate effectively and always from a place of love through those strange years. My aunt Minnie made the love of music normal. I mean taking a liking to some artists can sometimes be confusing! It is good to keep a music lover such as yourself around! My mom… My beautiful, strong mother showed me that life is full of tests, but that each one brings you closer to God. She continues to show me results from this lesson and I continue to take notes! She is a woman that knows how to walk gracefully through the fire and I admire that.

My father had a family of his own and chose not to take care of me. So I was blessed to have such a sweet network in my own home: beautiful people to claim me as their own because I was all theirs. I consider that a privilege and a loss only for my father. Everyone from each part of my family: in the home, in my church, and within my schools, all rose up to fill potential voids that could have easily taken my life in another direction.

Lesson #2: Live by high standards.

It was Spiderman that I was watching when I first heard, "To whom much is given, much is required." I didn't know until later that those same words are said in the Bible. But as I heard that line from the movie, it was as if Peter's uncle was speaking to me. I don't exactly remember where I was within the journey of my life, but for some reason, I took that as my cue to step up!

"But that's not fair!" I thought back. "Why does someone else's 'average' have to be so menial in my scope of things? Why can't I simply relax and be 'normal' like anyone else?"

Then I felt that my response to that is because I have been gifted with such a simple and blessed life that it is my responsibility to share it with others. It is my responsibility.

I've watched so many people in my village share their talents and gifts. It has been held a standard for me since I was young. If you can sing, you sing in the choir. If you are a good reader, you read aloud to friends. If you are a great hugger, you hug any and everyone who will allow you to! Because someone gave to you, you have to give to someone else. We all would not expect anything less!

Some may pity you or say that living with elevated standards can be demanding or stressful. I get that this may cause you to serve outside of your bounds, but I've learned three major things on my own as I've gotten older: 1) boundaries are important, 2) all things that are good aren't God, and 3) you have to learn to say no occasionally. With all of those things considered, I know how to move forward effectively and touch lives, deep and wide, outside of my family circle, as I was born to do, and just as it was done for me.

Lesson #3: Have a deep appreciation for your children's father.

My husband has been a glowing example of what a father should look and love like. I am sometimes ashamed to admit that it took me awhile to genuinely love my children and not be filled with jealousy whenever I saw the way their father interacted with them. What I witnessed then was everything and more of what they deserved to receive as children, but it was hard for me to not feel just as worthy of the love and affection he showed them.

My husband is not a very vocal being. He is the exact opposite of what I saw in my future years ago. I imagined that my spouse and I would be the life of the Christmas party, best dressed, and dancing and mingling all through the night. However, I got exactly what I needed in 2001 when I met my husband, and he has been more than I could ever need to this day. He is a straightforward, unconditional lover. He has taught me about loyalty, what it is to love, and what it means to love someone no matter what.

So when we had our first baby, something shifted. I couldn't quite put my finger on it, but it didn't become prevalent until my daughter was born. A beautiful, baby girl was the center of my husband's eye. He danced for her. Sang for her. Talked to her and there was no thought, expression, or word that was said from her that was unaddressed from him. It stung a bit. I was seeing a different side from him that wasn't because of me, but because of this sweet, baby girl. So things got uncomfortable for me. I sometimes looked at her with disgust. I sometimes felt anger towards her with no rhyme or reason. I soon took the time to realize that what I was feeling was jealousy.

It was a struggle that lasted for years until it was brought to my attention and I asked my heavenly Father for forgiveness. He changed my heart to see a kind and loving father was there for my children. Since then, I cannot thank Him enough for giving my children such a wonderful father. Once I released the ill feelings in my heart, more love was allowed to flow in. I now see the love that my husband has for me and I am no longer jealous of anyone nor do I expect him to fill any thing that the child in me was looking for more than thirty years ago.

Lesson #4: Give the love you didn't receive and even more will come your way.

As I mentioned in the previous lesson, "once I released the ill feelings in my heart, more love was allowed to flow in". Some say that being a fatherless child will leave you feeling a void in your heart. I beg to differ. I have been shown opportunities to love more, love bigger, and to love harder each and every day. Anything I may feel that I lacked then, I acknowledge is coming into my life to be received presently.

The hugs I may have missed without a father comes through my sweet, affectionate son who leans in at any random moment to put his arms out for an embrace or to ask me if I'm okay. The words of encouragement I may have received from a father, comes from my supportive, inner circle. They lift me up in affirmation consistently through my trials and achievements.

Words of affirmation are my love language. This can be a hard one to find for yourself. However, I have become proactive the past three years and have establish simple habits to be affirmed in my life daily.

Just think for a moment, what are some words that you would enjoy hearing every day? Words that will speak life into you no matter what? Start out with some as simple as setting a daily alarm on your phone that says "You are beautiful!" You will be amazed at how it will give you a sudden boost of self-esteem within your day. And this bring us back full circle! When you are feeling good with yourself and you feel that all things are well with you, your attitude of gratitude will spill over and you'll be ready to show love for others.

One thing that we like to do as a family, in the spirit of sharing love, is visit those in nursing homes that do not receive visitors often. Do you realize how much that can brighten someone's day? You just don't know whether the current condition you are seeing them in offers any light of hope, but you can! You can be that bright, beacon of hope to light up their sky of darkness.

Lesson #5: Independence!

So after living at my grandmother's home with my mom for about ten years, my mom decided that it was time for her to move out on her own. Within all of those years, I watched my mom graduate from nursing school, work full time, attain her own apartment, furnish that apartment, later purchase a house, provide for my every desire, supply for my every need, and more!

It may seem silly, but can you imagine how hard this made things for me within a marriage with a man who has been taught to be a dedicated provider and care taker? I use to take so many things personal in our marriage that had NOTHING to do with me, but dealt with what my husband believed were his duties as a husband. It took me years to ask my husband for help with anything! I also realized that I would ignorantly snap back and ignore his efforts of showing that he cared when he would attempt to do things that I was not use to when we first got married. It took me years to allow him to take groceries from my car into our house or to not be annoyed when he called so often when I was out of town. He was calling because he genuinely cared, but my reflexes always convinced me of otherwise.

I remember talking to my grandmother once about being upset that my husband would not give me the time to complete certain chores before he completed them himself. She sweetly looked me in the face and called me a fool! I was sitting there complaining that my husband wanted to do his part to help take care of things around our home.

Growing up in a home with a woman who "took care of things", made it hard for me to learn how to be a wife. Submission and teamwork are things that I still have to work hard on each day. However, I am proud of who I have become. My mom's independence has influenced me greatly, but I am also proud of the balance I have received through learning what I can through my marriage.

Reading back through parts of my story, it could be misunderstood that I am standing on the front line of defense proving a point that I didn't need a dad growing up. I cannot say that I would not have gained certain benefits with having a father in my home. I am so grateful that my children have their father to experience life with. I just wanted to take some time to celebrate the themes and values in my life I can stand stronger on because of what I have experienced.

Before I end, I must be sure to acknowledge that no one has to consider themselves as a fatherless child. Despite not having an Earthly father, one of the biggest treats I received as an adult was falling in love with my heavenly Father. I had known of Him through the lyrics of church songs I sung as a child, but while living life day to day and fellowshipping with other believers, I have learned more about living and walking with Him. My life has become more and more beautiful as I have become more intentional with living out His legacy.

No matter what your religion is or what you believe spiritually, please believe that you were never created to do life alone. If you feel that you need help finding consolation with anything you are dealing with in your life right now, seek out help. Until then, I pray that my words have offered some light and hope into your current situation.

"He gives us the strength to move forward even though we feel weak."
- Crystal McDowell

Wellness Pursuit: Trauma Recovery
T.J. Robinson

I don't tell my story to boast or brag. I don't tell my story to be pitied or patronized. I tell my story to help. I tell my story to heal. I tell my story because that's what it is....it is my story. It's not scholarly, it's not academic. It just is. Words stating what happened, what was, was is, what will be...ME.

She sat. The cold wall against her back. Oblivious to all around her except the knife in her hand and the pain in her heart. "I'm just tired of feeling. Even numb is a feeling. I just want it to be over". These are the words she thought to herself looking at the knife. A burning desire that every pain, every moment of despair, every memory, every thought would be gone. Nothing would be left, but traces of her life in the memories of her friends and loved ones. As the knife pressed against her flesh, she heard a voice. "You don't want to do this. You have a destiny and purpose in this life. You are loved beyond measure and your life has purpose". Hearing this she grabbed a pillow. Through the tears she slashed. Anger, grief, sadness, depression, anxiety, slashed in the pillow. The pillow was a turning point. Seeing the shredded fabric was a visual of her shattered heart. In need of repair, of salve, of healing. This is a story of a woman who thought she was broken. Who thought she wanted to die. This woman, was tired. Physically, emotionally, psychologically, spiritually, mentally tired. She thought she was broken.

I thought I was broken.

I discovered, I wasn't broken. I hadn't snapped. I had stopped believing. I was over it. Over life. Or so I thought. I was empty in need of filling. This is my story. A story of faith, healing, love, and support. A story of God's spirit filling my soul, of tapping into powerful passion driven by a desire to live and live well.

Healing is a process. A marathon, a journey. Healing is an intimate deep committed relationship which requires, tenacity, patience, perseverance, humility, discipline, gratitude and grace. For me, healing required me to no longer suppress the effects of experiences in my life which led to PTSD, anxiety, and insecurities. I had to deal with my mess. By the age of 25, I had been molested, hit by an ex-boyfriend, raped, and suffered a miscarriage. Always a busy body, I had been known for helping others, organizing, watching children and being a tomboy. Often, I would go home and drink away the pain I held inside. I would stay awake for days in attempts to not relieve these experiences in my dreams. Music, or some type of noise always on in futile attempts to drown out the sound of the assailant's voices that played like the song that never ends. The seconds, minutes and hours would drag on as I willed myself awake. Eventually, sleep came.

I wish I could say that moment with the knife in my hand was the only time I had contemplated suicide or had even been close. Unfortunately, it wasn't. Suicidal thoughts began when I was raped. I wanted to die the moment I saw the gun and knew what was happening. I was mad at myself. After being molested at age 8, and hit numerous times by a boyfriend in high school, I told myself I would not allow myself to be hurt anymore. And here I was, trained in boxing, kickboxing and Taekwondo, frozen in fear at the sight of the gun, phone dead, knowing this was happening again.

When I returned home the flashbacks began. Every day I would recall sounds, smells, phrases, feelings and the sound of the gun when he fired the blank. The actions of this officer of the law brought up memories I had repressed and some days it was just too overwhelming and I no longer wanted to live. Yet, I continued to live, never allowing myself to end it. Something would stir my soul and reignite a will to continue life. I knew I could not live like this however. Anxiety attacks and periods of isolation began to keep me from the things I loved. Singing, basketball, eating, going to the beach, hiking. I couldn't even pray. In the midst of this my best friends began to show their love for me. They talked to me saying I needed therapy, they prayed for me, they called and texted me. Never judging me for how I coped but telling me I could get heal, be wealthy, and be well. Finally, I made the decision to heal.

And to therapy I went.

Three sessions into therapy I dealt with church hurt. Someone I trusted and asked to pray for me while going through therapy tried to violate me, claiming we both felt the same thing and there was a deep love that was inexplicable. As a PK, I knew not to place people with high positions in the church on pedestals and that people especially those who go to church still have vices, and may lack integrity. Yet, my faith was shook. The next time I saw this individual preach I felt numb. Sitting in the congregation I wanted to scream, I wanted to cry. And so I did the only thing I knew to do. I wrote.

Sitting
Sitting here thinking
Sitting here wondering
Sitting here listening to your words
Your words about Jesus
But I do not hear
I do not see…

Yet as I sit here
listening to you preach
I can only think that I should forgive you
Well….maybe one day I will
But for now I will sit
I will sit and listen
Listen to you preach and focus on the words you say and not the man you became on that day.

While this experience halted my progress, it did not stop my healing. Little by little I began to pray again. Step by step I read my Bible again. To this day I have not immersed myself completely into a church building, but I am happy to say, my spirituality, my relationship with Christ has continued to grow. For it was after this I faced the biggest challenge in my therapeutic healing journey.

"I don't want to go." "It's too hard and causes me to hurt" "I just want to sleep". These are words I stated every week when my third therapist started me on exposure therapy 3 years ago. By this time, I had been medicated, gone through Image Rehearsal Therapy and Cognitive Behavior Therapy. When she told me, I would state what happened to me every week for 12 weeks and listen to the recording every day while exposing myself to different triggers, I wanted to choke her. While struggling to decide if I would embark on this journey a friend asked me "Do you want to heal"? Another friend asked, "Are you willing to exercise your faith in God? Let this test be your testimony"! So, in the first semester of a PhD program, teaching as an adjunct professor less than a mile from the home of the man who raped me, I began exposure therapy. 12 weeks of torture. Daily, I would cry, daily loved ones asked if I ate that day, tell me that I was safe. Daily, telling and hearing my story would unearth grief, anger, pain, and horror I had tried to hide for so long. Not just from one experience, but from all of them. I had to hold myself accountable for destructive habits I developed because I held onto painful experiences for so long. I had to learn how to live and be well. I had to teach myself I was not defined by others and their actions but by my faith, my culture, my family, and ME. Nothing nor no one else would dictate my life. I would dictate my life. I decided to be well.

Wellness does not come over night. 12 weeks of exposure therapy did not cure me. Did not heal me. It was the catalyst to the healing. It was a propeller forward. It forced me to confront and fight. Fighting beyond surviving, fighting beyond living, but fighting to wellness in every sense of the word. Fighting looks like eating, fighting looks like singing, fighting looks like praying, fighting looks like coping. Fighting is. My fight is in the poems I wrote, the songs I sang. But it wasn't just fighting, it was resisting and agency. One day my fighting was staring the rapist down when he pulled up next to me while I was driving to work. Another day fighting was going to the beach and sitting by the ocean because I wanted to. Fighting is asking for help when anxiety and PTSD are triggered and none of the strategies are working. Every day I fight. Every day I exist I fight. I don't win every day. Some days I have no fight in me, and I isolate, and sit on my bed and forget all strategies. But those days are few and far between now. I fight with grace. Grace for myself. I am not perfect and I will not win every day. But the losing days have dwindled. One day my fight was writing a letter to those who attacked me and sending them to a friend. I wasn't ready to send it to the attackers, but it felt good getting it out. Then a few weeks later, I confronted one of the people. I stated everything I felt, how I wasn't ready to forgive, how mad I was. The response left me in tears. The response was one of pure arrogance and left me emotionally drained, but I knew I had said my piece. I knew I said what needed to be said.

At this stage in my journey of wellness, I can say the anxiety attacks are less. Every morning I wake up and go through a morning routine. The routine of the morning allows me to center myself and get my day started. This is especially helpful after nights of nightmares from what has happened. Yes, I still have them even after all this therapy, and praying and crying and singing. I'm grateful they aren't every night anymore.

Throughout the day I take myself through breathing exercises and practice mindfulness, (I am so grateful for my calm app). When I'm in the car I pray, and I sing. On my phone I have affirmations I go through that I can look at when the need arises. I also use sage and essential oils in my home. It is important for me that my home be a place of peace. I have a prayer closet where I go and sit and pray. I think about loved ones who have passed and think about what they would say to me. I read my Bible. I journal and let the racing thoughts flow out rather than letting them fester in my head. All of these strategies may not work for you. It's important you do not use my healing process as the blueprint. Rather let it be a source of encouragement for you. You are able to heal. You are able to be well. You must commit and go through the process. It is not easy. You will question if it's worth it. That is a question you must answer for yourself. What I can say is, I'm glad I have gone through my process and I will continue the process. For I am worth healing, wellness, and living for me.

"To live is to suffer, to survive is to find some meaning in the suffering."
–Friedrich Nietzsche

The Nightmare
Amanda Molina

It took him less than nine months to destroy every aspect of my life that year… A mere 266 days of pure evil.

I was at work when my phone went off. I looked down and it said NEW FRIEND REQUEST… I thought, "Eh, ok I think I knew the guy in middle school, what harm could it be to answer?" As soon as I accepted it, He messaged:

Hey cutie, you probably don't remember me but we went to middle school together.

This is how it started. And for the rest of the day, he was in my Facebook messenger throwing random compliments out and blowing up my phone. Most of which I tried to ignore because quite frankly I still had no idea what he actually wanted at this point; but I was definitely intrigued.

I mean I was operating on autopilot it seemed. I was going through a divorce from a marriage ended abruptly. My happily ever after – really didn't last that long and it threw me for a loop. As I was trying to keep myself busy and not let it overcome me – here was a familiar face from my childhood showing up right in my messenger inbox. Somewhere in between the "hey cutie,"and the compliments I had agreed to let him drop by and hang out. I guess you could say my guard was down. I was on the road to divorce and I didn't feel like rejecting someone else after my life had just flipped upside down. So after a 14-hour shift, I headed home but the anxiety started to kick in. I swung by Taco Bell to grab something to eat, and as I sat in the drive thru my thoughts started to race, "Why did I agree to let this guy come over? I really hope this guy doesn't show up. I really just want to go to bed."

My wish did not come true and I received a text

Is it still ok to roll through?

I immediately thought, "Who talks like this? I must not be current on my preppy boy slang." This was probably sign number 232 that this was not supposed to happen but to my dismay, half asleep I responded,

Sure.

More than an hour later, as I had fallen asleep at this point, I heard a loud obnoxious vehicle outside. I got up to check the peephole, as I don't live in the greatest neighborhood, just to make sure someone wasn't going to break in. Outside I saw this broken-down clunker of a truck parked in my spot, I swung open the door and yelled out, "Um, hey! That's my spot! Could you move?" That is when I realize that it is him. He casually strolled up my driveway nonchalantly, looking NOTHING like his profile picture, with no shoes on.

"Uh, sorry about that." He says noticing me staring at his feet, "I just got back from the gym and I guess I forgot my other shoes."

Not one to judge. And in a season of auto pilot, sleepily I invited him in. That night we watched some random scary movie but I could tell he was distracted. Every few minutes he would look at his phone and make a face. He claimed that it was his mom saying he needed to get home and started making his way to the door. I walked him out and immediately, I fell asleep on the couch knowing that my alarm would go off in a few hours for work.

But sleep was not on the agenda that night.

Moments later, my phone went off way too early to be my alarm for work; I looked down to see a text message from him.

Hey is it cool if I come crash on your couch my roommate locked me out.

I don't think I even responded but shortly there after I hear a loud pounding on the door.

"Seriously," I think to myself, "my kids are sleeping and it's two in the morning? Who does he think he is?" I rushed and opened the door as not to wake my kids and at that moment I let him in. I let him into my house. I let him into my... Life.

As if the night was not weird enough. That next morning set the ball in motion. That morning I left for work at about 4AM. I left him asleep on my couch hoping that he would be gone first thing in the morning. I mean most guys work right? So, I sent him a text around 8Am.

"Don't you have to work or something?"
"Nah they let us have the day off."
"ok, well lock the door on your way out, I don't want anyone stealing anything."
"Oh, is it cool if I just chill here?"

       …..

I let a few moments pass because I wasn't sure how to respond to that. All I knew is that I didn't want to leave work just to have to kick him out. So I left it alone or so I thought. A few minutes later he texted me again,

I need to go do some odd jobs for a friend so I can make money for my car insurance, I will be back in a few hours so I am just going to leave it open.

The crap you are! How much do you need? You aren't leaving my house unlocked."

He said "$200."

Two hundred dollars?! yea ok, $200 in car insurance for a truck that is older than I am.

And that was the beginning of the incessant need for money and housing. He told me the next day that he was going through a rough time, his roommate kicked him out, he lost his job, and his mom wouldn't let him stay with her. He was on his own and needed help. I rolled my eyes. But my need to feel needed at that time of my life was riding hard on my back and I responded to him with, "Look, you can take the back room while you get yourself figured out."

But that invisible urge to help him… almost ruined me.

Two months into this roommate situation. Yes, roommate,that is what it had turned out to be. A dependent houseguest who never left my house from the moment he walked in. I had opened my door and here he stayed. He came over to "hang" and ended up being the guy who took advantage of me and cost me nearly $20,000 and my car. In the months that transpire, I made mistake after mistake. I ended up leasing a new car so that he could have my other relatively new car; and even still he somehow ended up driving the brand new car while I drove the older one. He didn't leave this house except to go chill with his buddies or his mom. I paid for everything. No rent money. No grocery money. He was just a permanent house guest who was full of excuses as to why he needed help financially with something every day. I was in a world wind of auto pilot. He was comfortable using me. I was comfortable feeling needed… until I wasn't.

So a month into this roommate situation my mom called me to tell me she found a tube sticking out of his wallet with white residue. I was stunned.

So I asked him, "Have you been doing drugs in my house? "WERE you snorting drugs in my new car?" He looked completely shocked, "Uh why would you say such a thing?" "Well for starters the white stuff on your nose kind of gave it away." Silence. Dead silence.

After moments passed he pleaded, "Look. I'll stop, I'll pay you back, please I have nowhere to go."

"FINE!"

I don't know why fine ended up being my response to something so serious but for months everything did seem fine. He seemed to be okay. He was out of the house more and I took it as him trying to find a job and get his life together. So, I didn't regret giving him that second chance to make things right. But eventually with no job in sight and not a dime paid back we were back to where we started and I was done.

Here I was giving chance after chance and I had even picked up an additional full-time job to make ends meet. I was trying to provide for my children and pay myself back for what this 'roommate' had already taken from me. That night, fed up, I went text and told him that he had to go.

You have go. You have to get out. I've had it!
Please. I have nowhere to go.
No. I don't want to see you again. I don't want my money back I just want you gone.
Please. No. Give me one more chance. I'm different. I will show you. Come with me for Thanksgiving. I will show you.

He pleaded and pleaded. Guilt trips blew up my phone. The excuses and the begging wore me down and I eventually agreed to spend Thanksgiving with his family. Thanksgiving ended up being a disaster. He made some kind of family drama excuse and after that day he was gone for two weeks with my new car.

All I saw was red, he had my car. I had planned on selling that car so I could stop working so hard. I was working nonstop those days, 20-hour days, sleeping in my car in between jobs... 2 weeks of not seeing my kids at all and he had taken my car. Finally after two weeks of calling him nonstop and getting excuse after excuse he bought the car back to me.

But not before dropping the bomb of guilt, "I have been living in the car. I have nowhere else to go."

I was trapped. I felt stuck. In the months that followed. I continued in this downward spiral, my life became centered around his leeching erratic drug addicted behavior. I sold the car. He convinced me to give him the money. He pleaded daily that he had nowhere to go. So I let him back in my house. My mom refused to let him and his drugs stay. So I paid for a hotel room where he ends up charging hundreds to the room. I told him to get out but and it only got worse. He was now taking pills, not just one, but the whole bottle.

This cannot be my life.

I sat in the hospital room at my wits end. His mom refused to come and get him and I was the only one there. I wanted out but I couldn't leave. He blamed me. He became violent and irrational. And I stayed.

That day they were able to resuscitate him but no one came to resuscitate me. I was in a coma. I was bound to a guy who had turned a Hey cutie into a full on mind manipulation. We went from can we hang to me being called every curse word under the sun. I helped and he hit me. I gave and he lashed out. I stayed and he continued to bury me in debt, guilt, and shame for the mental, physical and emotional abuse I was accepting.

From drugs, lies, a marriage of convenience for medical purposes, to cons. But the truth is it was the same cycle over and over - marriage papers or not. No romantic love. No consideration for me. I screamed. He threatened me. I appeased and he used me. I had morphed into him. I was becoming suicidal trying to find a way out. I was depressed following him into a downward spiral. I pleaded with him to go to rehab to get help. He agreed and days later after faking a panic attack he was released back to me and I was out of $70,000 in medical bills. I was hemorrhaging money for helping. The episodes of our existence together were endless and every situation ended up with me... in pain.

What happened next was all a blur
I wasn't prepared for what was to come next...

He overdosed.

I went to the funeral home to see his cold lifeless form laying there.
I cried.
I cried for the 266 days that I had endured.A
And then I cried some more.
How did a random friend request on Facebook end up in death and the death of a piece of my soul and strength? How was this my life?

I remembered thinking even after the funeral when would this nightmare end. I was still paying for him months later. Funeral bills and medical bills were placed on my shoulders. And even worse was the emotional debt that I had racked up. I was hurt and depressed.

Even after death his family continued the abuse he must have been genetically inclined to. They spread rumors, hit me up for more money, and blamed me for the whole thing I realized at some point it was all starting to happen again and I cut the whole family off.

Yet, still, previous sins of his followed me around. And I was determined to believe that this would be a nightmare I would never wake up from.

Then suddenly almost as fast as he had come into my life and left; a shift happened. One day his best friend reached out to me to see how I was coping. He was genuine. He was concerned. He cared. Someone was there to help me. His best friend came in to pick me up. It was a shock. It was needed. Here he was. Finally, here was someone who actually cared about my wellbeing with no ulterior motives.

It hasn't been a smooth ride, I've dealt with night terrors, constant panic attacks, and extreme depression. But almost a year to date, I am ok! My confidence is coming back and my life is looking up for the first time in a long time. I never thought this would be my story. I never thought I would be that girl. But it did happen. And I survived it. When I look back today, I see a girl who just wanted to help. I wanted to be there for someone so I opened the door. That door was filled with pain, guilt, depression, abuse, and naivety. But when the door finally closed nine months later I was left with a woman who is capable of love. I am a woman who is strong and a woman who is a true survivor with story to tell to help others know the nightmare doesn't have to last forever. You can open your eyes and dream bigger than your current situation.
There is help and there is love on the other side of the pain.

"If you don't like something, change it. If you can't change it,
change your attitude."
-Maya Angelou

Shiny Sparkly Pretty Bits
Seranie Manoogian

It is funny how things work out. I am a 40 year old Armenian woman (but please don't tell anyone I work with). I have just been promoted to being the producer of a primetime animated show and I am single and childless. This was not how I thought 40 would look. When I was little, 40 seemed like it was so far away it would never happen, but it did and here I am. In all of my thoughts and projections of what 40 would look like, it was always shiny, sparkly and pretty. It was me with a husband and one or two kids tops. I thought my husband was going to be a businessman, a good provider, a loving father and a doting husband. We would get dressed up regularly and attend balls and benefits. I would have had a big wedding with a bigger dress and all of my friends and family in attendance. There would have been 300 people and I would have gotten married in the small church in Fresno my parents were married in. Yeah none of that has happened, and quite frankly in the event a husband, wedding and marriage are a part of God's plan for me, that is not the way it will all go down.

It was all so simple. I grew up the youngest child of two in an Armenian family in San Diego, the baby of the family and the only girl. I was one of two children to parents born in the 1930's. By the time my parents had me, my father was 45 and my mother was 40. They are a full two generations older than me. It doesn't sound like much, but I believe those two generations have made all of the difference in how differently we see things and they have also played an instrumental role in shaping me into the woman I have grown to be.

Since my parents had my brother and I later in their lives, especially for those times, they were happy to have us with them all of the time. There was not an event or a trip that they attended without my brother and I in tow. We were a close knit family of four that lived in our own little world. Our extended family lived in Fresno, a six hour car ride away from our bubble in sunny San Diego. That was where we spent all of our vacations and holidays.

Once I went into seventh grade, I was attending school at the same school where my mom was a counselor. We drove 15 minutes every day from Pacific Beach, our suburban community, to Southeast San Diego, a much more diverse part of the city, so I could attend a math, science, and technology secondary school, none of which were of any interest to me. This was not a family decision, but a parental decision. Once enrolled, it took me a few years to find my tribe. Luckily for me, I have been able to hold on to these women and walk through life with them. We have crossed that sweet milestone where we have been in each other's lives longer than we have not.

Being of Armenian descent in San Diego in the early 90s, in a family that did not attend the one Armenian church in San Diego meant the only Armenian people in San Diego I knew were my immediate family. It also meant I was the only Armenian person all of my friends from school knew. Most of them had never even heard of a country named Armenia to be able to associate Armenians with. We weren't a novelty back then common to everyone and their mother...this was after all long before the world knew of a family of Kardashians. While this was my reality, it was not the upbringing my parents had.

Both my mother and father had been raised in Fresno, California, a farming town in central California with a large Armenian population, and they had both grown up attending an Armenian church. This afforded them a life where the majority of their friends were Armenian like them. They went to school with Armenians, they dated Armenians, they birthed Armenians who then repeated the cycle. For my little family of four, that cycle will likely end with my parents and for me it can all be traced back to their decision to send me to school in Southeast San Diego.

My school didn't have a lot in terms of non-academic extra

curricular, but what there was, I was involved in. I was in student government, chorus and drill team and that is where I found my tribe of women. I was inducted into a small group of girls, all African American and I was their token other. Of course it wasn't like they needed a token or to show diversity, after all this was a small high school clique. But nonetheless there we were, a group of seven young ladies with backgrounds that were all very different and we formed our own little family.   These girls helped influence my ideas of everything during those formative years from music and fashion to of course boys. We were always together, always laughing, always having fun and always talking about boys. We might have all been just a little boy crazy, but that was ok and even maybe a little expected.

As far back as I can remember, I have always liked boys and wanted to have a boyfriend. When I was four I had a dream that Beau and Luke Duke from The Dukes of Hazard came to visit me at my grandma's house and I so desperately wanted Luke Duke to be my boyfriend. As I went through elementary school, I can recall always having crushes that didn't like me back. There was Michael and Jason and Josh, all little white boys that never had any interest in me. When I got to middle school there was an Aaron and a Mike again two white boys that also never returned my interest back. In fact, I think Mike was the last white boy I had a crush on. The next crush I had was on another Mike, and this one was actually white Mike's friend and he was you guessed it, not white but African American. For the first time a boy I liked actually liked me back. He was never my boyfriend, but there was definitely something there and so it began. From there forward, all of the boys and then men I was attracted to have been African American.

It took until my junior year in high school before a boy reciprocated my feelings enough so that we could move into a relationship. Our young love began at a school dance and one week later we were boyfriend and girlfriend. He also went to my school and was a senior. My mom was his counselor and she had plenty of dealings with him, and none of them were positive. As soon as she realized what was going on, there were issues between she and I however as hard as I try to remember, I cannot recall when or how she actually brought her issues and concerns to me. There had been mentions here and there of him not being the best student and that he was always in trouble, but those things didn't matter to me. I was an A student with plenty of extra curricular and a bright future but the thing that mattered the most to me was how I felt when I was with him and how he spoke to me and about me. From the time he and I began talking, he had clearly placed me on a pedestal above and beyond everyone else. It didn't make a difference that the person he was with everyone else was so different than the person he was with me. The only thing I cared about was how he was with me. I had found someone that would put energy into me and us and for my 15 year old self that was enough.

There was very little discussion between my mom and I during this time about this relationship, but that changed. One afternoon, my parents came home from Costco where they had done some shopping but also picked up a package of pictures I had dropped off to be developed. As customary, before they even left the store they opened the pictures and flipped through them. In those pictures, they found a picture of me with my boyfriend at the time. In the picture, we were at school in the music room and it was the night of our annual December concert. I was dressed for a performance and he and I were hugging and with his hand that was behind my back he was flipping off the camera. According to my mom, when my dad saw the picture he lost it.

Like he lost all of it.

He apparently got very angry and was yelling at my mom, questioning who was the guy in the picture, what was I doing with him and did my mom know who he was. Of course she had all of the answers to his questions. As explained to me, the thing that had apparently set him off was the middle finger to the camera.

When my mom brought this to me, she let me know they had seen the pictures, I would never see them (I still have not), and my father was not amused by what he saw. She stated that it was now time for me to stop talking to the young man in the picture. She again reminded me of the grades and the behavior he demonstrated with everyone and how his unbecoming behavior had now surfaced in an image my parents did not want to see. . To them, the picture represented a lack of respect for me. The picture was evidence that he didn't think highly of me and was a display that contradicted all of my feelings about how he treated me differently. To me, it was a high school boy being a high school boy and not a demonstration of a lack of respect. I disregarded their comments and continued my relationship.

Of course as most high school relationships end, this one did as well. It had nothing to do with my parents and their wishes. It just ended. There was no discussion with my mom when it was over. I just moped around until I moved on. This young relationship would in turn influence how I would deal with my family during all of my relationships. As I had suspected, and would find out in later years, the issues with my first boyfriend had plenty to do with him not being the best student and a bit of a troublemaker at school, but it also had something to do with him being African American. This was the part that was somewhat confusing to me. All of my closest friends at that point in my life were African American girls and boys. My best friend at the time basically lived with us. None of these things were ever an issue. My parents had several African American friends and not just the ones you mention to verify you aren't racist, actual friends. They would come over for dinner and we would go to their houses for dinner. This really was about not wanting me with anyone that wasn't Armenian. They were after all born in the 1930's and if you looked at any group born during those times they would also have similar feelings.

A year later, I would be told having an African American date for my high school prom was not acceptable. The joke was on them. I had four African American dates for my prom, of course they were all my girlfriends as a bunch of us had decided to go in a group without dates, but somehow, I don't think that is what they were talking about or the dates they were worried about. After that warning, there was little discussion about the boys/men I was dating. I had other boyfriends after that first one and there was no mention or discussion about them with my mom or dad. In fact, the only discussion my dad and I have ever had in relation to men was the warning about my prom date.

After high school, I went away to college in Syracuse, New York. Something about being 3000 miles away and out from underneath my parent's roof and rules empowered me to continue keeping company with the men of my choosing. During those four years I had one long term boyfriend and dated various other men. Once college was over, and I moved back to California, I began dating my first grown and professional man. He was an accountant, which to me seemed like the most grown up job ever. He had a college degree, so clearly he was educated, he was handsome and very well spoken.I clearly remember thinking he was one of those guys you could take anywhere and he would get along and fit in with anyone. Being with him was refreshing. He had thoughts, goals and dreams and I wanted us to grow together and support one another. Dating him was the first time I felt like I could possibly share this part of my life with my mom. He seemed to check off all of the boxes.

Before I ever had that chance, she and I were running an errand one day and in what seemed to me to be out of the blue, she asked me, "Are you dating anyone?" Before I had a chance to answer, she followed it up with, "I certainly hope you aren't dating anyone because every time you do it turns this family upside down." I had no idea how to respond, and to be honest to this day I still don't. I believe I told her I was dating someone and I gave her the highlights in an attempt to acknowledge her question and end the conversation.

It worked.

During the course of that relationship she would occasionally ask questions which I would answer but not give any extra details. As an adult, it was much more difficult to ignore the idea that your parents don't approve of whom you are dating. My mom and I spoke several times a week and sometimes several times a day. To this day, relationships are still not on the table for discussion. I wholeheartedly believe this breakdown with my family has contributed to me being 40 and single.

I am a woman who strives to make everyone connected to me proud. I never want to be an embarrassment to my family or my friends. This is what is so difficult about this situation with my family. I believe they would be mortified by my choices in men, all men of substance (just not Armenian substance), based on their wishes for me to live their Armenian dream. But that dream is not my dream. I dream of a husband that supports me emotionally and can provide for us. A husband that if the sh*t hit the fan, without a second thought he could jump in and take care of us and the household. I dream of a husband that is loving and doting and doesn't raise his voice during an argument, a husband that may already have kids, because at 40 I don't necessarily know that my body will be able to have kids. I also dream of a husband that would potentially be ok without kids because at 40 I also am still not sure if I want to be a mother. It just so happens that in all of these dreams the variations of my husband are never Armenian and that is the issue for my parents.

Now that I have dreamt out loud about my dream husband, I believe it is important to mention I am also ok being a single woman. This last year I have spent more time dating then ever before. I had been a serial monogamist. And to be honest, I prefer the comfort of a relationship, but this last year has brought me to a place where I am comfortable in my singleness. I know there are married women that dream of being single so they can have the peace as well as control of the remote I enjoy every night. I still don't share stories with my family about the men I date, but that's ok too. As long as we are all still here, we all have the opportunity for growth so that one day we may be able to discuss the man I keep company with. This story, my story, my life…it is still progress. It is still happening every day. Pieces of it may look shiny and pretty from the outside while others, not so much. I'm really ok with that. The not so pretty bits are the pieces that build character and strength and foster growth…the growth that will then turn into shiny, sparkly and pretty bits.

"A woman in harmony with her spirit is like a river flowing. She goes where she will without pretense and arrives at her destination prepared to be herself and only herself."
-Maya Angelou

A Continuum of Consciousness: "Quantum Consciousness"
Jessica DeWalt

"Relax and count backwards, starting at 10", said Dr. Steams, my head and neck surgeon who was to perform the Sistrunk Procedure that was needed to eradicate this huge "thing" from my body. "I'm going to need you to put your head into position before the surgery for me. The human head is actually pretty heavy, and hard to position during surgery."
I instantly obeyed.

"10, 9, 8, 7......," was all I remember, until I was awakened by the aesthetic nurse on shift. I was still sleepy, slowly regaining consciousness. Asking the nurse, "what happened? How'd it go? Everything ok? Where's my husband?" all at once, but my voice was not coherent. My voice wouldn't work properly, I couldn't talk. The Sistrunk procedure was a rare removal of remnants left over in the thyroglossal duct from the development of the embryo. The Branchial Cleft, also a reminiscence of the embryonic stage, would be left intact indefinitely at the recommendation of the surgical team. The risk is too great. "Sit back and just concentrate on breathing, that is all I want you to do, your husband is on the way," was the only response I got from the nurse.

REALITY

My story is my reality. It is also the reality for many unseen and unheard souls. It is the reality for people that have been suffering under controversial symptoms for decades. The medical community and others minimize symptoms and struggles. When concerns are minimized, it tends to feel condescending. The constant condescension that the individual faces paints their life on a canvas of non-acceptance. With the perception of non-acceptance, further interaction leads to sustained dejection. Dejected and unseen, many unheard people face ostracism within our society silently. Often alone.

Society often speculates, which is something that can't be controlled. Speculations are hurtful to the soul, whether believable or not. It was this step that resonated in my soul. It was here with the speculations of what was wrong with me that I decided to move on. I had to move on from the life that I complacently assumed I would live. From the life that society had molded me to live. I couldn't run from it anymore, the obvious had not escaped me this time around. It had found me. I am different, and my differences are not convenient. What is convenient, sometimes is not always true. And what is true, is not always convenient. I wanted to believe them badly. But in this moment, that was not quantitative. And what was true needed attention. This was real.

TRUTH

More often than not, assigning blame is a reaction that many seem to exude. The only problem with that is you still have real time symptoms to address. The symptoms have their own plan, sometimes it is all consuming, tiring mentally and physically. It's hard to see the bigger picture of what in effect is happening. Over time, clarity will arise. However unbeknownst to that individual, *their struggles will assign their reality.*

I couldn't tell you what was wrong with me, and that is my truth. My truth was not society's truth, and society's truth about me was not the authority. No one believed me, and eventually I believed them. I believed that I was a bad person. As the time went on, it was hard for me to continue to hold the idea that society held about me. And after awhile, it was impossible.

To conclude negatively about an individual, the premise must first be prejudged untruths. If society believes you are untruthful, perhaps what you've seen reflected in society was not love and friendship after all. My interpersonal interactions became conditioned. "Never complain, never explain," became my meditation, day after day for a very long time. I learned that when in need, I would be alone. My concerns were prejudged untruths.

Many people were around me, and yet I was alone.

Soon I became lonely, and attempted to fill the spaces. I was grasping for another soul like I was grasping for another breath of air. I had to face societies conclusions, and they were hurtful. So I hid.

Eventually I was blessed with a gift, this gift came to me in the form of sight. An overview of sight, I guess you could say, something like a bigger picture. The cinema was the world, the initial loss was holographic, the subsequent gain was tangible knowledge. Moving forward I realized there was no love loss, and only knowledge gained. If greatness isn't going to be perfection for me, then I felt I could make greatness a depth.

Humbled, shaking and feeling alone I stepped out and confidently walked in the way that was my own truth. My truth was that I was struggling with my symptoms. I had to be honest with myself. *The only person who could care for me in the way that I yearned for, was me.* I was in constant companionship with myself. I was the person that I sought to fall in love with. I wanted to remember me.

I wasn't alone. I realized Jesus has already chosen those that are to walk with you on this journey. Step forward unshaken and accept His glory. I had to let people back in - all while holding and honoring my space and truth.

People are going to tell you who you are, but the question is, are you going to believe them? I wanted badly to believe them, I tried, and was unsuccessful. Maybe what is wrong is not to be explained. Maybe there isn't anything wrong, only what is perceived. Maybe what's perceived is the reflection of a misunderstood mirror. In that misunderstood mirror maybe you see your personified shadow.

The topic of self acceptance is fallacious, because your divine acceptance is a birthright. Unconditionally, so that your natural state is unconsciously and effortlessly of love and solace. It is so that we are here, and so it is. It is not to judge. It will be neither good nor bad. And it will be. It just is.

PERCEPTION

It is important to understand; assumptions are only thoughts of what is known. Assumptions reflect nothing about the subject, and much more about the thinker. Specifically, the thinker's growth and development. You may find that you personify your genuineness and nobility onto society, and that means you are a good person. The toxic behaviors that you did not perceived before, display that you didn't intend maliciousness. If your intentions can be displayed by your perception, then I was unaware of societies non-acceptance.

I know life tosses stones at you. It's a thing. It is neither bad nor good, it happens to all of us. Perception of these events is your distinct reflection. The stones will not weaken, nor harm you. They will build you analter for you to stand on in order to display what humility and strength looks like. Remember not all strength is all powerful. Some strength lies within the will to remain humble in the face of uninvited adversity. This i know to be true.

We will all ail in our health a bit grim. Some sooner, some later. Pay careful attention to the ego you cultivate, and how it embeds in society. Sustained humility and knowledge embeds a sustainable future in the present. The present will soon be the past. Sustain your energy in the present, do not expend your energy on things that will fade and pass. Cultivating an inverse perspective, I uncovered a long forgotten love. I got to fall in love with myself. I got a chance to know a person that I would have just walked away from. While hiding we walk away from a great friend in ourselves. While hiding we hide our light, our humanity, our humility, our strength, and our beautiful shadow. We are hiding our soul. But it's not ours to bombastically hide.

A recollection from within the soul will lead you as if you already knew where to go. You will feel your footsteps with every sense of your soul. No other soul can see it, because it is ancient within you. So it will be up to you. You have to sense your path. You are the only person meant to see you in the way that you yearn to be seen. Look your way, and see the glory within. The all knowing and innate within you is so common to you that it is undetectable, like the warmth you feel when you touch your own hand. Walk in the way that you feel led to do.

Absolute power is a fallacious dream sold to the perceptive human condition, to each and every one of us. Power will only reflect the soul underneath. Power should not corrupt absolutely. There is no true form of power. The only true form of power, is the power from within. All other forms of power are a fallacy. That power from within will speak to you. **Trust in that power within you.**

In this life, you get to choose your sequence. You get to choose who you become, line by line, code by code. You are a crucial piece to His puzzle, your path will be yours to recognize. Don't assume that there will be a place to which you will stop. What if the journey was the only thing that we came here for, not the destination?

Assuming that there was a designation in life to be attained, I asked my grandmother about her dreams. "All I ever really wanted to do was this," she would reply. My perception was short sighted, her response sounded so simple. Juxtaposing my perceptions now, I can equate her message. She made me understand that my ultimate audience is our future adult children.

REALIZATION

My husband and I have stepped forward together on this path bravely. With every evolution of our souls, each step resonates with our senses together. We moved forward together again and again, just as we did before, but on this path we realized ourselves. Our marriage became our mirror. A mirror and a whisper, with eternal echos. He took time to educate me and nurture me. He held space for me, made sure the space was inductive to peace, health, and growth. We had to grow as individuals, in order to understand the magnitude of our "together".

Realization has feeling. Respect that realization has a feeling in this consciousness. Consciousness is the realization of itself. Respect and value all souls as consciousness. Because it is not only "human consciousness," it is simply just "consciousness." All souls have consciousness.

Free will is important in consciousness, because it is like an agreement of self realization. An agreement of a self perceived reality. The will to be free, in conjunction with all wills, allows a cascade of blessings to happen around you. All because of free will. All because of your choice. All because of you.

You freely chose in His trust, and bravely walked forward.
Before long, you've willed your freedom to move closer to Him.
Don't worry if your path leads you to walk home early, Jesus has exponential pathways planned. Just go. You just go peacefully, and trust in His plan. Walk into the will of Jesus and He will lead you to the next step.

As you walk, understand that you are the Spirit realizing itself, over and over and over again, infinitely, as you grow and evolve through multiple lessons. Elder ship does not come with age, it comes with sustained knowledge and wisdom. Relax and trust your divine innate. Relax into the teamwork of Jesus and understanding will happen.

You are the strongest flower that ever grew, understand that when the weather changes, things are just seasonal. The seasons will reflect a mirror to you. The mirror that you see reflected to you, is your own. May that reflection be glorious in your beauty and shine an abundance of peace. An abundance of peace that is rightfully yours. Set out to follow His lead and create new stories.

"Greatness is the perception that virtue is enough."
Ralph Waldo Emerson

"The best time to love with your whole heart is always now, in this moment, because no breath beyond the current is promised."
-Fawn Weaver

Blessings in the Brokenness
Anita L. Withrow

Divorce is not something that I ever considered going through for a second time. But there I was, moving in to my own rental house, with furniture that I had bought on my own, and doing the work by myself to make it happen. Clearly this was not what we had planned. To be honest, I really didn't think that God would allow this to happen to me yet again.

Scott and I met on Christmas Eve of 2009, and our relationship got serious rather quickly. We had common goals and dreams, enjoyed many of the same activities, and both had children from our previous marriages. It was certainly challenging to blend so many personalities together, but we did the best that we could. He asked me to marry him on Valentine's Day of 2012, but told me even then that he was petrified to get married again and that he didn't think that he would be ready anytime soon. I knew that I loved him, so I decided that I would do my best to be patient and loving because God had a plan for us.

On August 10, 2012, our whole lives changed in a complete instant. While on a family vacation in the Outer Banks of North Carolina, Scott went into full cardiac arrest while we were having breakfast and planning our day of sightseeing. This was completely out of the blue and unexpected, because at the time, Scott was only thirty-nine years old. He was airlifted to a cardiac hospital for care, and had emergency surgery to open up the blockage in the main vessel that supplies blood to the heart. After surgery he was on a ventilator, in a coma, and his body temperature was kept at approximately 92 degrees so that his organs could rest and his heart could heal. Doctors were very unsure of his prognosis, there were some pretty severe medical complications, and most of the family seemed to be preparing for Scott to die. I said throughout the following weeks that he was going to recover, because God had been telling me that everything was going to be okay. I stayed at his bedside most of the time, was there when he woke up, and helped him through his rehabilitation process in the months to follow.

Scott and I got married on August 10, 2013 (yes, on the one year anniversary of his cardiac arrest!). He had made a near full recovery, and we had decided as a couple to celebrate that day instead of being sad about it. We had a beautiful and intimate wedding at a beach house in the Outer Banks, surrounded by our closest family and friends. Our children were all there and involved in the wedding as well, and we were all excited to begin a new chapter in our lives together.

Now mind you, our relationship had not always been sunshine and roses. He had two teenage daughters from his previous marriage, and I had three children from a previous marriage and relationship as well. I cannot possibly describe to you what types of challenges we faced when trying to blend our families together. There were lots of arguments, tears shed, hurt feelings, and silent treatments throughout the years of our relationship. We all tried really hard to make things work, but there were a lot of differences that caused us to struggle. We joined a church as a family, prayed a lot, and pressed onward.

s if blending the families wasn't enough of a battle, Scott went through a job loss right after his cardiac arrest. He decided to begin a new career as a nursing home administrator, which meant unpaid training time, finishing some college classes, and taking certification exams. Once that part of the work was over for him, he had to search for a position in a new field, and that was really hard. He interviewed for a job in a small town about three hours away from where we were living then, and he anxiously awaited a call from them with an offer. We talked about what would happen if he was offered the job, and decided that for a while, my kids and I would continue living in our current home for a while because I had a steady job there. We didn't want to move the kids right away in case the job wasn't quite the right fit for him. I asked Scott if he felt as though they were concerned about him working there and living separate from his family for a while, and he said that one of the people had mentioned that during the interview. While driving to work the next day, I felt as though God was speaking to me directly, and telling me that I should go with Scott if he was offered the job. I called to tell him that, and within the next hour, Scott called and told me that he had been offered and accepted the job. Then we began the search for a home and a job for me, and everything literally feel right into place.We bought our dream home, I secured a position in the therapy department of the same skilled nursing facility that Scott would be working in, and we packed up our lives to start all over again.

I am a very social person, and our new home was in a very rural location. We were almost an hour away from any major cities, and we didn't really have any neighbors our age. His children had decided that they would rather live with their mom in Pennsylvania, but my children were living with us. About six months after our move, Scott lost his job. He was devastated, of course…and struggled for nearly a year to find another position. It was really hard for us to keep things going on my income alone, and Scott became severely depressed because of a second job loss in just a little less than two years. I tried to help him, tried to be supportive, tried to find job listings that I thought would be a good match for him…but he sunk deeper and deeper into the darkness of depression. There were days that he wouldn't speak to any of us, days that he didn't want to get off of the couch or eat, and times that he just stared at the television without really watching what was on.

I have always had a tremendous amount of faith in God. He has been there with me always, and I have felt His presence and His hand in situations too numerous to count. He spoke to me throughout the entire time that Scott was in a coma after his cardiac arrest. God told me throughout that ordeal that Scott was going to be okay, even when others said that they didn't think he was going to make it. God had always provided for myself and for my family, even when I had no idea how I was going to put food on the table during the years that I was a single parent. He had always led the right people to me at the right time in my life, and I prayed to God every single day that He would help my husband to find a job.

After a few months, Scott's depression had not really lifted. He was still searching for a job with very few leads that could lead to an offer of employment. His sadness was hard for us to handle, and I often tried to bring him out of it. I will admit, I probably tried TOO hard at times, and it likely appeared as though I was just a nagging wife. I begged him to talk with someone about the depression, and to try to eat better in order to take care of his overall health. We began to argue a lot, and he disengaged from all of us even more, often yelling at the kids for making too much noise or not doing something right, and that had never really been his style.

I felt helpless, scared, and so alone. I couldn't fix this for him, and I couldn't seem to get him to see that he really needed to talk with someone before things got worse. I didn't know how I could afford all of our expenses alone, but I didn't want to bring things like that up because it just made Scott sink deeper into the darkness. I had nobody that I could really reach out to nearby, and I know that my best friend Jenny probably did get tired of me calling her in tears because Scott and I had had yet another fight. I began to feel myself becoming more and more anxious, sad, and disconnected from my husband. I was going through the motions because that was the only thing that I could do at this point.

The arguments and tension got worse. The kids started to exhibit behavioral symptoms because they could feel how things had changed within our home. I couldn't eat, sleep, or truly enjoy my life. The worst part of it all was that I couldn't get Scott to enjoy anything about his life either. I was losing touch with who I was, how I wanted to live my life, and what I wanted for my family. I knew had to stop this downward spiral somehow, and that was a tough pill to swallow.

A year passed and I made the incredibly difficult decision to separate from my husband. I had sworn that I would never go through another divorce again, because the first one had been the most difficult and bitter experience of my life. I needed my kids to feel comfortable and happy in their home, and I needed the same thing for myself as well. I told Scott that I didn't want a divorce, but I felt as though we all needed some time outside of the negative and tension-filled environment to regroup and figure out where to go from there. He was so angry, and so bitter…but I felt as though this was truly the right thing for me to do.

When the kids and I moved to our new place, something inside of me changed. All of my adult life I had hated being single, and I rarely was because it was so hard for me. I found myself enjoying the single life, even though I felt guilty at times because I wasn't as sad as I had thought I would be. I spent time with my kids, decorated our home, discovered yoga and meditation, began going for long walks in nature, and just did the best I could to go to bed happy at the end of every day. God spoke to me often, and assured me that it was going to be just fine. I wrote a lot in my journals, read some amazing life-changing books, attended church, and really devoted a lot of time to self-care and things that made me feel good. I stayed in touch with my husband, tried to be supportive of him even though we weren't together, and tried to gently bring up the difficult topics from time to time in an effort to begin the journey of possibly repairing our marriage.

I do believe that I knew even then that this wasn't the end of our marriage. I didn't move out of our beautiful family home because I wanted to…it was because I needed to. I was losing myself in my husband's depression, and I feel as though my children were starting to get lost too. That home was quiet, solemn, serious, and sad. I want my children to grow up in a home filled with love, laughter, security, and faith that God always does incredibly amazing things for us all. Living as a single parent again was difficult financially of course, but I knew that God would meet all of our needs. I focused on truly living a present and faithful life so that my children would see that example and do the same.

Scott and I spent some time together, and talked about our plans for the future. He did find another job, but lost that as well after about six months. I was supportive then as well, but it was so horrible watching him to suffer that blow to his masculine ego once again. He continued to search for work, but was not having much luck. He called me one day to tell me that he had been offered a job as a nursing home administrator in Pennsylvania, near where his family lives. He said that he was going to rent out our home and take the job. I was hurt because I felt that he had made all of these decisions without talking with me about them, and it was so scary to imagine him being that far away. How would we truly work on our marriage then? I didn't want to stop him from leaving because I knew that he needed the work and the experience while building this new career for himself. On the other hand, I didn't want him to just disappear and to have us just continue to grow further apart.

I had Scott come over one evening before he was scheduled to move. I told him that I loved him, that I truly did not want our marriage to end in divorce, and that I did not feel that our story was over. I told him that I would move into our family home again, that we would continue to talk about the struggles in our marriage and do the work to try to make things better. I also told him that I fully supported him taking the job in Pennsylvania, and that I would be here waiting for him whenever he was able to come back. He was happy to know that I would be taking care of our home and excited that we could take our time to work on the marriage without a ton of pressure. It really seemed to be a good plan.

Scott is doing well as the administrator there in Pennsylvania. We talk daily, and are continuing the work on our marriage. I spend time daily in prayer and meditation, and write in my prayer journal as well. We both attend church and are using the teachings from God to help to repair our marriage. I truly believe that this is the path that we are supposed to be on right now, and that God knows exactly what He is doing for us. Even though we live apart we get together whenever we can make it happen, and we are truly closer right now than we were before the separation. We have faith that we will get through this season in our lives, and have a stronger relationship because of the challenges that we have faced. We have a strong love for each other, for our children and families, and for God who helps us through it all. We will get there, and we will do so together. We trust in God's will, His timing, and His purpose. Of course, there are times that we wish the road was a little less rough, but we have faith that it is all perfectly planned.

"Be on your guard, stand firm in faith; be courageous; be strong.
1 Corinthians 16:13

Bus Stop Secrets
Brandi Allen

Sometimes I feel like I live a double life; where I've been and where I am now. I battle my present with my past when I am triggered by a memory of my past life. Triggers can be as small as I'm laying with my husband at night and he holds me to tight; that was a trigger for me. When I am alone, that is when my thoughts wander back to my past. When I watch the movie "Taken", I cry every time. It is a good cry because the daughter was rescued by her father who never gave up on her. It is a bad cry because I am taken back to where I was held captive.

When I was sixteen-years-old I met a man over the telephone who said he dialed the wrong number. Instead of ending the conversation, I continued to talk to him. He wanted to know my name and how old I was. I told him I was sixteen years old, and he told me he was 19 years old. We continued talking on the telephone for weeks before we laid eyes on each other.

When we did finally meet in person, he came to my school. We talked on the telephone all the time. He was someone I could tell my problems to and not worry about any repercussions. I confided in him and told him everything about myself. It was the unvarnished truth, from the eyes of a sixteen-year-old. He shared his life too; so I thought. I felt we had a true friendship which was blossoming into a relationship.

After our first in-person meeting, he would meet me at my job off of school campus. I liked talking to him, and there was no pressure. We never went anywhere together, but we would meet somewhere and talk. This was the one person that I was going to discover on my own, without interference from family members and friends.

I was living with my aunt, but she was pulling away from me emotionally. I felt that I was the reason why she was not talking to me anymore. When I told him I was thinking about running away he was all for it. I wasn't running away from my aunt, I was being bounced around from house to house until my mom was able to come and get me. I no longer wanted to be a burden on anyone, so my solution was to run away.

He shared he was having similar issues with his mom, and he was going to move to   to Los Angeles, California. He said he would come to San Diego during the week, and we could talk some more about the challenges we both were facing. He picked me up and we went to a neighborhood park. We talked at the park, and when it was time for me to meet my aunt, he offered to drive me back home. I noticed he was going in the opposite direction of where I needed to go. When I told him he was going the wrong way, he drove faster and then he hit me. That hit took me by surprise. I remember looking at him in total shock. Who was this person? How do I get out of the car?!

I tried to open the door, while the car was moving, and he grabbed me to prevent me from getting out the car. What happened? This was beyond me. He had been so nice. He never showed anger. This caught me off guard. I was in over my head away from my family and alone.
The drive was the longest drive I have ever experienced. He drove me to Long Beach, California. Every mile he drove was against my will and every mile was further away from home.

At our first stop we stayed a few days at one of his friend's house. He didn't let me out of his sight; not even to go to the bathroom. He would not let me use the phone, or go outside. I was in a fog of confusion. I was praying to God for deliverance. I needed to be free from whoever this person was.

Our next stop was at a motel in Los Angeles, California. Nothing happened the first few days, but he kept a close watch over me. I couldn't go to the bathroom without him. He would not let me use the telephone or go outside. Then he became concerned about how I looked; my clothes; my hair. I still did not comprehend what was going on. He met up with a friend and his girlfriend. This is when I realized the reason he was interested in how I looked. His friend's girlfriend was assigned to me. She was an older woman with a child. This was my prostitution class and she was the Street Walker Teacher. She was told she had to go with me, and if I did not come back, they would keep her child.

She knew all of the established rules:
Always use protection
Never kiss the person
How to identify a police officer
Never talk about money
Let the Trick touch you to determine if they are Law Enforcement or not

She was thorough with her teachings. Although she missed one rule or maybe she thought it was self-explanatory. You had to have intuition and common knowledge. It wasn't that simple; at least not to me.

I remember one evening I was dropped off at a bus stop, and I noticed a guy who looked to be my age. I started telling him I was on the streets, but I wasn't supposed to be on the streets. I was crying and pleading for his help. I wanted to go home.

One of the girls in the group told on me. He pulled up, and dragged me into the car and beat me. He kept saying, "you don't talk to anybody else on the street". I learned the Pimp's golden rule: If you talk to another Pimp, you become his property. This was my initiation into this world of the street, the players, and their rules.
After that incident, I didn't go back outside for a few days; my bruises had to heal. I felt very discouraged. I felt like everybody was in on this scheme to keep me from going home. It seemed like he had eyes on me everywhere. Where was God? I was talking to Him and looking for Him in anybody I could find. I needed deliverance.

One day he picked up a girl he knew. She was about my age, and she liked him. She was also willing to prostitute for him. She became his new spy. I could tell she was extremely jealous of me.

He took us to the friend's house with the girlfriend/Street Walker teacher who had the child. Initially, all the women were in the room together. The new girl had stepped out. As soon as she left the older lady gave me money. I was never allowed to have any money. No dollars, dimes, nickels, pennies. She told me to put it away and to ensure that no one ever knew where I got the money from. I placed the money in the sole of my shoe. She told me I did not belong there. She said I should get far, far away and promise her I would never tell where the money came from.

A couple of hours later, he took me to the top of the building, a few stories high. He told me take my shoes off. He took the money from out of my shoe and began to beat me up. "Do you think I'm stupid? I have eyes everywhere." It was the new girl that told him. The older woman had the same fate as mine. Her baby daddy beat her too. She didn't give me any more money after that. She tried to take me on dates with her or take me with her to her main clients. She would have sex with her clients, and have them pay for the two of us. Money was the driving force. If you didn't bring in money you got beat, and if you didn't bring in enough money, you got beat.

Was the first rule explicitly stated? I learned the 2nd rule: You always had to get in a car. You would sit at the bus stop, but if you didn't get in a car in a certain amount of time he would come back and threaten you.

One day, I got in the car with a guy who was a doctor. I remember crying and asking if he could take me to a Greyhound train station. He said didn't want to get involved. Wait, he was already involved, but that was at the transaction level not the compassion level. He also feared for his life. He just gave me the money, but the money was only in my hands for a few minutes. As soon as I got out the car, he was there to collect it.

Rule #3: No black guys, because they don't want to pay.
One day he said I could finally call home. I had my mom's number memorized. I called my mom at work and as soon as I said, "Hello", he snatched the phone from my hands.

My hopes were shattered.

He would always threaten he to hurt my family or kill me if I left. I had divulged so much information, he knew everything. He knew my relationships. He knew my dad was a police officer and that our relationship was nonexistent. I told him my dad was going to put him in jail and he laughed and beat me. He always made sure he did not hit me in in the face, because nobody would want a pretty girl with a messed up face.

When he dropped me off on Sunset Blvd in Los Angeles, he would either walk up and down the street or walk on the opposite side of the street or watch me from his car. He would sit in the car and watch my every move. He would spit out truths he learned from his mother. "As long as you have a woman, you should never be broke". It was obvious his mother drilled that saying into his head. Unfortunately for me, he believed it.

The bus stop was considered the spot. Instead of walking up and down the street and attracting the attention of the police, the bus stop held all the street secrets. At the bus stop spot, women and young girls would tell their stories about how they got into the life. Their stories ranged from being a runaway, sexually or physically abused or both, sold by their pimps to other pimps, raped, robbed, stabbed, and losing close friends to violence. Some of the girls and women were in my situation; they were forced into this life, and made to do whatever their pimp wanted them to do. Other women and girls were doing it on their own for their own reasons.

One day, I met a grandmother who was prostituting to feed her grandchildren who were in her custody. She would become one of the individuals that would look out for me. Nights were frightening.

He would hold his hand around my neck while he was sleeping, so I would always wait until he was sound asleep and snoring before I would go to the bathroom and pray for God to help me.

I would wait for the moments when he would cry when he beat me up. He would always say, " I don't want to do this, but this is what we have to do now." He told me his stepfather use to beat him and his siblings when he was younger. He would also say he really loved me and no one would ever love me " the way" he loved me.

My Mom taught me about love as a kid, I was able to tell the difference between real love and his version of love. In my mom's attempt to protect me from the world, I didn't have any knowledge of the real world. He was trying to break my spirit. He would say things like, "no one is looking for you, no one cares about you, and no one wants you". He wanted me to believe that he was all I had. He hated it when I said, "yes, they love me and they are looking for me".

I would beg him to let me go. I promised not to tell anyone, if he just let me go. I tried to convince him that this was not what he wanted to do, but it never worked. Everyday was like the day before. If the Police were in the area, he would move to another area. Not only was I supposed to provide sexual acts for Johns/Tricks and bring in the money, but I had to sleep with him every night too.His friends had moved to an upgraded Motel. There were a lot of guys from out of town, drinking and smoking. There were no other girls with us. I kept coughing from all of the smoke. He only allowed me to go out to the hallway to get fresh air because he was drunk and high. When I was out in hallway, I was praying and trying to come up with a plan to get away. I thought I could jump out the window, but there were no trash cans below to break my fall. The motel room was in the middle of the building, and the stairs were at the opposite end of the building. On the other side of the building, there was a window, and stairs near the elevator. I ran so fast to the elevator that by the time I reached it I was out of breath. I let the people in the elevator get out before I got in. It seemed like it took forever for them to exit the elevator.

Just as the elevator door began to close, he put his hand inside the door and pushed it open. He dragged me out of the elevator and started beating me. He knocked me to the ground choking me with one hand. While he was choking and beating me two Security Guards walked up the stairs. They told him they had a complaint about loud noises and we needed to keep the noise down. He apologized to the Security Guards, and said we would keep the noise down. There was no way out.

He seemed to know everybody and anybody that could help me escape. I prayed continuously. I prayed whenever I was alone in the bathroom, and any opportunity I got. I did not let go of my faith even during the times he tried to break my spirit. One evening he left me alone for a brief moment. I called a cab and asked them to pick me up and take me to the nearest bus station. He returned just as the cab arrived. He then began to threaten me, and he point a gun in my face. I started begging and pleading for him to let me go. I told him I would not tell anyone. In desperation, I lied and told him I was pregnant. He let me go.

This experience could have destroyed me, but because of my faith and belief in God I survived it. Even in those darkest moments, God was right there and I was home.

We are all meant to shine, as children do. We were born to make manifest the glory of God that is within us. It's not just in some of us; it's in everyone.
- Marianne Williamson

The Assignment
Sequita Myers Carlisle

I was going to be 40 soon and we both knew we wanted to have children. I was concerned that it could take a while for us to get pregnant. Boy, God had a plan for us! We were blessed to conceive the first month we tried. WOW! We were so excited when we found out the news. Would the baby be a BOY or a GIRL? Who would he or she look like? Would they play sports? What would they become when they grow up? All things as a parent you think about when you're about to bring a bundle of joy into the world. I had weekly OB check-ups as well as Maternal Fetal Medicine check-ups since I was "AMA" (advanced maternal age) to make sure both me and the baby were fine. I literally had an amazing pregnancy, no morning sickness, can you believe it? God knew the plans He had for me so he made sure I experienced a pretty uneventful nine months.

Then on the night of December 27, 2008, my entire world was tossed and turned upside down. My husband and I arrived at the hospital to begin the induction process. Full of anticipation and excitement. I remember feeling nervous, excited and literally scared to death, is all of that even possible at the same time? I mean after all; I do not know the first thing about what to do with a newborn. Will I be able to breastfeed? I was literally freaking out! The what if's kept coming to the point of it making me more and more terrified and maybe, I don't want to have a baby. Oops, it's too late, it is happening whether I'm ready or not. Well, the time is upon us…and the staff gets me all checked into my room, hooks up the monitors and starts to administer the induction meds. The evening is uneventful until around 1 or 2 AM and I'm awakened by a nurse quickly placing oxygen on me telling me the baby's heart rate has dropped as well as my oxygen levels. Now, I'm officially scared to death, I mean what on earth is happening here? Am I going to be okay? What about my baby? What is next, what is going on?! How did a simple induction plan turn into a possible emergency cesarean section? I'm terrified and I'm sure my husband is as well but he of course is cool under pressure and knows exactly what to do to calm me down. We pray and wait to see what happens. They continued to monitor me and the baby and finally the decision was made to take me to the operating room. William Thomas Myers-Carlisle is getting ready to make his grand entrance into the world.

What happens next is beyond my worst nightmare. I mean why was this happening to me? To my baby? God, I did everything the right way, so why are you punishing me? I just do not understand what is going on? Why? I am moved to recovery and William is brought in by his wonderful nurse, I hold him briefly before she notices something is off with his color. She takes him away and the next person that comes to the room is one of the Neonatal Intensive Care doctors to tell us that he believes William has Down syndrome. Wait, what? What was the point of weekly check-ups with the Maternal Fetal Medicine physicians, I mean they have specialized sonogram machines that can detect almost anything. I do recall reading some of my progress notes after Lil Will passed away that indicated thickened nuchal chord, which is a possible indicator for Down Syndrome, why didn't the physician say anything? I mean it wouldn't have changed anything but I think it would have been nice to know ahead of time but I guess that is not what God intended. So, despite our best efforts, our beautiful baby boy was born with Down syndrome and severe heart defects. What a blow! Not to mention the fact that you think you are going to have a healthy baby and suddenly your world as you know it is forever changed. Everything from that point on happens so quickly. I ask to see my baby and I am rolled down in my hospital bed. He doesn't look like my baby, he is extremely puffy, what happened? We are told they had to give him fluids. I remember thinking this cannot be a good sign. The next day we are told he needs to be transferred to Children's Medical Center, because he is extremely sick but ultimately he wasn't transferred until December 30, 2008. William goes with him and I am stuck in my hospital room crying, in total disbelief and wanting to be discharged but of course I couldn't be because I had just had a caesarean section.

All I could do in my cold, lonely and dark hospital room was cry out to God. Why my baby? Why oh God, why? Why did this happen? It is just not fair! I had three other friends who were pregnant at the same time and all of their babies were just fine. I was jealous! Why me? Why my baby? It wasn't like I wanted anything bad to happen to their babies but again, God, why me? I did everything right, I ate right, I exercised. My God, I waited for the man you wanted for me and you do this to me? I was SO angry, hurt and scared to death. I call William constantly to check on Lil Will, he really couldn't tell me much except they are working on him trying to get him settled in his new room on the PICU floor. William couldn't see him until this was done. So, all I could do was sleep, cry, sleep and cry. The next morning, the lactation consultant is trying to teach me how to nurse. I want to scream at her, lady my baby is NOT here. He is at another hospital now leave me the HELL alone. My doctor came to see me and I asked to be discharged. He was reluctant but agreed to let me leave. I get to the other hospital and see my sweet baby for the first time in days. He is less puffy and intubated. I can't hold him. All I can do is kiss him, pray over him and hold on to my husband.

Sometimes in life, we are dealt with circumstances that we cannot control.

It is how we react to those circumstances that will ultimately define us. We choose to stay strong while Lil Will was in the hospital because we wanted to share his story to help other people. God is still awesome even when you do not like what storm He is taking you through. He will give you hope and strength to endure. We gave God all of our fears, our sadness and trusted in Him that He would take care of us. And you know what? He did. When we put God first, He controlled our feelings and everything fell perfectly into place. Some may say, how did everything fall into place perfectly, Lil Will is gone. It did because God's PERFECT will was done through Lil Will. It wasn't easy but you can't live in joy and hate. You have to choose joy. Now, I was very angry with God, I asked him many questions and He answered every one of them;

not necessarily when I asked but over time. His will and His way was shown to me through His grace and His mercy in my life.

Throughout Lil Will's life we encountered trials during the storm, it seemed like one storm would pass and then another would come. My sweet boy had so many procedures that we were warned he could die on the operating table because of his heart and kidney issues. But God was always there, holding us, imparting His wisdom upon us to make the right choices and to be the best advocates for our son. He was intubated for most of his life. I learned how to take care of him despite all of the equipment he was hooked up to. I made him a lullaby cd to listen to, I read to him, sang to him and prayed over him every day. As the days went by, I was unable to hold him until one day finally in January, I got to hold my baby boy, my Lil Will. The last time I held him was the day he was born. This was such a tremendous milestone and I thanked God for the amazing gift. Soon after that day, we hit a stumbling block. Lil Will needed to have a tube placed so he could have kidney dialysis. Here we go another surgery, its two steps forward and five steps back. You know I was thinking about how far God brought us and Lil Will... AND how Lil Will was a living testimony to everyone he came in contact with, on a daily basis. His kidney surgery was on January 8th, 2009. I cried and cried that day, I had a knot in the pit of my stomach, I was afraid but I prayed. I asked God to cover my baby and keep him safe. He did! God did this for our family on numerous occasions, surgery #2, surgery #3, heart catheterization, ear tubes and the list goes on.

There were three occasions when Lil Will coded and had to be brought back; it seems he always did this when he was moved to different floors, it was like the little stinker was testing the physicians and nurses on each floor. He was actually giving his mom and dad some major stress. I remember one early morning the phone rang and it was the doctor saying Lil Will was having some trouble and we needed to come to the hospital. My heart sank and I am scared. What is going to happen when we arrive?. We get there and the physicians are straight, they tell us Lil Will needs to have a tracheostomy placed. We agreed and the next day, he received his trach. It was so beautiful, I could hold him more, and it was much easier. This plan also started us to our journey of leaving Children's and going to a rehab hospital to bring our boy home! Yes! Soon baby boy you will be home with us. Now, we have to learn how to administer his dialysis, change his trach and manage his oxygen settings. We are smart we can do it and so the learning begins. I was still yearning to bring him home and to get a picture with him smiling. After all by now, most of my friends had lots of smiling pics of their babies. Just not fair!

Finally, I was able to get that picture! It was once we had moved to the rehabilitation facility. Lil Will put that smile on my face on July 14, 2009..For months and months I tried to get a picture of him smiling. Never could I catch it! He would grin, but no smile. Just two days before he went to heaven, he put that smile on his momma's face! See how God knew what to give me when I needed it? What if he had allowed me to get the picture months earlier? Would this one have been as special? I would say it wouldn't have been, no! God did what only He can do. That picture is one of my most favorites and I can only imagine all of the things Lil Will was thinking about as he smiled while he was drifting off to sleep. Was he playing with the angels and listening to God tell him that his work on earth was almost done? Was He telling him that soon you will be home with me? Was He easing his mind and letting him know that He would come and take him home to heaven when we were not with him so we could let him go? Whatever he was thinking, I take comfort in imagining what the conversation was between Lil Will and God.

July 16, 2009, I took a day trip for work. I planned on stopping by to see my angel prior to my flight but God told me that He had him and to not stop. The night before, He had told William to come home and get a good night's rest, He had Lil Will. God knew if we were there and Lil Will had any issues we would want all actions taken to save his life. God always has a plan that far outweighs our desires and He knows what is best for us. As I'm in the middle of a staff meeting my phone rings, it's the rehabilitation hospital saying I need to get there as Lil Will is not doing well. I tell them to call my husband because I am out of town. I pack my things up and honestly, I am unsure how I made it back to the airport. I was able to get on a flight and God sent me a special angel to sit with me as I flew home knowing my baby boy was gone. He was gone and I wasn't there to hold him, to love on him, to fight for him. How could I have taken a day trip? Why did I do it? I land, my new friend ask to call me a cab, I don't need one, and I will make it on my own. My husband and my baby were waiting for me in a small, dark room just outside of the emergency room. There was my baby, all swaddled up laying there lifeless. Lil Will was called home at 11:02 AM by our Father. He was all alone, we weren't there with him. But God reminded me, He was there, after all Lil Will was His son and his work here on earth was complete. He touched so many lives including ours while we were blessed with his presence. He taught us how to live one day at a time and depend on our Father no matter what the circumstances. He was our lil angel on earth. We miss him dearly but we must all remember God gives us our children for a time, they are HIS, on loan to us. To love, to cherish and rear in the way the Lord wants us to. I still miss Lil Will every day, there are some days where I miss him so, so much. Thoughts of him are heavy on my mind and my heart is heavy with sorrow, with sadness, not without hope but I guess it is just the normal grief process.

Grief never ends.

This week I thought a lot about what ifs? What if Lil Will had died in utero? How would I have felt? How do mothers feel when this happens to them? I can only imagine how I would have felt, never being able to hold the precious gift you carried in your womb? How do you heal from that experience? What if Lil Will had died shortly after birth? Yes, as the mom, you would have held your miracle but you would never be able to make any memories with your angel. During the midst of all these "what ifs", God reminded me that, if we live in a "what if land" we are not allowing God to just BE in our lives. God met me where I was during this time, in my "what if land". He told me, you carried Lil Will to term, he was born and lived, yes, I only gave him to you for 201 days, four hours and 17 minutes but you were able to create wonderful memories, I strengthened your relationship with me, I helped you mend broken relationships, I allowed Lil Will to minister to many. You will never know but through him My work was done. I chose you and only you, you were the only mother who could give Lil Will what he needed while he was doing my work. I chose you because I knew when it was time, you would give him back to me freely without question. I want you to rise up, I want you to grieve but do not grieve like there is no hope, no tomorrow for I am with you even until the end of the earth.

Through my baby, a ministry was born within me, to help those moms, parents who have lost children. To show them how to navigate the choppy waters they will encounter on the journey no parent wants to go on and come out on the other side a stronger person. God knows what is best for us always. I encourage each of you to live to the fullest potential that God has for you. Never allow fear to overtake you. Stand strong and firm in your beliefs. And know that God is our friend, so talk to Him like you speak to your friends. Develop your own language with Him, our God is awesome and He has a super sense of humor! Each day is an awesome opportunity for us to grow stronger in our faith! I know God is able. He will not fail you. You may say, well, Lil Will is gone now, so God did fail. NO! He did not! He gave Lil Will an assignment, Lil Will fulfilled it and God came and took him home.

"...when you let go and learn to trust God, it releases joy in your life. And when you trust God, you're able to be more patient. Patience is not just about waiting for something... it's about how you wait, or your attitude while waiting."
- Joyce Meyer

I Choose Joy
Angela Mountz

My phone rang around 10pm.

Which led me to pick my daughter up from a crime scene. Real life crime scenes are exactly like they show in the movie. Confusing, emotional and clogged with people walking around. When I arrived on the scene I had to park my car down the street and walk up to the house. Going around police cars and fire trucks to begin to look for my child. People were crying…nobody paid any attention to me. And then I saw her. My baby who always made me laugh, coming towards me…and I felt rage. A rage beyond any rage I had ever felt. How could she use heroin? How am I here at a crime scene instead of at home in my bed…how - am - I - at- a - crime - scene? And who is this person that I thought I knew? My baby girl who loved tutus and painted toenails. She is high and crying and unable to string words into an understandable sentence. And I slapped her.

I was so angry.

Angry at her choice to stick a needle in her arm. Angry that she chose to be with this boy who treated her like his own personal punching bag. But mostly I was angry that I couldn't control the situation. I couldn't control her decisions. The past year with her was a struggle. She skipped school, didn't come home and when she was home she was difficult to be around. She graduated high school and decided that staying with friends was better than home. I knew she was doing drugs but not heroin. I detoxed her twice before this night. Once she came home beat up and high. We went to the hospital. She went back to him less than a week later. The second time she threatened to kill herself. I forced her into the mental hospital. That lasted maybe a month and she was back with him. So as my hand connected with her face I felt rage.

Rage that she would throw away a family who loved her. Rage that she rejected the life that her father and I had worked so hard to provide her. As I was then talking with the police officer I learned that he had personally revived her from overdose at least twice before this night. You are probably wondering why it was a crime scene. The boyfriend overdosed and died. All of my wishes and nightmares coming true in the same moment. The next 48 hours were a blurry nightmare. Going to the hospital, setting up detox, working on finding her a rehab and emptying not only my bank account but her dads as well.

We put her on a plane to Mississippi to one of the best rehabs in the country. I watched my broken daughter board a plane by herself trusting in the Lord that He would guide her ways. My ex husband (her dad) and I drove seventeen hours to see her for family weekend together. We both have really supportive spouses. We felt good. We felt like we did the right thing. She looked good and she was making progress. The decision we made felt like the right thing. The right thing cost $140,000 plus about $800 a month for six months. But she was clean….until she came home. She came home and I remember the moment when I knew she used again. It was like ice cold water had been dumped over me. I was pulling laundry out of the dryer and a needle cap fell out. And I began to make all these reasons up in my head. It was from before. It was missed in her stuff. Is she diabetic? Of course I knew better. She had used.

Needless to say I was plunged into a really bad place emotionally. In the beginning I was numb. I walked through my day in autopilot and in the middle of the night I wandered the hallway looking for a magical answer and reliving every single moment I spent as a mother to this child wondering where I screwed up. Where were the mistakes that I made? And how could I fix them? I became obsessed with this. And because I was so ashamed of the situation I did not reach out and talk with people. I didn't go to meetings. I didn't ask for prayer at church. And when I did tell people there were prejudices that I had to deal with.

"Just kick her out of the house."
"Just make her stop doing drugs."
"Force her into rehab."

The suggestions go on and on. Well-intentioned people who think they have the answer to my problem. But there was no answer. I forced her into detox twice before, and this was before I knew she was using heroin. I received an ambulance bill from her overdosing and almost everyone I told commented on why I keep her on my health insurance policy. Really? Because providing insurance must somehow be enabling her. So now my circle of who I talk to is really small. Less than 5 people and even with them I am selective of what I share. And then there are the comments that people make during your everyday normal activities. The comments about how Narcan shouldn't be distributed or used. That these deadbeats should just be allowed to die the way they deserve. Which is fine except the deadbeat they are talking about is my child, who despite her addiction, I love her. The other response I get is the thinly veiled suggestions that somehow I had failed as a mother. How did I raise her? Didn't I correct her enough, or love her enough? Or that maybe I was too strict and she was somehow rebelling. There is a multitude of suggestions, comments and innuendos. Because peoples have perceptions of the type of parents that raised addicts. The common misconception is that addicts have crappy parents. They are either disconnected or they have raised these kids to be drug addicts. This added to the depression I was in.

I went through the typical stages of grief. Disbelief, Bartering, Anger. I haven't gotten to acceptance yet and I stayed in anger for a long time. In fact, it is where I have spent most of the last year. Angry. Angry at myself, angry at God, angry at the drug dealer, angry at the dead boyfriend and his family. You name it I was angry at it. I lost a best friend over my anger. I would lash out at people. My fuse was short and I avoided interacting with people. My work suffered. My relationships suffered. Because inside of me I was dying. You could physically see me age each day. The lines grew deeper each day. I began to not take care of myself. It was a dark time. I would read the bible and the words were lost in my mind because I felt God had left me. I thought I was being punished for my sins. Because of who I am and who I was. You see, I am an addict myself. I have struggled with sexual addiction as well as alcoholism. I grew up in a home where abuse, alcoholism and poor life choices were the norm rather than the exception.

Growing up in this type of environment I had a distorted idea of who God was and what His plan for the people of earth was. I felt that God was a horrible God because He allowed children to be abused and horrible things to happen. I went into my young adult life feeling conflicted and again angry. I used sex as a tool to gain power and control rather than within a covenant relationship. I didn't care about consequences of my actions or who I hurt. And then the moment came when God reached out to me during a particularly trying time of my life. My mother was dying, my marriage was a wreck and I was really making poor life choices. God gave me the choice to continue to screw up my life or to give Him a chance. I certainly could see that I screwed up my life, so I gave my life to Him.

In a matter of months, I became a new person. My anger went away, and I was devouring the Bible hoping to learn my purpose in this world. I thought there was nothing that could shake my faith. I also had the illusion that because I was a Christian my life would be easy and without conflict. Boy, was I wrong. In the past thirteen years as a Christian I have gotten divorced, had several life altering medical issues and of course my children. My oldest has kidney disease and my youngest is a heroin addict. "Lord, don't I deserve to have a good life? Haven't I suffered enough? This has been my questions almost everyday for the past year. Why my child? Wasn't I a good enough mom? Haven't I been a good enough Christian?". I worked so hard to be both. I made a life with my kids that was full of stability and love. I played with them and read to them and helped them with their homework. Their father and I modeled good work ethics and were honest. We spoke with them honestly about drugs and peer pressure. We were good parents.

And the anger so prevalent in my youth resurfaced. And every time I tried to return to the peace I had as a Christian something kept me from it. The constant drama that goes along with having a drug addict in your life. The everyday life issues that were amplified because of my stress.

My therapist must have offered to send me to a vacation at the mental ward at least six times in the last year. She was worried about what would finally break me. But I didn't break. A few months ago, I was in my car driving home on a Friday afternoon. The week went like a bad country song. My car broke down, my cat died, and I had three doctors' appointments and none of them went well. On top of that there is the tension that is always present surrounding the issues of my daughter. And I was sitting at a red light thinking about my week and the Lord said to me, "choose Joy".

Simply, choose joy.

And in that very moment, I realized that joy was the only choice. I had zero control over my daughter. I had zero control over the diagnosis I received. I had zero control over death. I wasn't in control. God was. And despite the long list of issues I had, for the first time in over a year I felt hope and peace. Because I have a big God who knows the outcome. I have a big God who will give me strength to fight another day. I have a big God who will give me wisdom to make the right choices. And yes I have a daughter who suffers from addiction. I still feel a sense of panic when the phone rings wondering if this is the call. But then I give it to God because He is in charge. At the end of the day you must have faith in the Lord and recognize that He doesn't make mistakes. He has made us all fearfully and wonderfully made. We are residing in a fallen world and in this world there are horrible things. But we are called to be the light. We are not responsible for the outcome, or the decisions that people make. We are responsible for choosing joy.

I keep her picture on my desk. The picture of the day I brought her home from the hospital full of hope. I look at that picture and I lay her at the feet of Jesus and I again remember that hope and remind myself that I choose joy.

I am fascinated by people's flaws and delusions: all the messy
bits of human nature we all try to pretend we don't have.
- Hattie Morahan

Feels Like Home
Kirsty Farrugia

Life is messy. Humans are messy. Whether it is from our own making or by circumstances that life brings along, life gets messy. I love that Jesus came to be with us in our mess. I adore this concept because I need it! He never shames us in our mess and will sit with us in our mess until, we together, figure a way forward. He never leaves us in our mess and never condemns us in it or to it. He loves us in and through our mess and with grace call us to grow and learn through the mess of life.

I am Professional Organizer (think Peter Walsh from Oprah) and I am so privileged to sit with people in the mess; the mess of their homes, their minds and their hearts. I feel like I am walking into sacred spaces each and everyday. I too have to be OK with their mess, to be OK with them, and to help them see that it is possible to move forward. Just like Jesus did and continues to do for me!

One of the many messy areas of my life that Jesus has sat with me in and through and called me to grow and learn from has been my physical space, which has led to a change in my heart and mind as well.

So you might think that because I am a successful Professional Organizer and Podcaster (The Art of Decluttering) I am therefore super organized and my house is always perfect. You might think I have always been super organized and my life has always been decluttered, a minimalist and full of grace. You might think that this decluttering gig comes easy to me, its natural, instinctual, flows easily, that I never procrastinate, that I am never late to anything, and that I never lose my mind at my kids or my husband, right? Full of self control, right? This is what you would expect from a Professional Organizer right? You would think that this is the gift that God gave me to share with the world from birth, right?

Wrong!

I was born a Red Hot Mess (still am some days to be honest!)! I grew up in a home where the focus was on hospitality. We would welcome in anyone, anytime! It was also a large family of 5 children. Our house was never dirty. My parents priorities were on people rather than possessions. Feeding their children and strangers rather than riding their children to keep their rooms and spaces neat and tidy, were their focus.. Add into this mix that fact that I am convinced that I am THE laziest person God ever created! I will procrastinate until the cows come home, in fact, I will procrastinate long after they are home as well! So it is not in my nature to be organized. But it is in my nature to spend all of my money on ALL. OF. THE. THINGS!! Which means I have not always been a good steward of the money I've been given and it also means that I'd have a lot of things that I didn't appreciate or look after well. So clearly you understand now, it was not in my nature to be decluttered.

17 years ago my now-husband entered my life. You now how opposites attract right? Well, he is my absolute opposite in many ways. He is naturally neat and tidy and he is naturally great with money and he has never liked clutter. While we were dating, Simon would come into my room and tidy it up, he would find a place for everything and make my room look amazing! Now I am sure you also appreciate how things that once were endearing during courtship can become a frustrating rub in marriage. This was certainly the case with us. Simon would be frustrated by my lack of putting anything away and I would be frustrated by having my things put away before I had finished with them! Oh the joys of partnership.

Something had to give. I could have dug my heels in and chosen to deliberately antagonize my husband but instead I decided to act in grace and ease. I saw how he did life as a better option for me personally and for our marriage. So began the process of transformation within me.

But transformation is hard.

It's never easy, is it? And it is messy! To be perfectly honest, this process is still occurring and has become one of lifestyle habits rather than a one-off transformation. What started out as a change to reduce my husband's frustrations has actually been transformational to me as a person and has been pivotal to being able to start and grow my business.

When I chose to put Simon's need to have a clean and tidy house above my own desire to be lazy, it was hard. When you have been selfish for 27 years it is hard to change. I used to get mad and frustrated that he wasn't changing instead! Seriously, I wanted him to be more lazy. What was I thinking? I know through speaking to many of my friends and nearly all of my clients, that my experience is not exactly common. It is usually not this dynamic in play in most partnerships, where the male is clean and tidy and the woman not so much. I know many women who would love their partner to take more pride in their home, however in the beginning I was not very grateful, I was very frustrated. I wanted to live into Paul's words in Philippians 2:3-4 "Do nothing out of selfish ambition or vain conceit. Rather, in humility value others above yourselves, not looking to your own interests but each of you to the interests of the others." but it was very hard to start with. Ideally I wanted to put Simon's interest above mine, but my own selfishness was super strong. The (selfish) force was strong in me (it still is, somedays!)

However, this experience, means that I can totally relate to the people I am honored to work with as clients when they are feeling overwhelmed in their homes. I can totally empathize with them when they feel these changes are hard, when they are frustrated and when they want to give up. I was once where they are now. I hope that I give them inspiration that they can change, just like I have! I hope that I can give you hope that you too can do the hard work of transformation (with God's & others help potentially). For there is freedom, joy and grace in the process and definitely as a reward!

So what did I do to change?

I stopped procrastinating (most of the time!). That almost sums it up and is the biggest tip I can give anyone who wants to live in a tidier and more decluttered home. Just do it NOW. I started to deal with things as soon as they entered my home or as soon as they arose. I now deal with the mail when I get it out of the mailbox. I put the clothes away when I bring it in from the clothesline. I do the dishes after the meal is finished. I unstack dishwasher when it is finished. I put my handbag away as soon as I walk in the door. My kids put their bags away (with some nagging sometimes) when they get home from school. I put things away after I have finished using them. I finish projects or I give myself permission to let the project go completely. The list could go on but you get the picture. I used to procrastinate because I imagined that these tasks would take longer than they really do but I have learnt through practice that don't take that long. In fact, it takes more energy and time to procrastinate on a task than actually doing it. I've found that imagined mountain is in fact a molehill when I tackle it one task at a time. It is all about touching things once. If I aim to only deal with something once, then it frees my brain to cross it off my to-do list and move on to other things. This one change has seen me able to have and maintain a tidy home which brings us all joy.

The next thing I changed was that I gave everything a home. The reason I would have piles of stuff around my room and home was because I never gave a home to EVERYTHING. Yes most things had home, but not everything. So I started giving things homes, so that I would know where to put it when I had finished using it. It also forced me to find the best place for things. It made me think of the flow of activities around my house and to think about where I would look for an object when I needed it. It also helped me to keep like with like. There was no point in having similar objects in half a dozen places around my home if it meant I had to go to all those place to gather the items to use.

Those are some of the tips I now give to my clients. These are the habits that I practice every day and they help me keep the clutter at bay.

As much as my husband Simon was always neat and tidy, I wouldn't have called him a minimalist, so when we discovered the timeless philosophy of minimalism several years ago, it just gave our home and our family even more life. Literally! I love Joshua Becker from Becoming Minimalist definition of minimalism "minimalism is the intentional promotion of the things we most value and the removal of everything that distracts us from it. Minimalism brings freedom from the all-consuming passion to possess. It steps off the treadmill of consumerism and dares to seek happiness elsewhere. It values relationships, experiences, and soul-care. And in doing so, it finds life. It invites us to slow down, consume less, but enjoy more."

We have found all this to be true! We have significantly reduced our possessions over the last 6 years. We are more intentional of what we buy, what we consume and what we get distracted by. We are not perfect! We still get distracted by pretty things and things marketers tell us to buy. We also don't think that to be minimalist that you have to live with only 1 spoon, knife, fork and plate. Minimalism is about intentionality and when I look at Jesus, I see bucketloads of intentionality. When I look at Jesus, I see a man that was all about relationships, experiences and soul-care. I want to be a woman after God's own heart and so I want to be more focused on relationships, experiences and soul-care, than I am about my possessions.

By creating a vision for our family that we wanted to live in a decluttered and tidy home where our focus was on relationship, this has given us life and life abundantly! It literally takes me 30 minutes, at the most, everyday to stay on top of things. This includes, washing dishes, washing clothes, getting the kids to tidy up and put things away & dealing with mail. (The 30 minutes a day does not include preparing and cooking meals or doing the weekly clean.)

It means that I have so much time in my day to pursue other things. It gives me time to invite others into our home at a drop of a hat, it gives me time to help the kids with their homework, and it gives me time to help others, be available to others. It gives the kids time to play and be creative before and after school. We are intentional to not fill up our week with organized/paid after school activities. At the moment we limit our kids to only 2 extracurricular activities a week each, which means we are not out every afternoon and all weekend.

It has also allowed me to create and grow my successful business. Alongside being present for my children and my husband without feeling like a red hot mess of a Mumma (most of the time)!

You see, five and a half years ago I was full time stay at home mum with a 3 year old and a 15 month old. Before children I had worked as an accountant and financial planner but had always dreamed of being a stay at home mum like my own Mum. I was fortunate enough that Simon was very supportive of this dream and that he earned enough money to make this financially viable for our family. However, the reality of motherhood was vastly different to my perception of it, or at least my expectations of myself as a mother. Living the life of a mother was a very different reality of how God created me versus how I imagined I wanted to be. So one day I had picked up a magazine from a home storage shop and it had an article about a Professional Organizer in it and right there and then I discovered the next adventure I was to take with God. I turned to Simon and asked him what he thought of me starting a Professional Organizing business, to which he said "Go for it!".

I knew that if I, the biggest procrastinator of all, was able to change and be transformed, then I could be the champion of others transformations. I knew the freedom and joy that came from living with less and living in an organized home and I wanted to share my learning with others. Jesus came to bring freedom, not only freedom from death (John 3:16), but freedom to live life abundantly now (John10:10). I see my job as partnering with God to make space for Him in families homes, hearts and minds, whether my clients realize this or not. I don't go into clients home with the intention of converting them or even preaching the good news to them. I enter their homes offering them grace, love and freedom, the very essence of God!

Again, life is messy, humans are messy. And that's my job, to actually sit in the mess with them. To be OK with their mess, to be OK with them, and to help them see that it is possible to move forward. My job is to find beauty and blessings in the mess and to help them create a vision and a home that can bring freedom and joy with less clutter. I have learnt first hand, thanks to God's grace, the benefits of letting go, letting go of things and letting go of my old ways. I've learnt by giving myself permission to live the life I want to live that there is freedom and joy. To not live a life dictated by the things but by relationships, experiences and soul-care and so I am so honored, humbled and privileged to be able to share this knowledge with my clients and podcast listeners all over the world.

It is funny, sitting here only 13 years into our marriage and taking the time to reflect on the changes that God has made in me over that time. I am so very grateful for the partner he has given me in Simon. Without God bringing Simon into my life, I very much doubt that I would have made the changes to my everyday habits. Minimalism has been a gift to us both. Without it, we would have missed out of on a ton of growth and would have still been living with a ton of excess stuff. I would not have then been in a position to pass on this learning to others through my business and podcast. I am so grateful for the grace and freedom extended to me through the life of Jesus and the ability to show this grace and freedom to others. Life will always be messy, it's how we choose to deal with the mess that counts!

I pray that my story will join the others in this book to bring you joy, life and hope. Your story is part of the uniqueness of this world!

That you were made in an amazing and wonderful way and the world needs your unique gifts that only you bring to this world. Remember, no matter how messy it life is, you can always make it feel like home!

"A feeling of pleasure or solace can be so hard to find when you are in the depths of your grief. Sometimes it's the little things that help get you through the day. You may think your comforts sound ridiculous to others, but there is nothing ridiculous about finding one little thing to help you feel good in the midst of pain and sorrow!"
– Elizabeth Berrien

The Blessing Of A Grief Stricken Heart
Kayla Brissi

I could hear voices outside of my parent's house, far away voices, but every so often the voices would be louder from joyful shouts of children. It was a day where people could enjoy the sun with the warm weather of spring after being snowbound for many months. How could they be having so much fun when I was in our family living room struggling to stay awake from days without sleep, with the fan blowing on my face, my Dad's moaning piercing my ears, the loud hum of his oxygen machine drowning out my thoughts? I was holding his hand praying for peace and comfort while I looked into his lifeless eyes as he stared off into the distance while he took his last breath and, in that moment, I kissed his forehead and told him, "We love you Dad."

The tragedy of losing my Dad will forever change my life and the very actions I choose to make until it is my time to be called home to be with our Lord.

I was not able to prepare for death and this has single-handedly been the most challenging thing I have ever had to endure. It has shaken me to my core and I can honestly say I am not the same person because of it.

It's crazy to think this journey with my Dad started in April 2016. It almost seems like yesterday but also a lifetime ago. His blessing in disguise bought us another year with him, and I am so grateful for the day that he fell off of the ladder at one of my rental properties. Had he not fallen and been rushed to the Emergency Room his cancer would have gone undetected and we would not have had one more year to listen to his stories, hear him laugh, and create memories with him.

I always assumed that my dad would grow old with my mom. My son was always going to have his Gramps to show him how to hunt and fish and have him on the sidelines cheering him on at games.

223

Dad was my rock. He was always there. I thought he would always be there. Death is what happens to others, but not my dad. I'm angry that his time was cut short, but I understand that he's at peace and at home with our Lord.

I am glad that he is no longer suffering. My dad is gone. I didn't know grief could hurt this much. Sure, I have lost grandparents, and that was sad, but I quickly moved on with my life and kept their memory with me. But for my Dad, there's an emptiness that will always linger. No matter how hard I try to fill it, it's as if it's a bottomless pit. A vast, deep dark hole that will forever remain empty. Nothing prepared for me for his death. I didn't ask for this.

I feel empty.

I feel as if a piece of me is missing and no matter how hard I try to find it I can't. I look for signs that Dad is here, but he's not. I try to replace the emptiness of pain with something else, but it never seems to work. I attempt to go about my life and pray that I feel whole again one day.

There are times I still can't believe he's gone. It feels as if I am having a nightmare and I can't seem to wake up. It's my personal hell that I have been reliving for the last year. Every day I wake up and realize it's my reality and I realize how much I miss him. I can't tell you the number of times I have picked up my phone to call my Dad to ask him a question and then remember that he won't answer because he's not here. I have watched a video of us a thousand times just so that I could hear his voice one more time.

It has been nearly a year and the pain I feel for his loss has only intensified. They say time heals all wounds. I beg to differ. I think the scars will always be there. Life will eventually go on, but the pain will forever linger. And grief is such a fickle thing that strikes you when you least expect it. One moment you can be laughing and having fun, and the next minute a song could come on the radio that triggers a memory that leaves you crying like a baby, and you're instantly reminded of the pain that is deep within you.

It's is a life-changing experience that I honestly wouldn't wish on my worst enemy. And maybe we go through grief because we can't process logically how a loved one could be here today and gone tomorrow. I'm not sure. All I know is that grief is painful, ugly, and draining both mentally and physically.

Sadly, society expects you to be back to "normal" within a couple of months, but grief doesn't work like that. It doesn't know time as we do. Grief has no timeline and no boundaries.

Despite dealing with grief and uprooting my entire life for a year to be with my Dad while he courageously fought for his life, I have come to realize that my business has been one of my greatest blessings. Had I not started my business, I would not have been able to take him to and from his doctor appointments, surgeries, and chemo treatments for a year. I would have missed out on several hours of listening to his stories, hearing his laugh, enjoying meals with him, and creating memories that I will cherish for my lifetime.

I am so proud of my Dad. Not once did he ever let us see that he was in pain or scared to die. He accepted that it was his time to go and stayed brave for all of his girls. I will never forget the stories he shared days before he passed about his time in Vietnam. He was so proud to be a veteran and that he served his country. Even though his exposure to Agent Orange is what cut his time with us short, he told me that he would proudly serve again. He was a man of integrity who believed in his call to duty, and I am so honored to be his daughter.

Do I have regrets? Absolutely! Had I known his treatment wasn't going to work and he would be taken from us earlier than we hoped, I would have given him more of my time. I regret not giving him my undivided attention that he deserved. I regret working as hard as I did when I was in his presence. I regret not taking in every single moment with him for had I known it was going to be the last time I would have cherished it even more.

But my biggest regret though is not telling my Dad how much I loved him. I'm sure he knew it by everything that I did for him, but I would give anything to be able to go back in time to tell him, "I love you Dad." And maybe, just maybe, he would have said it back to me.

What I would give right now just to hear those words come out of his mouth. It's silly to think as a woman with a family of her own that I long to hear those words but you never really know what you have until it's gone.

Not a day doesn't go by that I don't ask myself if I'm making him proud. Wondering if I am holding up my end of the bargain with my promise to him to take care of my mom and sisters. The day he died, it is as if the weight of the world was placed on my shoulders. I know he chose me for a reason to be in charge once he was gone and I may never fully understand why but I guess that too is a blessing in disguise because no matter how difficult all of this may be it has taught me so much in the process.

To this day I honestly don't know how I managed to provide for my family, support my Dad during his battle for his life, and run multiple businesses. From the day that he fell at my rental property to his emergency hip surgery and three months of using a wheelchair, I was by his side. He never gave up even with all that he endured the last year of his life. He had perseverance and grit!

Shortly after his body was on the mend from the fall, he was headed to the VA hospital for a biopsy on his lung. Biopsy results confirmed he had limited stage small cell lung cancer. Once he received the cancer diagnosis, he was scheduled for surgery to remove the lower lobe of his right lung where the tumor was located. A short time later, he started his rounds of chemo and then brain radiation as a preventative in the event the cancer would come back with a vengeance.

The greater part of 2016 and 2017 my life was busy with taking him to and from appointments, surgeries, treatments, and more. Traveling back and forth up to four hours a day and sometimes multiple times a week. I spent many days that were full of appointments and nights at the VA hospital when he was admitted for various reasons during his treatment. My life revolved around my Dad and whatever he needed to get better.

I felt that whatever I had going on in my life was minuscule compared to what he was dealing with and as his daughter, I owed it to him to be by his side. Truth be told, I wouldn't have had it any other way either. There is no way that I would have been able to concentrate on work if I wasn't there with him.

My dad and I were always close. Growing up, I wanted to be with him every second I could. I learned how to hunt, fish, tie flies for fly fishing, and more so that I could be in his presence. Looking back on our relationship, he was my world and now that he's gone I see more of him in myself daily.

During all of this, I sacrificed my family, marriage, health, relationships with friends, and even my business to support my Dad and I have absolutely no regrets about that. My business has been my blessing because it allowed me to work around my priorities. It allowed me to create memories with my Dad.

Come the first part of 2017, my Dad was experiencing some pain that his oncology team couldn't determine the source or cause. He insisted it was kidney stones, but deep down I really think he knew it was his cancer spreading even though the scans he had showed no signs of active cancer.

Over the next couple of months, things started to worsen with his health. Finally, at my request, he agreed for me to take him to the local emergency room. I knew that something wasn't right, and my worst fears were confirmed while I sat in a patient room #12 with my parents. We learned his cancer had spread to his liver, kidneys, and into both lungs. I remember looking at the images with the doctor and couldn't believe how much cancer was in my dad's body.

As I sat there taking notes for my parents I saw the look on their faces when the doctor explained that his cancer spread. It was as if their brains weren't able to process the information. I repeated it again for them and maybe it was shock or that they really didn't want to accept the reality of what was coming. I'm not entirely sure.

The next day I contacted his oncology doctor, and I rushed him to the VA hospital for more tests and to be admitted for observation. The oncology team confirmed that in fact, his cancer has spread and that his time with us would be short.

As I sat next to my Dad in the hospital with my Mom on the other side of the room, I remember trying to hold back the tears because I didn't want my Dad to see how upset I was. The thought of losing him was unbearable.

When death is imminent, it almost paralyzes you. I wanted to scream out, and I remember asking God internally, Why? Why my Dad? I couldn't understand why he was taking him from us.

I looked over at my Dad. He sat there with his hands together in his lap, and he had a stoic expression on his face. Not once did he ever cry or show that he was afraid to die. In fact, over the next few days, he kept telling me he lived a good life and it was his time to go. I never saw such bravery than I did as I watched his life deteriorate before my eyes.

During our last hospital admission before I took him home to admit him into hospice, we had many challenging discussions about what to do next. On the Wednesday, before he passed, I was sitting in the chair next to his hospital bed, and after he gave me all of my instructions for after he was gone, he turned to face me and with an oddly calm expression on his face. He calmly told me that he only had 3 more days left to live. He passed three days later surrounded by his loved ones.

Was it pure luck or did he know? I guess I will never know until it's my time too. I remember this day so vividly that it actually gives me chills when I think about it. It's an eerie feeling that will forever be ingrained in my memory.

My life was chaotic and messy. Maybe I survived it because of the adrenaline running through my body each day to keep up or perhaps it was by the grace of God. Either way, I am grateful I didn't burn out but know that I am truly blessed that I was able to be by his side every step of the way no matter how difficult it was.

Dad's death has taught me a lot about myself, my life, and business. It opened my eyes to see what is truly important to me and how to shift my focus to align with my priorities. It could have derailed me both personally and professionally. I could have wallowed in self-pity and let my anxiety and depression take over. But I didn't. Instead, I let my grief inspire and heal me. Do I still have bad days? Of course! Grief will be a process that I work through for as long as it takes as we all grieve differently.

Grief changes you. I learned that I could choose to focus on the negative ways it has impacted my life, or I could choose to focus on the positive ways it has changed my life. Thankfully, I can find the silver lining in any situation no matter how grim it may be.

Grief has inspired me to modify my current business model to allow for more time freedom so that I could be present with my family while we create memories because life is too short to be working all the time.

It has helped make me a better leader and mentor for my community and my family. I saw where I was weak and where I was strong. I quickly learned how to play to my strengths and to work on my weaknesses so that I could empower those around me.

Grief even gave me a new outlook on life where I humbly learned that grief has no boundaries and it doesn't care if it strikes at the most inappropriate times. I wholeheartedly embrace crying and feeling any emotions that come because of the grief. I don't hide it. I just let it flow, and that was something I wouldn't allow myself to do before losing my Dad.

Through the process of grieving, I learned that I am strong! It has been said that you never really know how strong you are until being strong is all that you have left. This really couldn't be more accurate. My Dad always told me I was the strong one, but I never really saw it in myself until I was forced to be the glue that holds the family together during this tragedy. Like my Dad, I have perseverance and grit!

Life didn't get in the way of pursuing my dreams. Life and its unpredictable-ness inspired me to do great things!

****

I don't know what God has in store for me, and I am sure he will find a way to use this pain I feel for the greater good. But in the meantime, I'm ok with sharing my journey with others so that they can find hope and inspiration from my story. We all face adversities in our life and business, and it's how we react to those situations that shape us into who we are.

Use the adversities in your life to inspire you to create a legacy for those that you leave behind because one day they'll look to that legacy to hold onto with a firm grip to keep your memory alive.

"She is clothed with strength and dignity, and she laughs without
fear of the future."
Proverbs 31:25

My Journey, My Truth, His Way
Linda Malloian

I write humbly. I'm excited and grateful for this blessing to share my story in hopes of helping others. You see; not too long ago I was in the fight of my life. In the end, I won, but let me share with you the journey..

I was given the precious gift of life on April 23, 1968 at 7 am. I was blessed with 2 two wonderful parents and 3 siblings. I couldn't be luckier to have a greater, more loving, and caring family. Ever since I was a child I remember being sick quite often. As I got older things didn't improve, as a matter of fact I developed even more health issues. At times I wondered why hadn't my parents taken my health more seriously. Today I know the answer to this question- it's because they simply didn't know any better back then.

It was not until I was in my late teens that I went to the doctor on my own. My first surgery was at the age of 19, removing my tonsils. Shortly after I learned that I had an autoimmune disease, and thyroid issues. I remember being so tired, depressed, and achy most of the time. I couldn't understand what was happening, or why I was feeling this way. I lost the job I had loved, and worked at for over 8 years because of my illnesses.

Fast forward several years later I met my current husband, and we married 7 years later. One year later we wanted to start a family. There was not much luck in trying for a child naturally, and we both decided to try for one artificially. After spending so much time, energy, and money, we were once again disappointed with the results. Several months later I found out the reason for my struggle in conceiving- I had endometriosis. The disease had left no healthy reproductive organs in my body. The despair and devastation of this had me spiraling down into severe depression. The thought of the inability to bare a child made me feel like less of a women, and an imperfect wife. The doctors I had went to all told me my chances of carrying were not possible. Miraculously six years later, I became pregnant. Needless to say, this stunned my OBGYN's, and they couldn't understand or explain how this was possible, but I could. This was God. We were blessed with a true miracle- a beautiful baby girl, who was handcrafted by God himself.

My pregnancy was difficult and my daughter was born at six months. Her lungs were not developed fully, and she was not able to breath on her own. I asked the Lord everyday why he would do such a thing. I cried so many tears that my face swelled, and wet tears became dry. She stayed in the hospital and survived. One week after her birth, I was released, and came home without her. The image of coming home with my new baby girl was shattered. Six months after her birth, I had a complete hysterectomy. I felt robbed of my femininity. Eventually, after all our pain, my husband and I were able to bring our daughter home- healthy, and strong. Life was happy, and I was happy. I felt as if things were getting better. I would take my daughter to the park, to the beach, and wherever I went, she went.

I was so consumed in raising our daughter that I didn't realize the toll it was taking on our marriage. Our relationship suffered, but neither of us admitted it to one another. We started to grow apart emotionally, and physically. I found out that he was having an affair with women from his own work. They would make my daughter gifts, and give them to my husband for him to give them to her. I found out eventually, and was furious. Everything was going okay in our household, and it was smooth sailing until he decided that our marriage wasn't enough. I knew the vows I had made when I got married, and stuck with him, but once again-he had an affair.

This was my breaking point.

The amount of energy and support I supplied him with, meant nothing to our romance or friendship. The night I found out, I called some of my family members and his family members. I told them to " come and get their son." The look of confusion in my daughters youthful eyes made my heart shatter into a million pieces. I had always wanted a "white-picket fence family", and my dreams were crushed. My husband moved out, and jumped around where he would sleep for the night. Sometimes he would sleep at his parent's house, and at other times he would sleep at a co-worker's house. I was met with divorce papers on many occasions, but they were never followed through. He wanted a third chance, and so I gave it to him, and he moved back into our house.

By age 40, I had developed many health issues and took a plethora of medications. By the years 2012- 2015, I was prescribed, and ingesting 700 pills a month- Yes, 700 pills a month. How was it possible that I was still alive? My medical professionals failed me completely. At one point I stopped all meds, but the pain I endured was severe, and I replaced the pills with alcohol. There was one time where I obtained pills illegally. I was even arrested, and had to go to a drug rehab facility. The drugs I was taking consumed my mind, and I began to think irrationally. They eventually let me out of the rehab center because of the pain I was experiencing from other unrelated issues. I was a melting pot for poor health. The deadly combination of pills, alcohol, depression, anxiety, insomnia, poor diet, marriage problems, and surgeries, put me in a coma. My family was given little hope for me to survive. The thought of planning a funeral was starring my family in the face.

During the time I was in a coma, I was in a space that was beautiful beyond anything, anyone could ever imagine. It was peaceful, and time did not exist. I saw, and met with Jesus, and Mary. They stood beside one another, and radiated an indescribable bright light. Peace, and love surrounded them. I ran towards Christ, and couldn't wait to reach him. I remember being only a couple of feet away when Jesus put his palm up and said to me "Stop, it is not time for you to come yet." I couldn't understand why because I wanted and was ready to go despite what I would be leaving behind. It was a selfish thought, but I was in so much misery, that nothing mattered.

Waking up from my coma, I felt lost, confused, and thought I was tied down because I was unable to move. Little did I know, I was paralyzed from the neck down, and had stage 1 liver cancer. Labs would show that I was depleted from any vitamins, or minerals. I was unable to eat, speak, and my memory shut down. I couldn't recognize my loved ones. Weighing in at 85 pounds, my body was weak, and toxic. I lost my hair, lashes, brows, and nails. My body was so malnourished that it started to feed on itself. My flesh was exposed, and parts of my body looked as if they were decomposing. I had to be wrapped in bandages, as a burn victim would. My face and mouth were infected and surgeons had to cut open my face. I didn't look anywhere close to what was once Linda. I refused to let my daughter see me. What was truly worse than this, was feeling I failed myself, failed my family, failed my husband, failed my daughter, and most of all, failed God. I wanted to die, and not feel the pain of this guilt, which was by far worse than the physical pain I experienced.

I had hit my version of rock bottom, and I was willing to let go of everything, and everyone- to find peace. I went through a long period in which people would judge me. The burden of being a mother and not being physically there for my daughter laid a huge weight on my shoulders. I didn't know what else I could do to help myself heal. One night I was so desperate for God to take me that I fell down to my knees, and begged him to end it all. I was suffering, and my loved ones were suffering with me. Many times I was angry with God, and couldn't understand why this was happening. Had I done something so horrific in my lifetime, that this was the price for my sin? Instead of me taking my daughter to school, it was always someone else. Instead of me taking care of my mom, my mom was taking care of me. I had to relearn how to walk, talk, eat, and think. It felt as if I was one year old.

Because of all of this, my husband and I's relationship was essentially nonexistent. He didn't think of me as a romantic partner anymore. My daughter and I could sense that he was seeing someone else. This wasn't a big surprise to me because of our complicated history. In all honesty, I didn't blame him. I didn't have enough energy to blame him. When we got married we promised to stay together "in sickness and in health." This obviously was preached, but not practiced. He would come see me in the hospital, and although I knew he loved me, I often wondered if he was just waiting for me to die so that he could rebuild another life with another woman. Because I was so far away from home, I had no control over who he was able to see. He would leave our daughter home for an hour or two to go see his mistresses. I wanted to take control of my life, but I felt like I couldn't.

The first time I allowed my daughter to see me in my physical rehab center was very emotional. I hadn't seen her for several months, and it looked as if she had grown into a young woman without me. I gave her the biggest hug I had ever given in my life. My sense of motherhood returned, and it felt good. I took her to meet some other patients I had met at the hospital. We played bingo and some other games that the nurses hosted. We got to connect in a mother-daughter way and it was liberating. I missed that feeling. Although I wasn't 100 percent better I believe seeing my daughter helped me feel a little more normal, and motivated me to get better faster.

One day I remembered waking up in my mother's bed, as she was taking care of me, and I felt good for the first time in five years. This little light of hope felt as if God was finally answering my prayers. I knew I had to start thinking of me first. I knew I had to let go of trying to make sure everything at home was taken care of. It was extremely difficult to learn how to say "No" to other people's needs and wants. I also knew western medicine wasn't working for me, and had nothing to lose by trying eastern medicine. Instead of asking God to take me, I started asking Jesus to lay his hands on me, and carry me through my journey. I put all my hope, faith, and trust in <u>Him.</u> I started to thank him for all that I had been enduring. The more I thanked him the closer I felt to the Lord. I started to view my pain, and suffering as God's glorious intervention for me. I began to realize my life journey was not of constant positives, but of many failures, and with each failure came a great lesson and growing opportunity. I knew this would be one of my biggest trials, and I couldn't let my situation get me more down than it already did. I also knew God had a bigger plan, a plan to grow, and prosper. A plan to help reach out to others in any way possible. Sometimes my blessings came in mysterious ways- through pain, and trouble. Understanding my situation failed me, but accepting it kept me close to God, and I dwelled in his blessing of tranquility.

There was a moment when I felt an overwhelming presence of angels. At that moment, I accepted my condition, and knew God would be there to hold my hand, and carry me through. All I had to do to achieve so, is surrender to him. I had to let go of loved ones, and of control. Released everything precious, and important to me, to God. Simply rest in his arms where I am safe. From 2000-2015, I lived in, and out of hospitals, and physical rehab facilities. Slowly, but surely my health began to respond in a positive direction. I choose to refuse chemotherapy for my liver cancer, surgery, or any other form of medications. I chose the path that involved trusting God, and approached natural treatments, and therapies. That was the answer I had needed all along.

My journey has been challenging for many years. When I look back, and observe, I know why God had chosen me to walk along this path. I'm grateful every minute, of everyday that I was chosen because I am who I am as a result of my passage. I've been back at home, with my family, for two years now, and today I'm stronger, healthier, and at my best than ever before. Things are always roses and lollipops but I can see the growth in every situation. As I wrap up this story, , I am still fighting for my marriage. I am still showing up daily to love me the best way I deserve to be loved no matter who is in my life. I know it's up to me to love me - through all my pain, all my joys; whether I am healthy or sick.

I have my moments, don't get me wrong. But through this all, I have learned that happiness is a choice. You may not always control what happens to you, but you can control how you choose to look at the situation. In the moment that an incident is happening, you look at the negatives. I often look at people's ungrateful attitudes towards life. I would go through the hard times in life 20 more times if it were guaranteed I wouldn't end up like them. Sometimes I'm thankful that I can do somethings as simple as drive a car, cook a meal, or watch a movie with my daughter. I'm so grateful for the family and friends who stood beside me in some of my worst moments. They've become my rocks.

I am unsure of what tomorrow holds but I do know that I am surrounded by people who truly love and care for me. I do know that no matter what - my life is worth living and I want to show up daily. I now know that I have a special gift where I can see and feel God in everything I do. Anything is possible with faith, hope, and love in the Lord. Trust Him always and watch Him do miracles in your life His way. This truly is my journey and my truth, all done His way.

Out of my distress I called on the Lord; the Lord answered me and
set me free."
Psalm 91:14-15

Betrayed But Not Forsaken
Angelique Mosley

Sitting in the courtroom, hands folded in my lap, I waited. Sweaty-palmed and cotton-mouthed I glanced around. He's not here yet, I thought. Maybe he's decided not to go through with this after all. Adjusting my posture I sat up a little straighter. My stomach was in knots, I realized I was holding my breath. Breathe, I reminded myself, inhaling and exhaling slowly. Pulling my shoulders down and back I leaned against the hard bench and closed my eyes.

"Here's your copy of what was filed with the court," my attorney whispered.

I opened my eyes as she handed me a stack of neatly stapled papers. Reaching out for them I responded with a thank you. Smiling she said,

"It's going to be okay, I will do all of the talking."

She patted me on the knee and returned to her seat at the table in front of the room. Time seemed to stand still as the courtroom began to fill with people. Soon it was bustling with sounds of shuffling documents and hushed whispers.

I closed my eyes and prayed, "God please help me, give me strength." I turned and looked toward the door. My heart sank and I was gripped with fear as I watched my husband enter and take a seat on the other side of the room. He's here. He's actually going to do this. He is going to divorce me. And not only is he going to divorce me, he is going to try to take our daughter from me. Blinking back tears, I wondered, 'how did we get here?' I looked over at him. He seemed so detached and matter-of-fact. I on the other hand was utterly broken. How could he go through with this without ever trying to make things work? Why would he file for divorce without ever going to counseling? And in front of all of these people? He was a pastor after all, he knew that this was wrong. When did his heart become so hard?

I recalled an email I received from my Pastoral Counseling Organization several months back. It read, "At this time we do not believe your husband is a candidate for counseling." I was sad but not surprised. In order to heal your marriage you have to want to heal your marriage. My husband had been threatening to divorce me for a few years. He didn't think he needed counseling and had refused to go with me or on his own. Still I struggled to understand why he would put me and our daughter through all of this. But mostly I ached to understand how I could have been so foolish and weak.

I watched as he sorted through his papers and organized his files. He seemed so calm and dignified. Would the judge see the truth? Not likely. It was only after we'd married and moved in together that I began to see his true character. It took several years of living and serving alongside him in the church before I understood the extent of his hypocrisy.

A few years back I attended a gathering for pastors' wives where the facilitator asked, "What is the hardest part about being a pastor's wife?" I listened as the other women relayed stories about challenges with church members and frustration with the long hours their husbands put in at church. I yearned to share my truth but I was afraid. I wanted to tell them that being a pastor's wife was not easy that I too, had been hurt by people. But that I'd had little difficulty overcoming that hurt and continuing to minister to them with a sincere heart. No, for me, the hardest part about being a pastor's wife wasn't the people, the sacrifice or the loneliness. For me the hardest part about being a pastor's wife was being married to my husband.

A husband who was distant, harsh, dismissive, and detached at home. As Pastor and founder of our church he was faithful to Sunday services and engaging when he was there. An awesome preacher and teacher, his sermons were filled with love and grace and the people admired him. But at home he was mean, unforgiving, hard-hearted, stubborn and full of pride. He drank almost every night and denied that he had a problem. He checked out completely at home and sat in front of the television drinking glass after glass of wine until he passed out. He would ignore me for days on end and blamed me for almost everything wrong in our lives. When he drank, he was obnoxious and verbally abusive. This behavior had alienated our adult children and my parents refused to be around him when was drinking. At church everyone thought he was fabulous. He dealt with our daughter dutifully and with tremendous love and patience. He was kind and loving toward other people; always good for a joke and a chuckle. Whenever he was mad at me he would be overly affectionate with the women at church only to withdraw once we were at home where I got little or no affection, let alone conversation. Outside of church he was quick to anger; a symptom of which presented itself as extreme road rage. He was controlling, impatient and harsh in his dealings with me and our young daughter. He would snap at or be rude to wait staff, baristas, our neighbors and people in general.

I wanted to tell them that the way my husband treated me at home sometimes spilled over at church. He would ignore me or make dismissive comments toward me at ministry meetings. As a result some people at church followed his example and began treating me with disrespect. I wanted to share my truth with these pastors' wives but many of them knew my husband, and I didn't think they would believe me or even care. So I sat in silence.

For a long time, I brushed off his bad behavior by telling myself he was suffering from depression from all he'd been through in his first marriage and subsequent divorce. When we met, he explained how his first wife left him, took all that they owned including the house and turned their children against him. It pained me to hear how she "tried to destroy the church", that she was "emotionally unstable" and that he feared for his safety. I empathized with him and his frustration about having to start over with nothing. When we were married, I convinced myself that if I prayed more, loved him more, and focused on taking care of the needs of our household he would eventually snap out of this depression, stop drinking, and begin to walk in the kindness and love he so eloquently relayed in his weekly sermons.

In fairness, he made it clear from the beginning that he would have an occasional glass of wine. During our brief courtship, he told me that he drank wine and had no plans to stop. Because of my past relationships and the history of abuse at the hands of an alcoholic, it was a potential deal-breaker for me. He assured me that drinking was not a problem for him, that he didn't drink regularly and that he would never hurt me. I decided to get married after all. Not realizing that the occasional glass of wine would turn into a daily glass, and then two to three glasses and eventually turn into two bottles a night, sometimes more.

Over the years, I began to vocalize my concerns with him and communication between us broke down severely. Whenever I stood up to him, he became angry, resentful, withdrawn and bitter toward me. When he drank he was obnoxious, loud, sloppy and even cruel. Name calling was a technique he favored when he wanted to hurt me, once kicking me out of the house while shouting profanities. Worse yet, he wouldn't always remember the things he said or did. So when I would confront him the next day, he'd accuse me of over exaggerating or making things up.

He went to work every day and since he didn't drink before noon, he reasoned that he didn't have a drinking problem. And I covered for him. I kept our personal life secret. I didn't want to hurt him or the wonderful people I'd come to know and love in our congregation.
At one point I gave him an ultimatum, something he advised me never to do. I told him if he didn't stop drinking I would leave. He said he would stop but after three days he began drinking again. I was heartbroken, but I didn't leave. With no money, no job, and no way I was going to tell anyone that my pastor/husband had a drinking problem, I had nowhere to go. It was a turning point and from that time on I tried to encourage him to take a sabbatical.

By his own admission he was, "self-medicating" because of depression. I pleaded with him, telling him we needed to do something different. I even used his sermon fodder to drive home my point.

"If we keep doing what we've always done, we'll always get what we've always gotten," I said.

He finally relented and told me he would pray about it and consider moving to be closer to his family in California. For the first time in years I was hopeful. I began looking for jobs near my in-laws. If he were take a sabbatical we would need additional income, and I was happy to go back to work if it could save our family. I was offered a job within a few months but he said he didn't feel God calling him to leave yet so I turned it down. In the meantime, he continued drinking and things worsened at home. He threatened divorce several times and even left once. Our daughter, just four or five years old at the time was being subjected to the abusive language, arguing and overall turmoil in the house so when I got another job offer in California I began making plans to visit the area and meet with potential staff. He said he'd support me and help me move but he didn't. He never intended to take a sabbatical, he never intended to join me in California nor did he intend to go to marriage counseling. I would later learn that he'd been planning to divorce me for several months prior to my accepting the job.

When I moved to California, he told church members that I was on sabbatical and completely cut me off. He stopped taking my calls, drained our joint bank account, removed me from our insurance policies, filed for divorce and started seeing other women. I was devastated.

"All rise." The clerk's voice shook me to attention. Everyone in the courtroom stood. I slowly rose to my feet, feeling dizzy. I took hold of the bench in front of me to steady myself.

"The honorable Judge Brown presiding." The judge emerged from chambers. Oh no, I worried. It's a man, he's never going to believe me.

"You may be seated," the judge said taking his seat. We heeded his words.

Opening a file in front of him, the judge asked, "Are the parties for Mosley vs. Mosley present in the courtroom? My husband and his attorney stood.

"Yes your Honor," he said. My attorney stood.

"Yes your honor," she replied.

"Please come forward," said the Judge.

In a dreamlike state, I followed my attorney to the front of the courtroom and stood next to her at the bench. My husband stood on the other side of the courtroom with his attorney. I glanced at him. The expression on his face was unsettling. He looked directly at me, hardened his mouth, rolled his eyes and looked away. I felt like he was looking through me and I was afraid.

My ex-husband presents well. He's charismatic and charming in front of others. I was certain he'd have the judge wrapped around his finger in no time. He'd convinced many people that I was to blame for the demise of our marriage. I had always been silent about our personal life and hadn't been to the church in over a year so that wasn't a difficult feat. He told me not to speak to anyone at church because they didn't care about me and since no one had reached out to me since I left, I believed him. I later found out he asked the congregation not to contact me but to "pray for me."

Even before taking the job in California, I had "left" the church, I had stopped participating in church activities and settled into the position he asked me to fill. He asked me to be like his former pastors wife.

"Just sit in church and be quiet. Smile at people and don't engage, don't get involved", he'd said.

Because of this, I truly believed no one missed me or even cared. I now realize that many did care, but they were just doing what they were told.

Standing in front of this judge, I reasoned that there was no way he would be able to see my husband's lies for what they were. That his accusations of my abandoning the marriage and leaving with our child in the middle of the night to go to California were completely unfounded. I knew that my husband was going to deny that he had a drinking problem and deny any abusive behavior on his part.

Worst of all, he was seeking full custody of our daughter on the grounds that I was mentally unstable! I listened intently as my husband spoke to the judge. He and his attorney told lie after lie. I was shocked and angry at first, then so sad and finally embarrassed. As my attorney began speaking in my defense, I wondered if the story I'd just heard my husband tell the judge was the same one he'd told his family members and many of our friends who had forsaken me. 'I'd be upset with me too if those things he was telling the judge were true' I thought. But they weren't true.

As the judge questioned my husband, I remembered how utterly betrayed and foolish I felt after arriving in California. I had nowhere to live and hadn't truly secured my job. When he cut off contact with me, I reached out to my mother-in-law, desperate to understand what was going on and to figure out what to do next. She had been my confidant for years, my safe place to turn. As a pastor's wife I really couldn't speak about what was happening in my personal life for fear that it would affect my husband's career. But I felt safe talking to his mother because I knew she loved him and I thought she loved me. Speaking to her about our problems was helpful because I knew she would never use anything I told her against him. I shared with her about the drinking and the abusive behaviors. She would advise me and comfort me during those trouble times. As the wife of a pastor herself for many years, she understood the pressures of ministry and marriage. She confided that her mother was an alcoholic too and she often gave me advice on how to deal with my husband. I needed to hear her voice; once I spoke to her, I just knew she would help make all of this right. I never heard from her. Instead, I received a text from my husband. Sitting in the parking lot at my new job, I read the words that would send me into one of the darkest loneliest times of my life. "My mother has asked me to tell you not to contact her or my father anymore…they would prefer if you didn't visit them."

I was flabbergasted and full of despair as I read those hurtful words. The heart wrenching pain of betrayal is still with me to this day. I'd come to love my husband's parents and indeed, I had come to love his entire family. His mother had counseled me not to mention my husband's drinking to any of his brothers or sisters. I heeded her advice and kept the drinking secret. Although she and my father-in-law had spoken to my husband about it, he never stopped drinking and in fact seemed to become more defiant. Having moved to be closer to his family only to learn via text message that they no longer wished to speak to me was crushing. I couldn't have known it at the time, but I now realize that the betrayal signified a new beginning in my soul.

I was alone. Betrayed. "God, give me wisdom, give me strength" was my prayer at the time. I had no time to feel sorry for myself, I had my daughter to care for and I had a job. I would need to start work very soon. Over the next few weeks, I'd found a place to live, began attending a local church, enrolled my daughter in all day kindergarten, and went to work. During those first few weeks my daughter and I experienced such peace and tranquility in our new place. We no longer had to walk on eggshells, we could laugh, play games, dance, listen to music as loud as we wanted and come and go whenever we pleased. With this newfound freedom and the stark contrast to the dysfunctional home life I'd experienced over the past several years, I came to understand just how toxic and abusive my marriage had become and the traumatic effect it must have had on me and our precious daughter.

Although my husband refused to take my calls, he was still communicating with me via text messages and emails. He advised that he would no longer be looking for jobs in California and that he would not be taking a sabbatical. He told me that if I wanted to work things out I would need to return home. I was confused by his turnaround, and afraid that he was going to retaliate if I returned home. I sought counsel from the pastor at the church my daughter and I had been attending, and spoke to a few of my spiritual mentors. I was surprised when my pastor and each of my mentors advised me to remain separated. The thinking was that by going back to him, my husband would have no incentive to change. Over the next few weeks I wrestled with whether or not to return. Finally, I replied to my husband telling him, I didn't want a divorce but would not return until he stopped drinking and received counseling. He responded by filing for divorce. I was devastated. I reached out to him, hoping to change his mind. He actually picked up his phone and spoke to me! He told me he loved me and wanted to make things work but I would need to come home first. "Come back home and I will withdraw the divorce", he'd said. He said he wouldn't go to counseling unless I returned. I was afraid, but I loved him and wanted to make our marriage work so I returned.

"Your Honor, I'm certain you've read all of the documents submitted in this case", my attorney stated.

"Yes counsel, I have" the judge replied.

I listened with great sadness and embarrassment as my attorney recounted what my husband had done in recent months. The courtroom came alive with murmurs and whispers as she spoke, "Your Honor the Pastor has substantial income, yet he's provided no support for his wife since the parties separated.....as a result she has applied for and has been approved for full welfare benefits….she stopped working at his request... .now, he refuses to pay support"

Struggling not to cry, I took a deep breath and stood up a little straighter.

Closing my eyes briefly I prayed, "God please forgive us".

"The Pastor makes a number of assertions, my attorney continued, '...He alleges untruthfully that my client has a mental health issue. Well we've provided the Court with specific documentation …."

I wanted to disappear. The pain of it all was just too much. I'd returned home a few months earlier only to find that he was still drinking. He did not withdraw the divorce and did not start counseling as he'd promised. With no job, no money and no way I was going to continue to place my daughter in harm's way, I told him I was going to go to my parent's house. He responded with, "If you go to your mother's house don't ever bother coming back". I was saddened, but hopeful that if I left, he would do the right thing. Less than a week after I'd gone to my parents, he changed the locks on our home, disconnected my cell phone, closed our bank account and filed for full custody of our daughter on the grounds that I was mentally unstable.

Standing in the courtroom, I felt so exposed, so small. What if the judge sides with him and takes my baby away from me? "God, please help me, I need you " I prayed.

When I received the certified letter notifying me that my husband was attempting to have our daughter removed from my care, I was shocked. Being a mother and the special relationship I have with each of my children is what I value most in life. The idea that I might lose custody of my little girl and not be able to protect her from her dad's abusive behavior was almost unbearable. I cannot describe the depth of pain and betrayal I felt reading the declaration my husband filed with the court. With each word I realized that the man I married did not exist. Until that point, I still trusted him. I still had hope. In that moment, I realized that reconciliation was not an option. I knew that it was truly the end of our marriage.

Once my family and close friends found out that he'd filed for full custody of our daughter with me only having supervised visits, they rallied to help me find an attorney and then assisted with my legal fees. My attorney, a Christian was disgusted by the things she'd learned during the discovery process and it was apparent in her voice as she pleaded my case before the judge. After hearing from both sides the judge made his ruling. He ruled in my favor! He ordered my husband to pay spousal and child support and scolded him for closing our accounts, accusing me of mental instability and for putting me in a position to have to request financial assistance from the state. I was shocked at the tone the judge took with my husband. I'd never heard anyone stand up to him and certainly not in my defense. I felt so alone and broken standing in the courtroom that day. At the time I was still reeling from disbelief at what my husband was doing and too weary to speak. God had answered my prayers that day and I learned a valuable lesson. God will fight for you when you are unable to fight for yourself. He will reach down from on high and draw you out of deep waters. He will strengthen you, preserve you and grant you peace during trial.

My husband went on to file three separate motions with the court to reduce support payments and gain custody of our daughter, but each time he brought me to court, I prevailed.

Divorce is painful. During the year long process, God insulated me with family and friends who supported me every step of the way. But it was still a heart wrenching ordeal. I had a strong support network, and was meeting with my life coach and pastor regularly, but I was absolutely broken emotionally during the process. When my soul was weary and I could barely stand, God sent His people to fight for me. Time and time again I "won" in court. Each judge and commissioner in my case saw through my husband's deception and lies. My attorney fought for me when I was too devastated and broken to fight for myself. I had no money, but God provided for me financially through the generosity of others.

It was a very difficult year but a liberating as well. I am no longer living under the abusive and toxic authority of my ex-husband. My daughter and I no longer walk on eggshells, nor do we huddle together out of fear. Instead, we are free.

"The strength of a woman is not measured by the impact that all her hardships in life have had on her; but the strength of a woman is measured by the extent of her refusal to allow those hardships to dictate her and who she becomes."
– C. JoyBell C.

The End To The Beginning
Kendra Pierce

Strong willed, independent, bold and fearless were traits that summed me up for the first 17 years of my life. Little did I know the world as I had known it was about to crumble beneath me and leave me defeated, weak, and full of self doubt and self worth. There were so many nights that I would lay on my bed, after just getting in a verbal or physicals fight with my "abuser" and wonder how I let this happen?, how I let it get this bad?, and how I did not see this coming?. Which lead me to believe that I wasn't as strong as I once thought I was. As a result I become a victim of Domestic Violence.

Often times, I felt that he was so far above me and deserved someone that could love him in a way that I couldn't. Someone that could "obey" the way he needed. Someone that could make him happy. From the things he told me, I started to believe that I was incapable of loving him the way he needed me to. I started believing all the negative things that he had ingrained in me over all the years. Comments like "You're worthless, I don't even know why you want to live", "You're so ugly if I ever left you, you would never find another man that would love you". The constant remarks started to convince me that what he was saying was true. It got to a point that I truly believed I was ugly, worthless, untalented, incapable and not worth loving. It wasn't until I hit rock bottom, the very lowest of my lows that I knew something had to change.

There were only two places I could go from that point. The first and most prominent thought, was that I could give up, I could all around stop fighting to live. Thoughts consumed my mind, that maybe if I wasn't around anymore, my abuser would be happier. Maybe my children would get a "capable, smart, beautiful" mother and maybe my family and few friends that I was "allowed to have" would be happier without me. The possibility of everyone else around me living a better life because I wasn't around anymore seemed worth it to me. I knew it was only a matter of time before this road crossed my path. He was either going to kill me, or I was going to muster up enough courage to fight back. The only problem with fighting back was that unless I were to kill him in the process the plan would backfire and instead he would kill me. Several times I thought about the possibility and at the time it seemed like the only way out. But I knew, deep in my heart and sole that I was not strong enough to follow through. Despite the hate and anger that burned inside of me, I was not that person.

I wasn't strong enough to pull the trigger, I wasn't strong enough to physically take him down. I wasn't strong enough to live with that, even if it was self defense. At that point, I knew my two options were to continue to live in the situation I was in and wonder every day if it would be my last, or stand up and hope that I was strong enough to regain my self worth.

It was 3 o'clock a.m, as I laid in bed next to him, feeling my face pound with pain. Laying on a pillow covered in blood, still trying to get my breath back from nearly being choked unconscious that I realized now is the time to make that decision. I didn't sleep that night. I laid next to him knowing it would be the last time we would ever lay in a bed together. It would be the last time he kissed me goodbye before he went to work. It would be the last time he would leave our house feeling like he was in total control. I knew in my heart however, it wouldn't be the last time he hurt me. It wouldn't be the last time I feared for my life, and it wouldn't be the last time I would wonder if it would all be worth it. But I was willing to try, and if I died in the process of fighting for freedom then I will not have died in vain. If he was going to kill me, he was going to kill me standing up for myself and my children. Not as a victim of weakness, control, and hate. The thought alone, of what I was about to face, scared me more than anything I had ever faced up to this point in my life.

It scared me more then the look in his eyes when he would beat me. It scared me more then him turning the oven on broil and holding me in front of it, listening to him tell me how bad it was going to hurt. It scared me more then when he opened the oven and tried to put me in it. It scared me more then when he tried to push me out of the car going 85 miles down the freeway or when he beat me black and blue and drove me up the mountain and convinced me I was going to die that day. It scared me more then when he forced bleach down my throat when he found out I was pregnant with our second child. It scared me more than the many times I was choked until I passed out or almost passed out. It scared me more then having to go out in public with bruises all over my body. It scared me more then having the Department of Child and Family Services (DCFS) show up at my door and threaten to take my child out of my hands during a child abuse "investigation". It scared me more than having my face slammed into the passenger side window after mouthing to someone in the car next to me stopped at a stoplight to call 911. It scared me more than wondering how many broken bones I would have when I made it to the bottom of the cement staircase I was tumbling down. It scared me more then lying to the doctor at the hospital after yet another altercation. It scared me more then the first 5 minutes of him coming home after work and not knowing if the vacuum lines in the carpet were fresh enough, or if I had gotten all the fingerprints from our toddler off all the glass in the house, or if I had left any water spot or streaks in the kitchen sink after drying it. It scared me more then the gun that was held to my head. It scared me more than anything in the world but I was ready.

The alarm clock went off at 6:00 am and my heart was beating harder than ever. I tried to act as if I was asleep as he got ready for work and kissed me goodbye. I listened for his car to drive off. As soon as the sound of the car leaving became faint, I immediately called my mother. I was doing this! For the first time, with tears rolling down my face, I spoke the words I needed to speak for far too long…. "Mom, I need help!". She got my fathers truck and drove the 30+ minutes to our house. Together, we packed up all of my child's belongings and a few other things and we left. She drove me 60 miles away to my best friend's house.. It wasn't more than 15 minutes after we left my house that my phone rang and I knew he was home. My phone rang 134 times on that hour long drive and with each ring, I would again wonder, if I was making the right choice.

The next year was filled with mind games over the phone. Trying to figure out if we could make this work. In my mind I knew I could never go back to him. It didn't matter how good it sounded I knew it would go back to what it was. I was very emotionally and mentally unstable at that time and knew that there was a process to what I was trying to do and for the moment, distance was the only thing helping me stay firm and grounded.

A year and a half after leaving him, I moved back into the area that both him and I grew up. He didn't know where I was living, nor what kind of car I was driving. He didn't know where I was working or anyone I surrounded myself with. For all explanation purposes, I was still in "hiding". Slowly and carefully I was rebuilding my confidence and self worth while trying to make ends meet and continuing to be strong for my children. They were young, and the less they knew or had to see, the better.

I needed to prove to myself that I wasn't alone and that this road to safety was possible. I soon found and joined a local group that helped women in my situation. They provided different resources including classes and one on one counseling to help battered women stabilize. The classes seemed intimidating but I still went. I didn't speak but I showed up and I listened. Part of me was scared to even admit that I was victim enough to be there. However, as time went on I started feeling a little bit better about myself. I knew I still had a lot of rebuilding to do. I knew I was going to have to make sacrifices now to better our future. I was working full time but after paying for daycare, it was barely enough. So I enrolled in college. In order for something to change I needed to change what I was doing. Some days, I would drop my children off at daycare at 7am and pick them up just in time to get them home, read them a story and tuck them in bed. Those days were hard but I knew in the end it would be worth it!

Very rarely, I would hang out with a friend or two. While out one night I met a handsome, well put together gentleman a little bit older than I. We started casually dating and things were going well. I knew I had to be very careful about what we did, where we went together, or who we hung out with. He was patient and tried to understand the situation but I knew at times there was no way to completely explain why some things had to be how they were.

The city I was living in, about 45 minutes outside of Salt Lake City, Utah, wasn't huge but big enough I felt somewhat safe. The local agency I was working with highly suggested I live at a secure women's shelter until everything with my children's custody filing was finalized and things calmed down. I didn't think that was a good idea as I knew that meant putting a protective order in place. The agency pushed me to get a protective order but I didn't think it was a good idea. They would remind me very often that protective orders are there to protect me and my children. I fully understood that. However, what they or most other people for that matter, didn't understand was that a piece of paper saying that he can't come around us, is not going to stop him. Not at all. If anything it would taunt him. And for that reason, I respectfully declined.

As things went on without incident I started letting my guard down a little bit. Maybe I was obsessing. Maybe I didn't have to live in fear or in hiding as much as I had been. I invited the gentleman I had been dating over one spring day to come hang out. To my surprise, my abuser wasn't too far behind him. He all but walked in my front door before my abuser kicked my door in and attacked both of us. He was there all but about four minutes and in that time managed to turn my house into what looked like a deadly crime scene. There was blood all over the floor, blood on the walls and carpet, and broken glass all over the living room and kitchen. As I stood in the middle of the room after he ran out, I looked up to the top of the stairs and both of my kids were standing there. They had watched the whole thing. My heart broke into a million pieces.

All of the work I had put into trying to protect them from seeing "daddy" get mad, had failed. The hiding, the rebuilding, all of it, felt like it was in vain. Who was I kidding? Of course he knew where we lived and what we were doing. I should have known better. 911 was called and arrived a few minutes later. They took the gentleman to the hospital as he took the blunt of the anger that day. His arm was cut so severely when they were loading him into the ambulance, for the first time in my life, I saw what looked to be raw bone. The police came, and again urged me to get a protective order. Sitting in my kitchen, covered in blood. I respectfully declined. Something deep down inside of me was sure that I knew my abuser better than the law did and I was going out on a limb and doing something I hadn't done for many years, trusting myself that my decision was right!

It didn't last long. There was a case that was open due to the incident that left me with little to no choice. In order to show the court that I was doing everything I could to protect my children from violence (since they were present during the altercation) I was required to get a protective order against him. One for me and one for each of my kids. Tears streamed down my face as I signed all 3 of those documents. I knew we were in trouble. The judge however assured me this was the right way. The doubt set in…. The right way? How do they know the right way? Have they not read the reports? Have they not seen what we had been through? But it was done. I pleased the court and the case with the above incident was closed on my end.

The next week, I lived in complete fear. I knew he was going to be served the protective orders and I knew it was going to put my children and I in danger. We had come so far. I was terrified of what was going to happen. I kissed my children goodnight after tucking them in and I looked at them both, with tears in my eyes. I had a conversation that no parent should ever have to have with their children. I told them from that point on if they ever heard someone in the house fighting with mommy, the four year old was instructed to get the two year old and hide in the closet. I showed them how to pull the blanket in the closet down and cover themselves. I told them several times how important it would be that they stay as quiet as they could. It didn't matter what they thought was happening outside of their room. They were to stay there until I came and got them. I stressed that my oldest, the four year old needed to understand how important it was to follow my directions. I assured them I wouldn't let anything happen to them. He agreed. I kissed them again and went to my room. I layed there that night trying to come up with a plan. I needed a plan, I needed a way to protect myself and I needed a phone for them to keep in the closet. My son was young but he could call 911 if he needed to. I was scared to sleep that night, but feel asleep around 3 or 4 am.

It was still dark outside. I heard a noise but woke up just enough to hear that it was probably one of the neighbors heading to work. I dozed back off and was quickly awoken by my bedroom door slamming open with extreme force. There was just enough light shining through to see a figure standing in my doorway. It was him. At that very second all I could think about were my kids. The physical pain I endured that day is far too much to write about in this passage. But it didn't matter. The only thing I could think of was protecting the kids. My son was smart. I had hope he would follow our plan just like we talked about.

Four hours passed when he finally decided to throw me in the closet and shut the door. I knew he was probably sitting right outside the door. I knew I didn't have enough time to call 911 and even if I got them on the phone, I would need a few seconds to give them my address and risk him hearing me. Time was not in my favor. I turned the phone on. As soon as it registered to the home screen, I text a good friend of mine, "HELP! CALL 911" As I pressed send I heard him walking towards the closet I was in. As the door to the closet opened, I quickly fumbled to snap off the battery of the phone to disable it to ensure no calls, texts or sounds would come from the phone. I fell towards the door as it opened in hopes to confuse him and give me a split second to hide the phone. With the battery in one hand and the phone in another. I slide them under clothes that lay on both sides of the door.

I barely made it.

A few minutes later, there was a knock on my door. My heart was pounding harder than it ever had before. I was told not to answer it. After it was clear the person at the door was not leaving I was walked up to the door with a knife to my back and told to open it enough to tell them everything was fine and not to speak another word. I did as I was told. The police officer asked me to open the door a little more so he could see who he was talking too. The knife was pressed harder and deeper against my back. I refused. He asked if he could come in. The door was opened just enough that all he could see is a small part of my face. I looked directly in his eyes, fighting back the fear and tears that were surfacing and assured him everything was fine. I had the feeling in my stomach that I had learned to trust. The officer, looked me directly in the one eye that could be seen through the crack of the door, he was silent. I was nervous as I didn't know what was about to happen. I watched him carefully as I knew that any movement could result in one of us dying. He blinked. Not an ordinary blink. A slow, very distinct blink three times in a row and slightly nodded his head up and down with each blink. I blinked three times back. He turned to the officer behind him, and back around at me. He blinked once, he blinked twice and motioned he was coming in, on the third blink he rushed my door. I was thrown into the other officers arms so fast I didn't know what had happened. I was terrified of what was about to happen. I turned to the officer and as fast as the words would come out, came "my kids are in the closet upstairs, please help them".

I didn't know it at the time, but there were officers surrounding my house. They had seen through my back patio door that he was behind me. He was arrested (with incident of course). The officer protecting me walked me upstairs after they had removed him. I feel to my knees with my children in my arms. They were safe. They kept him out of our sight as they took him away. He was later charged with attempted murder, breaking and entering among many other charges and sent to prison.

Am I free? No. I will never be free. But I finally had time to heal in peace. I could heal knowing that my children and I were safe. I could heal knowing that once again, I had just lived through my greatest fear. No matter what it took, we were either going to successfully get away or I was going to die trying. Our freedom almost cost me my life that day, and if it would have turned out different, I would have died knowing that at least my children would be free…. but we survived.

It took giving myself a chance, to know that I am stronger than what my mind was "trained" to believe.
It took faith in not knowing what was going to happen, but taking the jump anyway.
It took trust in believing that regardless of how weak I thought I was, I had to be stronger than I was giving myself credit for. It took confidence in knowing that no matter how bad of a person I was made to believe that I was, I had to be better than the person making me believe those things.
It took courage in knowing that whatever life I lead from that point on, would be from my own decisions, not someone else making decisions for me. It would be my very own, to learn and grow from, to rejoice in triumphs and learn from failures.
It took responsibility to make a decision that day and a large responsibility from that day forward to accept the things I can change and let go of things I have no control over.
It took acceptance in knowing that the decisions I make will affect me and my children's future and trust in knowing it will all turn out okay.

The beauty in this mess of mine, is that I now have a much clearer idea of who I am and not only who I am but what I am worth. I started this journey we call life as a very shy, reserved and quiet person. As my teenage years came around I started gaining confidence and standing out for who I was. After having all of that taken from me in my late teens and early twenties I have been working on rebuilding the person I now know I am inside. The person I am today is not the person I thought I would be at this point in my life prior to this obstacle in my life. I don't know who I would have been or where life would have taken me. But I do know, for 100% certain, that the life I live and will continue to live is a life in a completely different light then it would have ever been before. I am on a continuous path to better myself and those around me. I believe in myself and others and strive to show that. I have learned to look past the physical scars and the damage to my face that shows ironically every time I smile. I have learned to fill the emotional scars with gratitude and peace. I have learned to trust more than most. I have learned that life is short and nobody knows what it has in store for us. I have learned to be happy. There is nothing in this world that should take you away from being happy. It's each of our lives to live how we want our life to be. We are in control of that, not anybody else. I have learned to trust myself, my thoughts, my feelings, my choices and my actions. I have learned to love and more importantly I have learned how to forgive. I continue to work on building self worth and self confidence and I hope that through my actions that I can pass the traits, strength and motivation I needed during that crucial time in my life, to others.

Nobody knows what people are going through. We all fall at some point in our lives. The most important thing is that we get back up. And when we get back up we hold our head a little higher and believe in who we are.

"There is no fear in love. But perfect love drives out fear, because fear has to do with punishment. The one who fears is not made perfect in love. We love because He first loved us."
1 John 4:18-19

When Love Broke Through
Walanda Johnson

March 2018 my heart was broken…again. I had basically been in love with my best friend the last 3 years of our 5 year relationship. I met him when my program worked next door to his job but we didn't really share space until a couple years later having to develop a working relationship. The first two years of our relationship were spent as co-workers. I already had the tough girl demeanor and, according to him, it challenged him to get beyond the walls I built. And, boy, did he work! I wasn't one to mix business relationships with friendships, especially with males. But the turning point came when a kid I worked with committed suicide. I asked for space from everyone to process the grief and although he respected it, he continued to check in with me, listen to my process and the rest was history. We became close friends, sharing intimate details of our lives and along the way, I fell in love despite my efforts to fight it. And so, 5 years later, here I was with my heart pounding in my ears as I hear him say he wanted to reunite with his ex. Imagine my shock and reaction when he told me this, granted he was with her when we met and they had agreed to take "a break as he completed Grad school but that information tore at my soul. You're probably wondering 'well, did you tell him how you felt?' And, despite the undertones of our conversations leading up to that moment, the truth is no, I didn't directly say it and the reason why is where the story of my journey begins.

My 20's were by far the most heart wrenching years of my existence. I had a minor rendition of job experience. In the course of 5 years, starting at 22, I, a certified daddy's girl, had lost her father to kidney cancer. At 23-25, I wrestled with losing who I thought was my "soulmate" after he cheated on me with a friend. A month before my 27th birthday my She-ro/mom had finally lost her short 8-month battle with glioblastoma, slowly dying before my eyes. Anyone who has lost a mom knows the pain of this loss. It's like no other. And to lose her and my father made me feel orphaned. I was left alone with the perpetual inner question of 'who do I belong to now!?' This question haunted me for years. It came up every time I would see my sisters with their husbands or children. It came up when I would see my friends with their mothers. Even when my godmother would try her hardest to console me and support me. My reactions to any of these scenarios would be to spit in their faces figuratively. The desperate anger of this question led me to spiral into a depression I had never known could exist. A depression so dark that it would float over and hover around me for a least a decade; a depression that would flirt often with the thought of leaving and never coming back (otherwise known as suicide); a depression that would build a fortified wall around my heart. Not just a wall but a stone one with barbed wires, poison ivy, and detonators all around it.

I accepted Jesus at 19 years old and since then really tried to live a life worthy of the call. I was devoted to God. So imagine my shock that this would happen to me. My father, I considered , to be like the woman with the issue of blood. He had struggled with kidney cancer since I was 10, my mom donating a kidney, him receiving treatment, all of that was much of my teenage life. Thus, when he hit that 12 year, I just knew that God would save him just like he did when I prayed before at 11. And when he told us he would not receive treatment anymore and began to whittle away, somehow I made peace with it or so I thought. I moved back home to help care for him and made sure that he accepted Jesus before he died. I didn't cry at his funeral and don't remember crying much afterward, only occasionally. I think in my mind I felt like I had 10 years to say goodbye. This was not the case when my mom passed. Hindsight tells me I stuffed my grief for my dad and balled it into the pain of losing my mom.

At any rate, I was living a devoted life to God throughout that time.

Well, I was trying.

It was tough. I cried and begged for God to let me die so I could be in heaven with my parents. I just wanted to be loved as much as I knew they loved me. I didn't feel that love from anyone, not even God and I just wanted to feel it again. My head told me that God loved me more and he wanted to be my parents but I was not trying to hear any of that news. No one understood the pain I was feeling. All my friends still had a parent and that fact made me hate - yes, hate - their lives. The wall was being rectified; the detonators in place. It was a dark time for me internally. Outwardly though I kept afloat, diving more into ministry and I believe that was the only truth that kept me afloat: knowing there was a God. Oddly enough, I was trying to cling to a God that I felt mostly anger toward and who I felt betrayed me. I felt as though he didn't protect my heart, so it was now my responsibility to make sure that I never felt the hurt and pain again. Stone by stone, vice after vice, I quickly built my wall.

The pain of loss dragged me into my 30s and surely left carnage along the way. A theme of 'you can't break my heart more than it broke already' kept me cold, distant, and lonely. Even my friendships didn't function healthily. The thought of being re-traumatized scared me so much that I didn't think I'd be able to survive removing one stone. But on the outside, on matters unrelated to the heart, I functioned. I completed my bachelors. Went on to complete my masters; trying to create something that made me look desirable, all the while not loving myself. Surrounded by people and desperately alone with all these aches in my soul.

It was a painful time. I was angry, bitter, depressed, suicidal, and hurt. I didn't realize that I was rejecting myself before anyone else could. I would like to say one day the heavens opened up and God whispered to my soul, but that was not my case. Even God was not welcomed behind my wall. And he tried. I would get close to him and then he would touch something that was too much like home and I would run away. The way that I functioned in my relationships was the same with God: get close then run away and never let anyone get behind the wall.

This was a long process to heal, quite possibly longer than it needed to be because I was unwilling to let go of my fear. Now fear, he was my friend. The only one that was behind the wall with me, warning me of when someone wanted to be closer and signaling alerts and waving red flags to detonate whenever someone got too close. He was the one that would whisper conspiracies and thoughts that people didn't have my best interest at heart. The one that would tell me that with him I would be completely safe, no one would ever hurt me again as long as he was near.

That was a lie of course. I was more alone that I had ever been. I would recall memories of my life before the losses of my 20s and remember being so happy and content and bold. God began to open my heart through children. He knew the love I needed to see had to be innocent, like his. And so for years, he used them and when my god sons had to move away and I realized that I would no longer be a part of his daily life, it tore at me. I felt myself battling with fear, with closing up my heart again. But this time, the battle was different; I didn't want to be walled up with fear. I wanted something more. I wanted to truly live.

I began to realize that I was not living the life that God intended for me. Granted, although I was still scared; I was ready. Let me say this process took a decade at least. I still wasn't the best at relationships: romantic or platonic, but I wanted to try. I would still run occasionally. My change did not happen overnight and I'm obviously sitting in a place of being broken. But my change is still happening and is coming, as cheesy as this may sound, with surrender.

What people didn't tell me is that surrender, like any other biblical principle, is the most oxymoronic word. When we think about surrender, naturally, we think about being in bondage to someone/ something else. But from the God perspective, it's completely the opposite. When I kept surrendering this place to God, when I kept telling him, I don't like this part of me, help me fix it, change it…he kept giving me more and more freedom. Looking back, he was willing to take whatever little piece I would give him. Maybe because being All-Knowing he knew that he would get the best of me one day. Every time I would ask 'what is this?' or petition him to help me or ask him to fix me, he was working. Again, the process continues. He is still digging up the fear that dug itself down deep into my soul almost two decades ago; the fear that kept my mouth quiet when I "should" have told my best friend how I felt about him.

You know what the beautiful thing is about this heartbreak is that I'm not mad, not bitter or fearful. I'm hurt, no doubt but when the other thoughts try and creep in, I religiously hear my Abba who I prayed to cover me whisper a promise to me. My heart has remained open to him and it will remain open. Somehow God, the All-Knowing God he is, knew that day in March was coming and because he knew he had been taking me on a love quest in search of him for months. Somehow during the course of that quest, he began to deactivate the detonators, Weed-X the poison ivy, snip away at the barbed-wire, and roll away the stones. Sounds like Lazarus, huh?

I remember the day after I received the news about my ex. I remember the first declarations out of my mouth was that I will not let fear win- not now and not in my future. Next time, I will speak up, boldly and with courage. Who wants to live a life in fear? No one, yet we all do at some point. And while we may not openly say "I'm afraid," we flirt with the "what ifs." This time, in this heartbreak, God is so close to me walking me through in His love. His perfect love that casts out fear; His love that covers. It is a different journey from the woman I knew 15 years ago.

Throughout the course of the past 15 years, I was like many women, wanting to be in full control of myself. I would constantly tell myself 'Don't be too emotional'; don't be too hardcore; don't let them break you or see you breaking. Take care of yourself; don't show weakness. Definitely don't let your heart be broken again.' All the while, I was breaking my own heart. I was preventing myself from experiencing the greatest gift: love, God's and mans. I was ultimately preventing myself from loving me. By not allowing myself the right to experience and give love, I was denying myself from life. Life is found in love.

And this is what saddens me the most; that this is the mantra some of us women take, the one we take to our little girls is the same one that leaves us hurting more than we would if we take the risk. When my heart broke that day in May, I told some of the teen girls I mentor and their responses were 'forget that!' They seemed cold; their responses made me sadder that these precious teenage hearts could subscribe to this energy. This is not how God designed us. Loving my best friend as deeply as I allowed myself - something I would not have chosen to do a decade before - was one of the boldest moves I've made in a while. And it was a scary, exhilarating ride, as scary as skydiving at times but amazingly beautiful. And while my heart aches and in the weeks, months ahead I'll vacillate between anger, sadness, disbelief, acceptance, and bargaining all of it is good because all of it is life and oddly enough, all of it is GOD!

I'm learning that being in my shell, hiding behind my walls, sinking my head in the sand and still trying to run my life course was the complete opposite of what God planned for me. His love for me has given me so much more life than I ever could've imagined. I am -we are- completely loved by Him on our best and worst day so to be able to share a smidge of that love to someone else is a gift. I was able to experience love in a vulnerable way and as scary as it seemed, I didn't die. It didn't kill me. I don't want to hide back in the sand! I don't want to be bitter! I will not rebuild a wall! Does my heart hurt? Absolutely! Do I look forward to the weeks and months coming? Not at all! But one thing I've learned about life is that perspective can make or break any moment. How we perceive our life experiences can lead us in victory or make us perpetual victims. For example, accepting the death of my parents opened up a bigger perspective for me. I would not be the woman I am today without experiencing the pain of their loss. I'd still be spoiled - I did mention I was a daddy's girl right!? I wouldn't have learned how to stand on my own or better yet stand with God. God would still be a faraway entity to me, not one that sticks closer than a brother. I can hear some readers saying, 'how do you know how you'd be?' and you're right I don't know. But what I do know is that suffering brings glory, patience, character, and hope. All of which are being produced in me in increasing measure.

The journey God is taking me on – because he always moves at our level of understanding – is me learning how much he loves me and once I can grasp the truth that He can't NOT love me as; I am in His creation. Once I see how valuable I am, how special I am to Him, how reckless His love is for me; how worth every nail, all the name calling, every ounce of pain was so that I could belong to Him, there's no way that I wouldn't love me.

Beloved, love is not an automatic; we have to work to accept it. Not to receive it, but accept it. Where there is hurt, pain, rejection, disappointment, mistrust – in part, we have to be willing to open ourselves up or at least, pray for the strength of God to help us open up. Love is always surrounding us, even in the darkest of pain. It's in the trees that give shade when it's hot, the water that quenches our thirst, the moon that gives light when it's dark the sun that gives heat when it's cold. It's there. It's even in the pain we endure because the pain challenges us to grow. It gives us a bottom to look up from: a hope that there is more than where we stand today. And isn't that the truth of God's word? That there's an exceeding abundance that is more than imaginable? Absolutely!

Inspired to join the movement?

First, let me just thank you for taking the time out of your busy lives to read THE BEAUTY IN MY MESS. As you can see, the ladies and contributors of this book have poured out pieces of their heart and soul on these pages. These stories are real. The pain is real. The joy is real yet what's even more real is the hope and inspiration that we want our stories to ignite within you.

Take these stories as life lessons learned. As fuel and truth that YOU TOO can live another day. And guess what? We want you to do more than just live - we want you to survive and thrive.

Our website has a "contact us" component in which you can reach out to any one of your favorite authors to ask for advice, to ask for prayer and or to simply just share. We are all here for you.

And not only that, we want to extend a personal invitation for you to join us in this movement. We all have a story to share. We all have something that we've endured. Something that we were born to teach the world - this is your time to tell your story!

I've put together a platform where women from all over the world can unite forces with other women and give their stories purpose and life. This goes way beyond money, or fame. This platform is so we can help change lives together. One person, one reader, at a time. We truly are better together and I would love for you to join us on future writing projects and beyond.

Check out the website at www.thebeautyinmymess.com and select "JOIN US". Here you will receive preliminary info and the application to become a publish author with us; all while taking the concept of "tell your story" to the next level. Your time is now and I'll be here every step of the way to guide you through the process of letting God turn your mess into something beautiful!

We want to hear your story!

Nicole Long ~ Author, Compiler and Coach

Acknowledgements

Thank you to all my fellow authors for entrusting me with your stories for THE BEAUTY IN MY MESS!!! You truly mean the world to me and we all share a special bond and experience that no one can ever take away from us. YOU are the very reason this book exists in its essence. I didn't realize when I finally became obedient to Christ and said yes - the magnitude of this project. But look at God!

As I keep saying ladies, we've only just begun but I thank you for your trust in the process, your patience, your encouragement, your prayers, your dance parties all along the way. Please thank your families for sharing a piece of you with me and this book. I thank you for freeing your stories with the world. Your gifts and contributions to this book - and movement do not go unnoticed. You are pioneers and God's precious daughters!!!

Special thanks to our publishing and editing teams. I've been the best consistent, always asking questions, giving my 2 cents partner /client you could ever have - but we did it ! Kayla, Jaclyn, Janna, and John- Thank you for shining your God Given talents into this project!

To our brand ambassadors and beta readers... you rock! I - We, appreciate you more than you'll ever know.

On average I went a little coo-coo at least once or twice a week (sometimes more) and my core: prayer warriors were right there. Thank you! Holly, Tae, Tiah, Janna, and Kayla you have been my go to ladies from the very beginning. We've shared tears, questions, strategies, doubts, fears, stalls and so much more. At times I felt like I was birthing and raising a newborn and I know one thing to be true: just like children, it takes a village to publish a book. Thank you for being my village people!

Chida, Amanda, Julia, Monique, Belisa, and Krista!!!! OMG!!! I have been so blessed to have you ladies guide me, love on me, mentor me, inspire me, and simply cheer for me through this project. I trusted you with this piece way before I was ready yet you showed compassion and insight to help it be something wonderful. Your reviews and forward were the icing on the cake! It's amazing how some of us started off as strangers and now we're extended family. Keep letting God use you and grow your ministries. Your labor is not in vain.

My children. Jyiah and Jyaele. You've dealt with me wearing so many hats that rooms went unclean, meals not as organic and fresh, and mommy simply not on her mommy A game but you've loved me just the same. Thank you for your sharp editing eyes, numbering pages, and graphic design insights. I do ALL this to show you: YOU can! You both are my inspiration.

And Mr. John Long Jr. - My dear husband. Thank you. Thank you for sharing me with this project. Thank you for understanding what it means to say "yes" to God even when you feel like everything in your life is saying "no, not right now". Thank you for healing with me and allowing me to be transparent through this project. My push actually came from you! I am blessed to be married to someone who allows the truth to shine through even when it can be uncomfortable and who has showed me through example on how to do the very same.

Thank you to my family support team. My Daddy, Father in loves, siblings, cousins and grandparents - even when it was unclear as to what I was up to… everyone of you have always cheered me on. Daddy - I am your little girl and you are my hero who taught me that anything God says is for me - truly is for me and there's no need to stress. Thank you for instilling belief and showing me what faith in action truly looks like.

Endless thanks to my mothers. Yes mothers! My Mommy and my mothers in love. Thank you for your special contribution to this book. Mommy (Ethel Sims); thank you for paving the way for your girls to take the ambition in becoming published writers just like you and never letting anything stand in the way of our

God given purposes. Thank you Cylnthia Long for always saying "yes"; without hesitation whenever I've needed you. Your gift of poetry needed to be shared with the world and I'm honored that I was able to do it within this book. Thank you Dee Bush for your prayers and your support for our nucleus of a family during our crazy moments. Every single one of you ladies inspire me daily to thrive to be a better me, wife, mom, business lady and above all - a God chaser.

I love you all!!!

About The Authors

(in order of their stories followed by our special collaborators)

Krista Pettiford
Foreword Author

Krista Pettiford the host of Called Women's Conference, the mom to four young adults, an author, and a speaker. She is also the women's ministry leader and a prayer leader at her local church New Covenant Tabernacle where she's been a member for more than eighteen years.

Krista has a B.A. in Biblical Studies from Southern California Seminary located in San Diego where she lives with her family. Her mission is to call God's daughters to the heart of the Father, to be shaped in their identity and the way they live their faith through the transformative power of His love, acceptance, and beauty.

Nicole Long
The Obedience Project

Nicole is a Certified Christian Transformation Life/Business Coach and Certifier. She enjoys working with women all over the world to help them find their voice, own their purpose and truly learn how to LIVE LIFE OUT LOUD! True to style, Nicole is also a collaborator and author of books and articles that empower women.

A native of San Diego, CA., she didn't venture too far from the beaches and currently resides north of San Diego in Inland Empire, CA. Nicole is a TV Production Major with a minor in Youth and Human Services from Pepperdine University. She has since furthered her education pursuits completing her Ph.D., and additional certifications from Grand Canyon University, Liberty University, Fielding University and the University of Canterbury.

When Nicole isn't working her business(s), you'll find her spending quality time with her hubby and best friend of over 15 years, and being a fabulous homeschooling, dance mom to her two extremely talented – God gifted daughters (one a tween and one a teen) – so extra prayers please. She finds solace in long walks on the beach, listening to music, shopping for purses and anything teal, as well as being an avid reader and learner.

Along with the special edition of being an independent publisher. You can visit Nicole's website at http://www.coaching4lifellc.com for tips and tools on how to grow and monetize both your coaching and networking businesses in minimal time.

Shawna Cook
I Once Was Blind

Shawna has always had a passion for empowering and encouraging women. She fills her passion by working with women one on one, or in small groups. She also teaches intimacy enhancement classes. Nothing is as fulfilling for her as ministering and supporting married couples with her husband through their true to life beauty for ashes experience.

Shawna believes that the power of prayer can change every area of your life by opening up the door for an intimate, growing relationship with our creator, who wants the best for His beloved children.

Shawna is a native of San Diego, CA. She is HAPPILY married and the mother of three children. Her favorite thing to do is engage is deep, thought provoking conversation but a lively, competitive game night with friends plays a close second. Shawna is currently writing a full account version of I Once Was Blind and also has a devotional book of daily prayers for marriages that will be released this year.

For more information and to sign up for her upcoming book releases visit: www.shawnacook.com

Cristin Germaine
Dare To Dream

Cristin was born and raised in New York, and relocated to Lancaster, Pennsylvania to attend Lancaster Bible College and eventually making it her permanent residence after earning two Associates Degrees.

In February of 2013, Cristin established H.O.P.E. (Helping Out Providing Encouragement), a single moms ministry through her church. In the first two years Cristin planned and organized the first Lancaster Dare to Dream Single Moms' Day Out. H.O.P.E. continues to grow and has expanded to two churches in Lancaster City and Stevens, PA. She is currently organizing Lancaster's third annual Dare to Dream as well as working to create a theme song based on her experiences where she will record the vocals. Cristin's next steps are to establish a nonprofit to serve single Moms.

Cristin has been employed in the health insurance industry as an Associate Account Manager and is a single mom of her fourteen year old son AJ.

Janis Melillo
Faith Happens

Janis Melillo is a widely sought out Health Coach and shares her passion of wellness through fitness and nutrition. Janis is a firm believer that every patient she coaches does NOT go on a diet but rather cultivates small changes to adhere to a healthy lifestyle change.

Along with her passion for wellness, Janis is also a #1 International Best Selling Author having co-authored eight books, five of which hit the International Bestsellers List, and of those five, three of which hit #1 International Best Seller and the other two in the International Best Seller Seller category. All of the books she has co-authored hit #1 Amazon Hot New Releases. Quite an accomplishment for a new author!

Janis has worked long and hard on her chapter for this Anthology. The purpose of sharing her tragic story is solely for the purpose of anyone who has suffered such as herself to take action in their own lives and continue to share the passion of triumph over tragedy.

Janis is very motivational and shares prayers and motivational scriptures on Facebook - Digital Life Ministries and motivational, gratitude and compassion quotes on Facebook: Circle Of Hope.

Tae McKinney
When Plans Change and List Fail

Amongst being a fit mom, a working mom, a business mom, and a healthy "as humanely possible with crazy schedules" mom... Tae also adds "author mom" to her many titles.

Tae has written Prayers for the NICU MOM after experiencing the trials of having a premature baby and also written a devotional entitled, New Me Same God. Both of her books can be found on Amazon. Tae is currently working on her latest novel all about the laughs, the tears, & the coffee that happens while raising her children. Follow her journey on social media @justacupoftae or @thenicumom to never miss a crazy moment.

Tae lives in Los Angeles, CA with her husband and two children and enjoys spending her days living out every definition of mom life.

Jaclyn Glaze
A Hot Mess

Jaclyn is a Jesus-loving wife to Matthew and mother to four beautiful children. As a high school Spanish teacher turned stay-at-home-mom, turned business owner, Jaclyn has developed a unique perspective when it comes to finding a balance between cooking, cleaning, laundry, soccer practice and business responsibilities. It usually means late nights, early mornings and several cups of coffee! In addition to running her household and Union28 Marriage Apparel, Jaclyn and her husband are also involved in Spanish ministries at their church. They share a passion for the Spanish language and culture. Another passion they share: Date night!

Jaclyn and her family reside in Houston, Texas.

Lisa Daniels
It Is Well

Lisa began leading worship at the young age of 13. She went on to serve as choir director and youth ministry leader at Victory Christian Center Church. In 2008, Lisa and her family were led to the City of Hope International Church, where she also served as the worship leader. It was a few years later when Lisa answered her call to teach and earned her minister's license.

In June of 2016, Lisa and her family were led to Bayview Baptist Church in San Diego, CA where she currently serves on the worship team. Through leading worship and teaching God's word, Lisa has learned that her feelings of inadequacy do not have a place in His presence and it is her mission to inspire and encourage everyone to believe in themselves and that they too are fearfully and wonderfully made.

Lisa is a loving wife and mother who loves to worship the Lord. She is a confident and inspirational game changer for her generation and generations to come.

Holly M Lopez
Crippled By A Spirit

Holly M Lopez is an accomplished speaker and life coach, who has helped countless people transform their lives. Sharing biblical truths through poignant and hilarious stories, she will make you laugh, cry, and learn. She draws upon a hard-to-believe wealth of experience: wife of 27 years; mom of three, ages 19 to 24; grandma to a child not in her life; survivor of a debilitating, life-threatening disease; and the list goes on!

Amanda Wood
Rebuilding The Walls

Amanda has always been driven to take things to the next level. Knowing that God created her and others for great things, she has always strived to be obedient, work towards living life to the fullest, and empowering others to experience the same. With this motivation, Amanda pursued her dreams of becoming an Organizational Life Coach. Her passion is to see others step into a life of freedom, purpose, boldness, and joy. Amanda is determined to help women who feel stuck in their clutter unleash their potential through transformational organization and simplification. As the Creator of Unleashed Life Coaching, Amanda loves to display her passion through personalized creations, and sharing the love of Jesus.

When Amanda isn't on the clock, you can find her exploring God's creation, creating an environment of laughter, enjoying a great book, and loving on dogs endlessly. Amanda holds her Master's Degree in Life Coaching.

Tiah Lewis
Covered Through The Storm

Tiah enjoys being a wife and a mom first. Her recommitment of her life to Jesus Christ began four years ago and she hasn't stopped being in awe by the power of the living word and its impact on her life.

A graduate of National University, Tiah holds a Masters' degree in Business Administration and has had her entrepreneurial spirit in high gear, ever since she left corporate America two years ago to become a stay at home mom. Tiah considers it a true blessing from God to be used to serve in whatever capacity He sees fits in hopes to encourage and change lives all over the world.

Tiah is a devoted member of Kingdom Builders Ministry in Houston, TX, and has witnessed and experienced the true love of God through outreach, evangelism, and prayer, serving over pastoral affairs at her church for the last four years.

In her spare time Tiah enjoys reading, ministering, and spending time with her loving husband of four years and her four beautiful children.

Tiah can be found on Facebook @TiahLewisAuthor

Omoni Williams
Tapped: Going from Tapped Out to Tapped In

Omoni is a military wife and special needs advocate and volunteer for her community. She is a mom to one daughter and three sons who have autism. In 2017 Omoni served as the keynote speaker for Arts for Autism Gala for the Autism Society of Northern Virginia.

In her spare time, Omoni loves to dive into a great book, go to the movies or hang with friends.

Em Desiray
The Redemption of a Lost Soul

Em Desiray has been a self-proclaimed, singer, songwriter, author and poet since childhood. Her work have been featured in newspapers, blogs, student journals, and social media gossip websites. She has also written many personal stories and essays, and in 2008, presented one of her essays at the National Conference of Black Studies in Atlanta, Ga.

Em is an avid social media user, and uses her platform to entertain, educate and empower her followers. Her writings, discussions and feelings can be painfully honest, brutally truthful and unapologetic - except when it comes to matters of her own heart, until now. Her mission is to use her testimony to help others can find the courage and strength to walk in their truth, just as she is still learning to walk in hers.

Em is a native of Philadelphia, PA and resides in San Diego, CA. She currently works as a social worker in the Adoptions department of Child Welfare Services for the County of San Diego. Em holds a Bachelors of Art in Social Science with an emphasis in African American Studies from California State University-Northridge.

Follow her at www.facebook.com/emdeebell

Joy Ada Onyesoh
Wings of Faith

Joy is a passionate, self motivated individual with a drive to succeed, having excellent organizational and interpersonal skills. Joy's purpose is to inspire others to find their life's purpose and live an impactful life. She creates opportunities for women and girls to find and own their voice.

Joy is founder of the Joy Onyesoh Foundation. She is also the President of Women's International League for Peace and Freedom Nigeria. Joy is a trainer, inspirational speaker and a researcher. Joy Onyesoh actively advocates for women's rights and substantive participation in peace and political processes at the international and national level including the United Nations Security Council 1325. Joy has earned several certificates in women and peace building, gender analysis, conflict resolution and transformation.

Teresa Shindle
God's Miracles

Teresa Shindle began her journey of writing short stories and poems as a young adult. It helped her overcome the obstacles of everyday life. Her passion for writing led her to pursue her dreams of writing and publishing her first children's book in 2015, titled, "If It Were Me... I Would Be..."

Always having a passion for teaching, Teresa also pursued her dreams of becoming a preschool teacher and graduated with honors in 2017.She continues that love for teaching into the weekends as the Director of Children's Ministry for her local church.

Teresa grew up in Glendale, Arizona and later made her way to Southern California. She lives in beautiful wine country with her three adorable children and loving husband.

She enjoys spending her time crafting, writing and being inspired by her kids. She will continue to pursue her passion for teaching and writing while inspiring young minds to pursue their dreams.

Chou Hallegra
I Found Life

Chou Hallegra, the founder of Grace & Hope Consulting, LLC, is a Christian Counselor, Life Coach, as well as a Mental Health and Disability Consultant. She has a passion for helping others achieve emotional wellness, reach their full potential, and live fulfilling lives. She combines her life experiences with her professional training to help others go from victims to survivors who thrive and enjoy life the fullest.

Chou is originally from Brazzaville, Congo and has been residing in Central Pennsylvania for 14 years. She is the devoted mother of Hope Nyasha, Gabriel Joseph, and Daniel Jeremiah. Find out more about Chou and her work at www.graceandhopeconsulting.com

April Johnson
In The Middle

April is a mother of two and wife of a courageous stroke survivor. She recently resigned from her job to become a full-time caretaker for her husband.

With an administrative and customer service background, April is a self-proclaimed chaos coordinator who is currently flexing her entrepreneurial muscles by building two online businesses and fleshing out the idea for a caretaker blog/forum.

When not spending time with her husband, volunteering or chauffeuring children, April can be found crafting, going on clearance walks, also known as, bargain hunting, or curled up with a great book and a piping hot cup of tea. April and her family currently reside in Inland Empire, CA.

Crystal Dixon
Daddy Issues

Crystal began a career in teaching and in her ninth year, realized her passion for teaching was no longer there. She made the bold decision to leave the classroom and losing what was her safe and secure identity. Crystal found herself in an unfamiliar place of not knowing who she was and entered a place of deep sadness and depression. It was in this two year period where Crystal reclaimed her self love and came to realize that many women had been through similar experiences. This discovery created an opportunity for her to share her experiences with others. Crystal wanted others to know they are worth their own happiness.

Now as a trained, happiness, life coach, Crystal is best known for her signature program, The Happy Plan Project. This is a group coaching program that helps women who have faded into the background of their own lives rebuild a specialized plan to make them centerstage again.

T.J. Robinson
Wellness Pursuit: Trauma Recovery

T.J. is the founder and executive director of Natural-WE Community, a non-profit under CCFEI in Los Angeles, CA. T.J. is also a certified Life and Spiritual Coach, and adjunct professor at several colleges and universities in the Los Angeles area.

She is a proud alumni of CSU Dominguez Hills were she earned her Master of the Arts in Africana Psychology. T.J. is currently pursuing her PhD at Claremont Graduate University in the Cultural Studies program. Her research interests are standards of beauty and the Spirituals. In October, 2015 her article, "The Healing Element of the Spirituals" was published in the Journal of Pan African Studies.

T.J. Robinson sings in several choirs including the Voices of Praise at her home church, New Providence Baptist Church.

In her spare time T.J. enjoys helping others, spending time with her nieces and nephews, friends and loved ones, playing with her dog Xena, and her bearded dragon Earl.

Amanda Molina
The Nightmare

Amanda Molina has worked in the sales industry for over 10 years, where she has gained experience in both management and leadership. As a seasoned sales manager, she is passionate about challenging the status quo and is always looking to advance her skill set. In addition to her love for sales, Amanda has a love for beauty where she serves as a Beauty Guide for Lime Life by Alcone. Amanda also enjoys photography, hiking, and spending time with her family.

Seranie Manoogian
Shiny Sparkly Pretty Bits

Seranie has spent the last 18 years living and working in Los Angeles, CA where she has been a contributing member to two Emmy Award Winning Primetime Animated Series. A graduate of Syracuse University's Newhouse School, Seranie shares her story of growing up in an Armenian family in San Diego, CA during the 90's.

In her spare time, Seranie enjoys providing color commentary for her friends and co-workers. When asked if she needs salsa with her breakfast burrito she always responds with "No thanks, I don't need it...I'm spicy enough."

Jessica DeWalt
A Continuum of Consciousness

Jessica is a person with intense passion, whom has learned how to develop this passion into positive personal growth and development as a hobby. She has found that remaining positive in difficult times is the key to longevity and a robust life. Managing a household while remaining aggressively happy in the face of adversity, has become a strategic blessing that has proven to provide consistent results, or you could call them miracles. Within each person lies the ability to maximize the innate. Using her words to create a string of evolving perspective, she provides her readers with a broad understanding and insight into consciousness and quantum perspectives.

Jessica can be found in San Diego, California exploring her children's natural talents and abilities through play, reading, and interpersonal connection. She is a loving wife and mother of two beautiful and gifted children. Jessica enjoys spending her free time at the beach, rain or shine equally. She enjoys meditation as a daily practice.

Anita L. Withrow
Blessings In The Brokeness

Anita L. Withrow has been in practice as an occupational therapy assistant for twenty years, and truly enjoys the work that she does to help geriatric patients recover from injury and illness. She is also a 200-hour YTT certified yoga teacher, and she even teaches chair yoga classes for the senior residents!

Anita also thrives in her work as a coach for women who are moving from codependency and low self-esteem, into a life that is purposeful and based on true self-love. She firmly believes that we all as people have an opportunity to pursue dreams and fulfillment, and encourages those that she comes into contact with to do just that. One of her core values is that every experience that we go through, both the good and the bad, is a part of what makes us who we are and helps us to become who we want to be.

Anita is a mother to three beautiful children, and a wife. She has four cats and a dog that are all shelter rescues. She lives in rural Virginia on a gorgeous lake!

Brandi Allen
The Bus Stop Secrets

Brandi McElroy-Allen was born and raised in San Diego, California and in 2012 she relocated to Charlotte, North Carolina. Brandi's journey began for her passion for youth and community service, from her work in the non-profit sector as holding multiple positions that include, Independent Living Skills Peer Counselor, HIV prevention and outreach and supervising homeless youth through Child Protective Services.

Brandi hopes one day to open a safe house and shelter for human trafficking victims. She wants her readers to understand that human trafficking is a worldwide problem that is happening in our own backyards.

Brandi is also a mother of four children.

Sequita Myers-Carlisle
The Assignment

Sequita has always used her genuine spirit and strength in relationship building to effortlessly connect with perfect strangers. Sequita was given an assignment that she didn't ask for, but was hand-picked by God to complete. It was this very important assignment that lead to her life calling. The calling to help empower, encourage and equip women with the necessary tools to be their best selves no matter the "assignments" placed in their lives. From this calling, Sequita along with her husband founded Myers Carlisle Coaching. that focuses on grief recovery, marriage, family and business coaching.

Sequita lives in Rowlett, Texas with her son and husband of ten years.

Angela Mountz
I Choose Joy

Angela Mountz has been around a few blocks in her life. Growing up in an abusive home where alcoholism and drugs were prevalent, she decided she wanted to travel down a different path. Although that path included her own addiction issues, a failed marriage and most recently a heroin addicted child, through it all she found her identity in God and seeks to find joy in the little things.

Angela holds a pastoral license from the Brethren in Christ and a Social Science Degree specializing in families and children. Her passions include identity in Christ, healing from woundedness, and loving people where they are.

Angela believes God has given her a second chance with an amazing husband she has been married to for seven years. Together they live in central Philadelphia with their 4 delightful cats.

Kirsty Farrugia
Feels Like Home

Kirsty is a professional organizer and a transformed messaholic. She is

passionate about helping others find space in their heads, hearts and home, Kirsty wants to share with others the freedom that comes from living a decluttered life.

Owner of Feels Like Home Professional Organizers, and co-producer of popular podcast The Art of Decluttering, Kirsty is on a mission to help those who are too busy, too confused, too tired, too stressed or too overwhelmed to deal with their clutter on their own. She works with clients to create order and make long-term improvements in all aspects of their lives.

Kirsty lives in Sydney, Australia with her uber-organized husband and her two gorgeous children.

Kayla Brissi
The Blessing of a Grief Stricken Broken Heart

Combine passion, hard work, and dedication, and you have Kayla Brissi. As CEO and Founder of Kayla Brissi LLC, Kayla takes on the challenging responsibilities of blending marketing and sales to deliver results for her clients.

Kayla is a master strategist, professional digital marketer, and skillful copywriter. With her impressive marketing and sales background, Kayla has impacted thousands with her teaching and transforms lives while doing what she loves.

Kayla holds a Master's of Business Administration in Finance, and a Bachelor of Science degree in both Accounting and Business Administration from Lakeland College.

Kayla has contributed to a number of different industry publications and online platforms such as Christian Women in Business, Today.com, and Skillshare.

In her spare time, Kayla enjoys reading, watching movies, and spending time with her husband Fiacre and son Emmanuel.

Linda Malloian
My Journey, My Truth, His Way

Linda was born in the Middle East, and at the tender age of eight migrated to the United States along with her family. Growing up, Linda always knew her her true passion was to help others. She practices holistic/herbal healing, and aids many to a new found health. Faith is another essential component to Linda's life, and she implements it into her family everyday, and to those who need it.

Linda is a full time wife, and mother to one child and currently resides in San Diego, CA.

Kendra Pierce
The End to the Beginning

Kendra Pierce grew up in Farmington Utah, a beautiful home town with a great childhood upbringing. She became a mother at the age of seventeen and a mother of three by age twenty two. Kendra is a survivor of domestic violence and has since worked to inspire others through her experience. She is an active domestic violence advocate, as well as positive role model in her community where she has organized several groups to help empower and encourage people to follow their dreams and live their best lives, regardless of what that might be.

Aside of co-owning a small business in the renewable energy industry, Kendra also teaches people how to earn income by building personal and business relationships, using appreciation marking. Anyone who knows Kendra can tell you how much she loves business and pursuing her career.

In her spare time you can find Kendra spending time with family and friends, enjoying life 40,000 feet in the air, or counting reps and sets weight training at the local gym. Her passions include traveling the world, cruising across the deep ocean at 24 knots per hour, exploring new cultures and exotic foods, meeting new people, and reading anything related to business, entrepreneurs, and self growth..

Kendra can be found on Linkedin (Kendra Pierce), or Facebook and Instagram @KillinitwKendra

Walanda Johnson
When Love Broke Through

Since she was a child, Walanda always envisioned her life would be in the field of helping others. From first aspiring to be a teacher then a neurosurgeon/pediatrician, her path led her to becoming a licensed psychotherapist. She is intensely passionate about empowering others to live their best life and truly holds to the truth that "His divine power has given us all we need according to life and godliness (2 Peter. 1:3)." Her vision and purpose are fueled in knowing there is a God-filled life obtainable to all.

Professionally, her current roles include working with military families and in private practice helping people overcome trauma, anxieties, stress, depression, and life adjustments. Working in ministry, she uses her degree in organizational leadership to inspire others to lead volunteers with passion, relationship, and consistency. She also leads the Healthy Families department which strives to bring mental, spiritual, and physical health resources to the Body of Christ and the community.

Ever-evolving, in her spare time Walanda enjoys working out, writing, spending quality time in relationship with others, listening and dancing to music (you will find her dancing in a store if she likes the music), developing herself, and sleeping.

The Purple Womb
Dr. Ethel E. Sims

Dr. Ethel E. Sims is an Author, Educator, Trainer, Ministry Consultant and Business Entrepreneur. Her first public book release, The Purple Womb, was 'fearfully and wonderfully' inspired by the heart of her Beloved mother, Rebecca, and one of her own favorite scriptures, Psalms 139:13-14.

She is prayerfully preparing for other literary releases for Fall/ Winter 2018.

'Dr. E' feels blessed with the husband of her youth and their union of 38 years that boasts three adult children and 4 grands. Ethel loves spending time with family and friends; the arts, theatre, shopping, walking, dining; and taking adventurous mission road trips.

She was raised in Grambling, LA - as the youngest of three- with strong, extended family roots - by her single-divorcee mother and grandparents, The Browns. These factors have influenced her pursuit of 'Royal Life Purpose' - to grow in the Lord, to share and teach His word, to serve and inspire others, and to foster healthy relationships – all for the sake of Kingdom Building.

She is currently an Independent Broker and Entrepreneur with over 30 years of professional experience and premier, client services in the area of residential sales, staging and investments.

Dr. Ethel Sims completed her Doctor of Ministry in 2016 after being commissioned in 2015 by Campus Crusade in Orlando Florida - with her husband, Pastor Dr. Thomas Lee Sims (a native of San Diego, CA).

As Church Planters of Christ CornerStone Church (2000-2016) The Sims continue to serve collectively as founders of 'CornerStone Koenonia Connections' and as Urban Mission Leaders with CRU .
The Sims also serve in Ministry Leadership at the Mesa View Baptist Church in Poway, CA.

Ethel's book The Purple Womb can be found on Amazon at https://amzn.to/2HdoFQa

Cylnthia R. Long Poet
Whirlwind of Life

Cylnthia a native of San Diego serves as the leader of the women's ministry and intercessory prayer teams at Bayview Baptist Church in San Diego, CA.

Cylnthia is married to Deacon John W. Long and has four adult children and seven grandchildren. She is a Christian and serves as a deacon's wife. Cylnthia has been a supervisor for San Diego Police Parking Enforcement for twenty years and counting.

In her spare time she loves writing, relaxing and spending time with her family.